The Rise of Market Society in England, 1066–1800

Studies in British and Imperial History
Published for the German Historical Institute London
Edited by Andreas Gestrich

THE RISE OF MARKET SOCIETY IN ENGLAND, 1066–1800

Christiane Eisenberg

Translated by Deborah Cohen

berghahn
NEW YORK · OXFORD
www.berghahnbooks.com

Published in 2013 by
Berghahn Books
www.berghahnbooks.com

© 2013, 2016 Berghahn Books
First paperback edition published in 2016

German Language © 2009 Vandenhoeck & Ruprecht GmbH & Co. KG,
Christiane Eisenberg
Original title: Englands Weg in die Marktgesellschaft, Göttingen, 2009

The translation of this work was funded by Geisteswissenschaften International –
Translation Funding for Humanities and Social Sciences from Germany, a joint
initiative of the Fritz Thyssen Foundation, the German Federal Foreign Office, the
collecting society VG WORT and the Börsenverein des Deutschen Buchhandels
(German Publishers & Booksellers Association).

Library of Congress Cataloging-in-Publication Data

Eisenberg, Christiane, 1956–
　　[Englands Weg in die Marktgesellschaft. English]
　　The rise of market society in England, 1066–1800 / Christiane Eisenberg ;
translated by Deborah Cohen.
　　　pages cm. — (Monographs in British history ; volume 1)
　　Translation of Christiane Eisenberg's Englands Weg in die Marktgesellschaft.
　　Includes bibliographical references and index.
　　ISBN 978-1-78238-258-4 (hardback) — ISBN 978-1-78533-217-3 (paperback) —
ISBN 978-1-78238-259-1 (ebook)
　　1. England—Commerce--History. 2. Capitalism—England—History. I. Title.
HF3505.E58413 2014
381.0942—dc23
　　　　　　　　　　　　　　　　　　　　　　　　　　　　　　　　　2013017838

British Library Cataloguing in Publication Data

A catalogue record for this book is available from the British Library

ISBN 978-1-78238-258-4 hardback
ISBN 978-1-78533-217-3 paperback
ISBN 978-1-78238-259-1 ebook

CONTENTS

Figures and Tables

Figures

Despite diligent research, we were not able to trace the copyright holders of all images. If notified, we will insure full acknowledgement of legitimate claims within the framework of the usual agreements.

Tables

PREFACE

This book is based on the study *Englands Weg in die Marktgesellschaft*, which was published by Vandenhoeck and Ruprecht in Göttingen in 2009, with a German audience in mind. In reediting the book for the English translation, I revised several passages for readers with an Anglo-American background and incorporated some of the literature that has appeared since the original publication. I would like to thank the two anonymous readers for Berghahn for their suggested revisions and Deborah Cohen in Berlin for her meticulous translation.

The translation was funded by the Börsenverein für den deutschen Buchhandel, the Thyssen Foundation and the German Foreign Office. The German Historical Institute in London and its director, Andreas Gestrich, also supported the publication, not least by including the manuscript in their new series, and I offer them my warmest thanks.

Berlin and Münster, January 2013
Christiane Eisenberg

Preface to the German Edition

This study takes up a question that grew out of two previous projects of mine. In a study of the early history of trade unions (1986) and another on the cultural transfer of modern sport from England to Germany (1999), I argued that the pioneering role that England played in these respective areas in the nineteenth century could be explained in terms of the early and thorough establishment of market relations in the country. This finding prompted the question pursued here of how this critically influential factor in English development came about.

I drew inspiration to pursue an answer from the community at the Großbritannien-Zentrum, an interdisciplinary centre for British Studies at the Humboldt University of Berlin, where I have been Professor of British History since 1998. I would like to thank my colleagues and students at the Zentrum as well as our British guest lecturers, who have all engaged with my topic in various ways. I am particularly grateful to Jürgen Schlaeger, our director for many years, for our discussions. Gerhard Dannemann and Helmut Weber answered my questions on Common Law and also commented on the relevant chapter.

Among those who closely read the manuscript are the editors of *Kritische Studien für Geschichtswissenschaft;* Jürgen Kocka also read through several versions. The questions and comments from this circle of scholars helped me to clarify and sharpen my argument. I would like to thank Heidrun Homburg, my friend since our Bielefeld days, as well as Karl Ditt for their intellectual generosity and constant encouragement during the writing phase.

Berlin and Münster, March 2009
Christiane Eisenberg

ENGLAND AND THE
PROCESS OF COMMERCIALIZATION

As the core country of the British Isles, England is regarded as a pioneer of modern industrial capitalism and as a model of an open society with a viable public sphere. Therefore, an examination of English history can be expected to yield fundamental insights into the preconditions for Western ways of living and doing business. It furthermore seems legitimate to reformulate a central question of historical social science, originally posed by Max Weber: 'to what combination of circumstances should the fact be attributed that precisely on English soil cultural phenomena appeared which (as we like to think) lie in a line of development having universal significance and value?'[1]

With reference to this question, English – and more broadly British – history has already been the subject of numerous comprehensive research initiatives. In the 1960s and 1970s, for example, it served U.S.-based modernization theorists as a preferred model and benchmark of Western development and inspired a large number of empirically rich comparative studies that juxtaposed it with the history of other European countries, the United States and Latin America.[2] The current debate about the 'Great Divergence' between Europe and Asia has rekindled this discussion. To determine when and for what reasons Asia diverged from the path of Western development, the protagonists viewed England and subregions of China as proxies for Europe and Asia, respectively. In this discussion, the stagnation of the Qing dynasty with its highly developed commercial economy is explained in terms of the absence of the structural preconditions that are presumed to have been present and effectively utilized in medieval and Early Modern England.[3]

_____

Notes from this chapter begin on page 15.

However, a century after Max Weber, historical social science is faced with the challenge of having to reorient its research agenda; for the state of our knowledge has changed, and the pressing problems of today, which give rise to the central questions, are not the same as in 1900. Most notably, the underlying research paradigm of industrial capitalism, which attempts to explain the dynamic of modern societies in terms of the Industrial Revolution, is in crisis, with far-reaching consequences for the view of England in historical social science.

Already in the late 1970s, British economic and social history began to move away from this paradigm. For one thing, the significance of steam engines and centralized production for economic growth was called into question, particularly for the period between 1760 and 1830, which had traditionally been regarded as the core phase of the Industrial Revolution in England. Increasing numbers of studies had found that the bulk of the mass production of manufactured goods taking place at this time was still being carried out in the traditional manner, i.e., by hand and in decentralized workshops. In 1850, factory workers still made up only 5 per cent of the adult male workforce, and, according to estimates, the machines utilized in factories represented less than 5 per cent of their capital stock.[4] For another, the rates of growth of the English economy between 1760 and 1830 were recalculated and revised downward, so that doubts arose as to the revolutionary character of the development. According to this view, what was specific about England as an industrial pioneer was paradoxically its extraordinarily slow pace of development. Today, most economic historians regard the industrialization of England more as the provisional climax of a process of commercialization and market rationalization that had begun centuries earlier than as the prelude to a fundamentally new phenomenon.[5]

Although the social sciences, with their contemporary focus, have not yet fully taken these reinterpretations of history into account,[6] they also reveal a paradigmatic shift in that they avoid referring to the concept of an industrial society. This research tendency, which emerged in the final two decades of the twentieth century and has since become generalized, can be explained in terms of the fact that precisely in advanced societies in the Western mould – beginning with the English region of Great Britain – a deindustrialization and shifting of economic activity from industrial production to services of all kinds can be observed. Alternative labels abound, with the concepts of 'postindustrial society', 'post-Fordism' and the 'information', 'knowledge', 'experience-driven' and 'risk society' all competing for attention within a social scientific discourse that has grown increasingly opaque. Where consensus does exist, however, is in the belief that, however it is described, modern and/or postmodern society is organized around the market economy, and that herein lies the key to understanding it.[7]

If one regards the above-outlined development of the historical and contemporary social sciences in context, one will relativize the weight of industrial society as the leading factor shaping conditions of life in the nineteenth and the greater part of the twentieth century. Precisely in England, the industrial pioneer, and later in Great Britain as a whole, industrial society appears – at the risk of overstating the case – as an interlude within a longer period of increasingly more efficient economic management, the locus of which lay outside of centralized production in factories. At the same time, it emerges that the specific characteristics of modernizing societies of the preindustrial type are to be understood against the background of the same process of commercialization that is also accelerating transformations in the present. The question therefore arises as to its structural preconditions, features and developmental dynamics.

The renewed interest in commercialization directs the attention of researchers to the category of the market, as well as to the economic and social effects of consociation (*Vergesellschaftung*) and societal integration. It thereby simultaneously marks the point at which historical social science must put aside the classical social science theorists, as they have virtually nothing more to contribute to the discussion. The best example is the above-quoted Max Weber, whose voluminous work *Economy and Society* contains but a single chapter – only three and a half pages in length and of little real substance – on the topic of consociation through market exchange (*Marktvergesellschaftung*). In this chapter, Weber elucidates several historical examples of social action in markets and mentions the use of money as 'the exact counterpart to any consociation through rationally agreed or imposed norms'.[8] How this mode of consociation arose and under what concrete underlying conditions it continued to function on a sustained basis remains unclear, however – a deficit that subsequent generations of social scientists have failed to overcome. Their general lack of interest in the topic is indicated not least by the fact that as late as 1968, the *International Encyclopedia of the Social Sciences* contained no entry for the word 'market' in its index.[9]

The present study will contribute to filling this gap in the research by investigating the formation of modern market society in England. This will be achieved by marrying a structural analysis with a process one. On the one hand, the specific social, economic and legal structures of the late Middle Ages and the Early Modern period that made it possible for market society to develop will be identified, and the concomitant changes to the living environment will be described. As such, this study is a contribution to English economic, social and cultural history. On the other hand, it attempts to reconstruct the commercialization of England as a process that unfolded over centuries. The driving forces underlying the universalization and consolidation of market relations shall be identified, and the developmental pattern and potential of this process shall be analysed.

This study focuses largely on the development of the domestic market in England. It shows how it came to be that in the late Middle Ages, certain types of markets – those for land, work and capital, but also for commodities such as use rights – developed and how the social relationships effected through the market were shaped over the course of the Early Modern period. In addition, attention will be paid to the creation of institutions and modes of communication, as well as to the ways in which contemporaries dealt with uncertainty and the risks involved in market activity. Foreign trade must also be considered, as precisely for England – the core country of the British Isles and of the coalescing empire – any distinction between the domestic and export markets would be artificial. However, foreign trade is not the primary focus of this study, as it was predicated upon and utilized the institutions and conventions of the English domestic market, without which foundation even the inner-British trade with Scotland would have been inconceivable.[10] In any event, it was only in the course of the seventeenth century – that is, deep into the time frame of this study – that the sails were trimmed for the transatlantic trade, when a large number of foreign merchants began to settle in London, establishing it as the hub of an English and/or British-based European trading network. Until that time, England's foreign trade activities had been focussed on Russia and nearby Europe.[11] Even towards the end of the eighteenth century, when trade with North America was in full swing and was bolstering the burgeoning process of industrialization, the bulk of the trading activity still clearly took place within the domestic market, which at this point in time accounted for 85 to 95 per cent of the value of all goods traded.[12] The words that Daniel Defoe had penned decades earlier in his advice volume *The Complete English Tradesman* still rang true: 'The Inland trade of England is … the support of all our foreign trade, and of our manufacturing, and … of the tradesmen who carry it on.' Defoe saw 'the foundation of all our wealth and greatness' as lying right here, in England itself.[13]

It goes without saying that the findings of a case study such as this one, which focuses on the English domestic market, presumably cannot universally be applied to other countries, nor was this my intention. The purpose was rather to reconstruct in an ideal-typical manner the rise, structural features and developmental dynamic of an early developing market society, which can serve future studies – be they historical or contemporary in orientation – as a basis for comparison.

In neo-classical economics, markets are regarded as places where fully informed economic subjects behave rationally and where the price mechanism keeps supply and demand in balance. This definition is of little use to social scientists and social historians, as it obscures the concrete cultural, political and other circumstances of social behaviour on various markets (those for goods, services, labour and other commodities). In this study, markets are therefore regarded as arenas in which scarce resources, goods and services are allocated by having buyers and sellers enter into a relationship of competition with one another. This definition focuses on the function of markets in brokering interactions between individuals and social groups but refrains from leaping to conclusions as to the effects of these interactions. However, it does implicitly assume that with the formation of a market society, these interactions necessarily solidify and thereby undergo a shift in meaning. This definition calls our attention to the fact that markets are not merely structures but also form 'ligatures' in societies (Ralf Dahrendorf), so that one can say that they coordinate and institutionalize mechanisms of consociation and societal integration.[14] This can be regarded as an effect of the power of the 'invisible hand', which, according to Adam Smith, leads each and every market participant 'to promote an end which was no part of his intention'.[15]

The reciprocal relations of exchange on markets are mediated through money. This second criterion for a definition of the market is indispensable for a study of this particular historical process, as only money made it possible for continuous exchange to take place. Under any alternative means of transferring ownership, e.g., gift-giving or robbery, it would sooner or later have stalled.[16] Monetary relationships can exist regardless of whether sufficient reserves of coins or bank notes are available as a means of payment, or just a monetary offsetting takes place. During the period examined in this study – the Middle Ages and Early Modern era – when coins were in notoriously short supply, the former set of circumstances generally did not apply, while the latter appertains to most transactions on world markets today. An important indicator of the continued development of a market society is therefore the determination of the value of the goods and services purchased in money or equivalent payment instruments (e.g., promissory notes).

Such monetarily mediated social relationships have existed throughout human history, and in England they long predated the Roman invasion.[17] Due to the quality of sources, qualitatively advancing phases of commercialization, which lend themselves to an empirically based process study, can be identified for the High Middle Ages at the earliest.[18] The present study investigates the time period between 1066, the year of the Norman Invasion, and the turn of the nineteenth century. As the Norman Invasion precipitated a radical upheaval of the political system and concomitantly also of the basic conditions of economic activity, it would seem inexpedient to set the beginning of the study any earlier. The decision to end the investigation around 1800 – or, more precisely, with the decades between 1780 and 1820 – is an equally pragmatic one. It is based on the consideration that the increasing weight of industrialization tends to make it more difficult for historians to isolate the specific effects of consociation through market exchange, so that distortions of the interpretation cannot be ruled out. Frequently, it is no easier to determine precisely what phenomena may be attributed to the process of commercialization and what to technical, organizational and other factors for the mid-to-late nineteenth century. What must be avoided above all are teleological explanations. The widespread notion that the process of commercialization gave rise to modern industrial society does seem plausible; in view of the crisis of this paradigm, however, it is necessary to subject it to empirical examination.[19] This consideration also speaks in favour of concluding the study with a snapshot of English market society at a point in time before the breakthrough of new production methods, i.e., before 1830–1850.

Thus conceived, the study covers a time span of 750 years. The example of England provides historians with virtually laboratory-level conditions for an analysis of 'pure commercialization'. With the exception of the Netherlands, whose development stagnated and in certain areas even regressed after the close of the seventeenth century, such a long and at the same time continually developing commercial prelude to industrialization can be seen nowhere else in European economic history, at least on the basis of our current state of knowledge. The case study of England therefore offers a singular opportunity to reconstruct a centuries-long historical process, the progress, pace and developmental dynamic of which have thus far not been the subject of an empirical analysis.[20] The primary objective of this undertaking is to identify the actors who drove the process along and to show how events and structures intersected. A further aim is to investigate the concrete contexts in which and social mechanisms whereby continuity was conveyed and path dependence arose.

The abovementioned discussion on the 'Great Divergence' between Europe and Asia also underscores the need for such a study. Researchers agree that markets and market relations in both of the representative areas investigated – England and the Yangtze River Delta region in China – were already highly developed in the Middle Ages and the Early Modern period; indeed, the observed commonalities between these two regions, which would begin to industrialize about 150 years apart, were not the least of the factors that spurred interest in an intercontinental comparison. However, there is still too little information – not only for the Chinese case but also for England – on how these market relationships changed over time and how they interacted with other aspects of societal development, such as population growth, the underlying conditions of communication or industrial production. In this respect, the intercontinental comparison operates with two unknowns, which makes it more difficult to formulate precise statements. The present study understands itself as a contribution to this discussion, although, in the interest of not overburdening the presentation, it abstains from making concrete comparisons to China.[21]

Similar difficulties in determining the historical significance of the market emerge with regard to some other subaspects of the research into the 'great question' of historical social science sketched out in the introduction. Here, as well, great gaps exist in our knowledge of the formation of the market economy and market society in England, the pioneer of modernization. In order to bundle these subaspects, this study examines the following two questions from the classical social science discourse in greater detail:

1. To what extent can the process of commercialization of the economy, society and culture in England be understood as a 'self-governing modernization' (Shmuel N. Eisenstadt),[22] which drew its strength from within? To what extent did external impulses from foreign countries play a role?

2. What form did the relationship between tradition and modernity take in the course of this process of commercialization? What concrete significance did the oft-cited extra-economic foundations of commercial activity – namely, the traditional legal, social and household structures as well as cultural influences – have? Could the English market society build on these foundations, or was it necessary to do away with them and create new ones?

The first question as to the external impulses inspired the recent discussion about transnational relations and 'entangled history', which lately has been expanded to include the preindustrial era.[23] Corresponding statements have been made in the debate, carried on since the 1970s, over England's special path to modernity, which has revolved around a broad contextualization and explanation of 'English peculiarities' (e.g., the early development of a constitutional monarchy) as well as the influence of such structural particularities in the long term. In this connection, Hans-Christoph Schröder, in a groundbreaking essay on 'Modern English History in the Light of Several Modernization Theorems' (1977), used the perception of an economically advanced Netherlands as an occasion to cast doubt on the autochthonous character of the commercialization process in England.[24] This study will have to judge such impulses emanating from outside whilst taking into account the chronology; for only with an understanding of the succession of events and developments is it possible to give proper weight to endogenous and exogenous factors.

The second question of the extra-economic foundations of market exchange initially revolves around the political and legal structures that stimulated and/or accompanied the process of commercialization. That this study begins in the High Middle Ages means that the specific quality of English feudalism needs to be taken into account in the interpretation.

Furthermore, the phrase 'extra-economic foundations of market exchange' refers to a series of further, so-called premodern traditions of a legal, social and cultural nature. Suggestions for their identification can be found in the general discourse on the relationship between tradition and modernity in the capitalist market economy, which has been carried on since the nineteenth century and has developed into a permanent topic of debate in the social sciences. 'From Status to Contract' (Sir Henry Maine), 'from Community to Society' (Ferdinand Tönnies) and 'from Mechanical to Organic Solidarity' (Emile Durkheim) are a few of the catchphrases. This discourse therefore appears to be an appropriate point of departure for the present study, not least since in the country under investigation, England (and/or Great Britain), it has thus far been carried out in a manner that is calmer or at least less excited than has been the case in other Western and Central European countries, such as Germany.

The German contributors to the discourse tend to emphasize the profound experiences of loss that go hand in hand with the process of commercialization and predict a longer-term development in the direction of a crisis, since in its triumphant procession, modernity has developed a tendency to destroy its own traditional foundations. This argument was formulated especially pithily in the *Communist Manifesto* (1848), in which Marx and Engels wrote that in bourgeois society – and by this they meant capitalist market society – '[a]ll fixed, fast-frozen relations, with their train of ancient and venerable prejudices and opinions, are swept away' and '[a]ll that is solid melts into air'.[25] Today the foremost representative of this direction of thought is Jürgen Habermas, whose dictum about the 'colonization of the lifeworld' is supported by the diagnosis of an exhaustion of the premodern foundations of the modern era, accelerated by market processes.[26]

British scholars have set different points of emphasis. In their writings, the formula 'invention of traditions' – a term coined by the social historians Eric Hobsbawm and Terence Ranger more than a quarter of a century ago, and which was illustrated with examples from the commercial mass culture of the late nineteenth and twentieth centuries – stands as the argumentative equivalent of the 'exhaustion of traditions'. The difference to the German view of things is not a fundamental one, as in general the establishment of new traditions goes hand in hand with the obliteration of the old ones. And yet British scholars express a pronounced basic trust in the community-building abilities of the market. With regard to the process of commercialization, they are less interested in the losses that may result than in its innovative power and creative potential.[27]

This positive viewpoint is – and already was in the late seventeenth and eighteenth centuries – presented especially emphatically for the preindustrial development phase of market society. Trade, acquisition and commerce had led not to a corruption of morals but rather to their refinement and tempering – as one can read in the writings of Montesquieu and other minds of the Enlightenment.[28] Since the economist Albert O. Hirschman resurrected the phrase 'doux commerce' (Montesquieu) some thirty years ago to recall this positive perception of 'capitalism before its triumph', it has been taken up by historians – especially those in the fields of intellectual history, the history of ideas and the cultural history of consumption – who have further elucidated it.[29] Thus far, no examination has been undertaken of whether and if so, in what manner 'doux commerce' helped shape the rise and development of the process of commercialization.

In view of the controversial treatment of the topic of commercialization, it might be surprising that it has until now been neglected in historical social research. Max Weber, whose scant interest in the market has already been referred to, was in this respect thoroughly representative of the classical sociologists. Not even Werner Sombart's article 'The Commercialization of Economic Life', which appeared in the *Archiv für Sozialwissenschaft und Sozialpolitik* in 1910, dealt with the market and market society. Rather, Sombart attempted to determine the function of the instruments and institutions of finance (bills of exchange, shares, banknotes, banks, the stock exchange) and sketched out the context in which each one arose. In addition, he led the reader on a wild ramble through the economic history of Europe, from Renaissance Italy to the seventeenth-century Netherlands, and from the English East India Company to Germany in the age of 'high capitalism'. With this essay, Sombart wanted to provide proof that '[i]n all the stages, the Jew was ever present with his creative genius'.[30]

Only since the late 1980s, after the conclusive failure of 'real socialism', have the social sciences discovered the category of the market for themselves. The acceleration of economic globalization in the 1990s fuelled this interest. With the 'New Economic Sociology', a special subdiscipline has since taken root in American business schools that is dedicated to the study of the 'culture of the market'. Building on an approach of the Hungarian economist Karl Polanyi (1886–1964), its adherents investigate the embeddedness of the market mechanism in concrete cultural and social, and hence also historical, contexts.[31] Thus, the legal and political conditions framing business activity, transaction costs, the symbolism of exchanging gifts, trust and emotions, conventions and rules, tax and feedback mechanisms in networks and other context variables are now part of the market discourse in the historical social sciences. But as this development is only recent, it is necessary for us to re-examine the basic presuppositions underlying the discourse.

Within the field of history, the topic of commercialization has likewise been largely neglected, although individual social historians have periodically devoted attention to specific aspects of the growth of markets in local, regional or branch-specific case studies.[32] The reason behind the reticence of the historical profession to undertake a comprehensive historicization lies in a methodological deficit: no guidelines for conducting a genetic, i.e., nonteleological, reconstruction of historical processes are available.[33] The recent interest in the phenomenon of path dependence, i.e., the influence of initial conditions in shaping the long-term development of a process, does not contradict this statement, as a discussion of the problem of path dependence – as well as of the developmental dynamic, inefficiency and dysfunctionality that might accompany it – only makes sense when we know how the process unfolded. As such, this approach, which has its roots in economic scholarship, offers historians a mere classification system rather than a general model.[34]

This limitation equally applies to the more specific process models and theories tailor-made for the social sciences – for example, those relating to democratization, nation building or modernization in general, with which historians have been operating since the 1960s and 1970s. As helpful as these might be in individual cases, such as in comparative studies with brief time frames, they ultimately allow only for a classification, or a specification, but not for the genetic reconstruction of a process or of the mechanisms that contribute to ensuring its perpetuation.[35] Especially with regard to the analysis of the invariably accompanying contingencies, ambivalences and unintended consequences of these processes, historians who utilize these tools therefore find themselves obliged to resort to supplementary, 'free-hand' interpretations and to their own intuition.

At any rate, no fully elaborated model of commercialization yet exists in the toolbox of modernization theories. Instead, the terminology used in the relevant studies derives – sometimes directly, sometimes indirectly via the works of their disciples – from the research on capitalism of the classical sociologists Karl Marx, Max Weber and Werner Sombart. However, for a number of reasons, this research tradition cannot serve as a basis for an empirical study of the commercialization of late medieval and Early Modern England.

Firstly, in recent research, the term 'capitalism' is typically used in a structural rather than a process context. This convention can be explained not least in terms of the desire for a typology of the national and regional 'varieties of capitalism' that evolved over the course of the nineteenth and twentieth centuries. Unfortunately, in many cases the historical depth of the classical analyses has been sacrificed to this – in and of itself welcome – research trend, since the analysis of the various types of capitalism is only insufficiently linked to the study of its historical development.[36] Rather, the protagonists make do with general statements on the genesis of the respective form or even risk drawing bold conclusions as to the manner in which a structure arose on the basis of its features. Evidence of this dubious method can also be found in the recent general discussion on capitalism, within which the English example continues to play a central role.[37]

A second reason for the decision not to work with the term capitalism in this study has to do with the complexity resulting from the fact that the classical social scientists had already conceived of it in relation to industrial production. According to them, its defining criteria included the presence of private companies and of 'free', i.e., contractually regulated, wage labour, as well as assumptions as to the purpose and method of doing business (profit, calculability). In addition, they took the resulting impositions on the workers (power relations and conditions of exploitation) into consideration, as these were major factors determining the distribution of income and way of life in industrial capitalism. Some theoreticians made additional assumptions as to capitalism's antecedent societal form, feudalism and – as with Marx – presumed a conflictual developmental dynamic. No deep previous knowledge of English society in the late Middle Ages or Early Modern period is required to see that for the investigation undertaken here, so comprehensive a term is, on the one hand, too loaded, and on the other, cannot adequately grasp economic activities such as trade and finance. It is true that the classical sociologists also classify markets among the invariants of capitalism. However, even if – by leaving out state capitalist arrangements – one is willing to concede that every capitalist society is integrated through commercial, i.e., market-mediated, relations, it would be rash to make the reverse conclusion: that relationships are always shaped by the capitalist profit motive. If, when and to what extent a market society can be described as capitalist is, rather, an empirical question. If this historical study did not consciously leave it open, this would distort the view of precapitalist particularities and the momentum of the commercialization process.

Thirdly and finally, the analyses of capitalism by Marx, Weber and Sombart demonstrate a specific weakness: They all have an England problem. Werner Sombart cultivated his pronounced resentment against 'perfidious Albion' – which, he alleged, was capable of producing only 'merchants' (*Händler*) rather than 'heroes' (*Helden*) – not only in his famous First World War-era diatribe of that name, but also in his scholarly work.[38] Karl Marx proved incapable of shedding certain inherited German patterns of perception and impartially analysing the manifest empirical reality of his country of exile. Central elements of his concept of capitalism – such as the 'the sale of labour-power' as a commodity, or 'class' – therefore fail to fully grasp the way in which English market society functioned.[39] For his part, in the framework of his investigations on the 'rationalization of all spheres of life', Max Weber showed himself to be thoroughly perplexed by certain English particularities, especially the legal system, which was based not on systematic Roman law but on case-based Common Law. And yet he never grappled with the obvious question of why precisely the country that was regarded as the most highly advanced in the area of rational – and therefore modern – capitalism retained such 'anachronisms' on a long-term basis.[40]

Against this scientific-historical background, it is not surprising that the term 'commercialization' is also used both colloquially and inconsistently, even in contributions that are expressly devoted to the topic. In the above-mentioned essay, Werner Sombart uses this term to characterize 'the dissolution of all economic procedures in commerce' and the 'stock-marketization of the economy'.[41] More recent historical contributions refer to the 'breakthrough of consumer society' or use the term synonymously with 'commodification', i.e., the transfer of goods and services in the form of commodities in the Marxist sense.[42] Still others orient themselves towards Georg Simmel's major work, *The Philosophy of Money* (1900) – a multifaceted collection of examples of commercialization phenomena of all kinds – and employ a terminology that is open to change, for example the expansion and consolidation of social relations based on monetary exchange, also outside of the economy proper. This is also the working definition that underlies this study, which – like Simmel himself – abstains from making statements on the mechanism or direction of development.[43] Nor does it conjecture about the multifarious interconnections between the various phenomena of commercialization, or their coalescence into a potential driver for societal development. The previously mentioned field of 'New Economic Sociology' has also contributed little in this regard, particularly as its upturn has had the paradoxical effect of causing the market to sink under the weight of its various 'embeddings' and threaten to disappear from view.[44]

Upon closer inspection, however, the dismal state of historical research on commercialization cannot be surprising, as it is highly dependent on the specific approach taken by the respective scholar; that is, on a subjective factor: how he/she relates and temporally correlates the various embeddings of the market to one another in such a way that they are recognizable as stages in an historical process. For the act of exchanging equivalents on the market through the medium of money is, as such, an ephemeral interaction in whatever cultural context it takes place and does not lay out any developmental direction. Researchers on commercialization therefore can and must recall the words of Friedrich Nietzsche, who cautioned that 'all concepts in which an entire process is semiotically concentrated defy definition; only something which has no history can be defined'.[45]

* * * * *

To grasp the historicity and process character of the commercialization of England between 1066 and the turn of the nineteenth century, this study attempts to concretely describe the economic and extra-economic motives of the 'opening' and institutionalization of specific markets, but also of their in selective cases clearly observable 'closure'.[46] In addition, it shall analyse the circumstances under which this social action came to be enshrined in rules and conventions and the mechanisms by means of which interrelations, couplings and synergies were created between the market-organized economy and other areas of society: the state and the military, law and politics, and the financial and the tax systems, as well as the social structure, mentalities and culture. In contrast, the further question – of interest to economists and economic historians – of whether and to what extent 'perfect competition' reigned in this market society and of whether laissez faire as an ideology gained the upper hand will not be explored in detail. Such questions would necessitate a close contextualization, which would be difficult to reconcile with the long-term perspective aspired to here.

The empirical basis of this study consists of studies in the fields of economic, social and cultural history produced by British and other historians since the Second World War, especially since the 1960s and 1970s. Originally conceived of as part of an effort to explain the Industrial Revolution, they are here reevaluated with reference to the set of problems around commercialization. These studies include investigations of the role of the state in Early Modern England, which, despite a widespread assumption to the contrary, played an active role in the institutionalization of modern market society.[47] In contrast, little if any use will be made of the general overviews by the 'big-name' scholars in the field, e.g., Marx, Weber, Sombart, Wallerstein, Polanyi and Braudel, as the ideas they contain about the English economy and social history are hopelessly out of date.[48] Because today's social scientists continue to draw their historical knowledge chiefly from such works – and indeed, in view of the opacity of the more recent empirical research, are obliged to do so – this book aspires to provide an updated basis for a revival of the now slumbering but once (i.e., in the 1960s and 1970s) lively intellectual exchange between history and the social sciences.[49]

The presentation is structured chronologically, i.e., it begins with the medieval foundations of the English market society, progresses through the phase of its Early Modern unfolding – when the market began to create reciprocal relations between persons and institutions and to generate synergies – and concludes with the turn of the nineteenth century, by which time commercial ways of thinking and behaving had clearly come to dominate the mentality of contemporaries. In depicting the consolidation of market relations over the centuries, the presentation itself becomes denser. This is only in part a reflection of the increasing differentiation of the source material over time. More to the point, the progressively more concrete manner of presentation mirrors the actual development of English market society; indeed, already by the late seventeenth and eighteenth centuries, it had developed extraordinarily subtle techniques of self-perpetuation, which in turn call for a more differentiated discussion. For the general architecture of the study, the systematic final chapter – which returns to the questions developed above as to the relationship between endogenous and exogenous developmental factors, as well as of tradition and modernity in the market society – thus serves to retrace the fundamental lines of development and to answer in a synoptic manner the questions posed at the outset as to the drivers, direction of development and dynamics inherent in the process.

The extended time frame of the study includes the years 1536, when Wales was formally united with England, and 1707, when the union of England with Scotland came into force and Great Britain arose; the union with Ireland followed in 1801. The political expansion of the territory under investigation leads in the later chapters to linguistic adaptations. Instead of England, reference is made to Great Britain, and the adjective 'English' is supplanted by 'British'. However, this does not belie the fact that the actual subject of this long-term study is England and not Great Britain; for, as shall be shown, the medieval foundations of market society, which in the beginning are analysed only for England, developed lasting formative powers and favoured a path-dependent development (figure 0.1). The question of if and to what extent the specific English context of development also continued to be felt in Wales, Scotland and Ireland remains to be investigated in future studies.[50]

Figure 0.1. Map of England, circa 1250. The map, which served as an itinerary from Dover to Newcastle, still lacked geographic precision in the modern sense. Scotland is conceived of as an island, connected to England via a bridge at Stirling.

Notes

1. M. Weber. 1988. 'Vorbemerkung', in idem, *Gesammelte Aufsätze zur Religionssoziologie,* 9th ed., vol. 1, Tübingen: Mohr, 1; the original quotation refers to 'the soil of the occident'. For a commonly cited if somewhat free translation, see 'Author's Introduction', in M. Weber. 1958. *The Protestant Ethic and the Spirit of Capitalism,* trans. T. Parsons with a foreword by R. H. Tawney, New York, Charles Scribner's Sons, 13.
2. For a summary, see H.-U. Wehler, 1975. *Modernisierungstheorie und Geschichte,* Göttingen: Vandenhoeck and Ruprecht. A list of over five hundred comparative studies can be found in C. Eisenberg. 2008 ff. *British History Compared: A Bibliography,* Berlin (http://www.gbz .hu-berlin.de/staff/staff/publications/bibliographien, last accessed 21 September 2012), although admittedly not all of these were inspired by modernization theories.
3. This debate goes back to K. Pomeranz. 2000. *The Great Divergence. China, Europe, and the Making of the Modern World Economy,* Princeton/NJ: Princeton University Press, and R. B. Wong. 2002. 'The Search for European Differences and Domination in the Early Modern World: A View from Asia', *American Historical Review* 107, 447–69. See also the critical contributions of P. Vries. 2003. *Via Peking Back to Manchester. Britain, the Industrial Revolution, and China,* Leiden: CNWS Publications; S. Broadberry and B. Gupta. 2006. 'The Early Modern Great Divergence: Wages, Prices and Economic Development in Europe and Asia', *Economic History Review* 59, 2–31; P. K. O'Brien. 2006. 'The Divergence Debate. Europe and China 1368–1846', in G. Budde et al. (eds), *Transnationale Geschichte. Themen, Tendenzen und Theorien,* Göttingen: Vandenhoeck and Ruprecht, 68–82.
4. Data from S. King and G. Timmins. 2001. *Making Sense of the Industrial Revolution. English Economy and Society,* Manchester: Manchester University Press, 51. See also M. Fores. 1981. 'The Myth of a British Industrial Revolution', *History* 66, 191; Field, A. J. 1985. 'On the Unimportance of Machinery', *Explorations in Economic History* 22, 378–401, as well as the studies by A. E. Musson. 1976. 'Industrial Motive Power in the United Kingdom, 1800–70', *Economic History Review* 29, 415–39, and G. N. von Tunzelmann. 1978. *Steam Power and British Industrialization to 1860,* Oxford: Clarendon Press.
5. For a summary of the state of the research, see King and Timmins, *Making Sense of the Industrial Revolution,* as well as P. K. O'Brien. 2000. 'The Reconstruction, Rehabilitation and Reconfiguration of the British Industrial Revolution as a Conjuncture in Global History', *Itinerario* 24, 117–34.
6. The volume by T. Pirker et al. (eds). 1987. *Technik und industrielle Revolution. Vom Ende eines sozialwissenschaftlichen Paradigmas,* Opladen: Westdeutscher Verlag, represents an exception to this.
7. For an overview, see W. Abelshauser. 2006. 'Von der Industriellen Revolution zur Neuen Wirtschaft. Der Paradigmenwechsel im wirtschaftlichen Weltbild der Gegenwart', in J. Osterhammel et al. (eds), *Wege der Gesellschaftsgeschichte,* Göttingen: Vandenhoeck and Ruprecht, 201–18; G. Kneer et al. (eds). 1997. *Soziologische Gesellschaftsbegriffe. Konzepte moderner Zeitdiagnosen,* Paderborn: Fink/UTB.
8. M. Weber. 1976. *Wirtschaft und Gesellschaft. Grundriß der verstehenden Soziologie,* Studienausgabe, 5th ed., Tübingen: Mohr, 382–85. An English translation is available in M. Weber. 1999. Essays in Economic Sociology, R. Swedberg (ed.), Princeton: Princeton University Press, 75–79, quotation 75. On the development of Weber's terminology with regard to *Marktvergesellschaftung,* see K. Lichtblau. 2000. '"Vergemeinschaftung" und "Vergesellschaftung" bei Max Weber: eine Rekonstruktion seines Sprachgebrauchs', *Zeitschrift für Soziologie* 29, 434.
9. Cf. D. C. North. 1988. *Theorie des institutionellen Wandels,* Tübingen: Mohr, 35; also V. A. Zelizer. 1988. 'Beyond the Polemics of the Market: Establishing a Theoretical and Empirical Agenda', *Sociological Forum* 3(4), 614 ff.; V. Vanberg. 2001. 'Markets and the Law', in *Interna-*

tional Encyclopedia of the Social and Behavioral Sciences, vol. 14, N. J. Smelser and P. B. Baltes (eds), Amsterdam: Elsevier, 9223.

10. This assessment of the chronological development is accepted even by authors who focus on the topic of foreign trade and thus generally have a higher estimation of its importance; see especially P. K. O'Brien. 1999. 'Imperialism and the Rise and Decline of the British Economy, 1688–1989', *New Left Review* 208, 53–57, 62; S. Pincus. 2009. *1688. The First Modern Revolution,* New Haven: Yale University Press, 82–83. For a survey of works relevant to this topic, see J. Mokyr. 1999. 'Editor's Introduction: The New Economic History and the Industrial Revolution', in idem (ed.), *The British Industrial Revolution. An Economic Perspective,* Boulder/Co: Westview Press, 67–75.

11. The formulation 'British-based' derives from S. Chapman. 1992. *Merchant Enterprise in Britain. From the Industrial Revolution to World War I,* Cambridge: Cambridge University Press, who was the first to refer to the international character of London as a centre of trade. See also D. Hancock. 1995. *Citizens of the World. London Merchants and the Integration of the British Atlantic Community, 1735–85,* Cambridge: Cambridge University Press; M. Schulte Beerbühl. 2007. *Deutsche Kaufleute in London. Welthandel und Einbürgerung (1660–1818),* Munich: Oldenbourg, 64–74.

12. The percentages are based on R. B. Westerfield. 1968. *Middlemen in English Business Particularly Between 1660–1760,* New Haven/CT: Yale University Press. 1915, Reprint New York: David and Charles Reprints, 123–24, and P. K. O'Brien. 1998. 'Inseparable Connections: Trade, Economy, Fiscal State, and the Expansion of Empire, 1688–1815', in P. J. Marshall and A. Low (eds), *The Eighteenth Century* (= The Oxford History of the British Empire), Oxford: Oxford University Press, 53–54. See also J. A. Chartres. 1977. *Internal Trade in England 1500–1700,* London: Longman, 9–12, as well as L. Gomes. 1987. *Foreign Trade and the National Economy. Mercantilist and Classical Perspectives,* London: Macmillan, 76–77. By 1825 the proportion of foreign trade as a share of general trade grew to approximately 25 per cent; see J. Mokyr. 1984. 'The Industrial Revolution and the New Economic History', in J. Mokyr (ed.), *The Economics of the Industrial Revolution,* Totowa/N.J.: Rowman and Allanheld, 21. Many authors who study the connection between industrialization and empire base their calculations on the impressive growth rates of the late eighteenth century, without taking the absolute numbers into account. The significance of the domestic market is therefore frequently underestimated, as, unlike with foreign trade, no customs records of the prices and amounts of goods traded domestically were kept.

13. D. Defoe. 1726 (1725). *The Complete English Tradesman, in Familiar Letters; Directing Him in all the Several Parts and Progressions of Trade,* London, 387. Adam Smith, according to whom foreign trade led exclusively to a slowing of the speed of capital circulation, shared this perception; see 1981 (1776). *An Inquiry into the Nature and Causes of the Wealth of Nations,* R. H. Campbell and A. S. Skinner (eds), vol. 1, Indianapolis/IN: Liberty Fund, 388–401.

14. Dahrendorf refers to the sociological significance of ligatures; see his 1991. 'Die offene Gesellschaft und ihre Ängste', in W. Zapf (ed.) for the Deutsche Gesellschaft für Soziologie, *Die Modernisierung moderner Gesellschaften. Verhandlungen des 25. Deutschen Soziologentages in Frankfurt am Main 1990,* Frankfurt/Main: Campus, 140–50. See also R. Dahrendorf. 1994. 'Das Zerbrechen der Ligaturen und die Utopie der Weltbürgergesellschaft', in U. Beck and E. Beck-Gernsheim (eds), *Riskante Freiheiten. Individualisierung in modernen Gesellschaften,* Frankfurt/Main: Suhrkamp, 421–36.

15. Smith. 1981 (1976). Inquiry, vol. 1, 456. See also M. Streissler's introductory chapter to her German translation of *The Wealth of Nations* (*Untersuchung über Wesen und Ursachen des Reichtums der Völker,* Tübingen: Mohr Siebeck), 15–16.

16. G. Simmel referred to this issue in his 2004 (1900). *The Philosophy of Money,* trans. T. Bottomore and D. Frisby, 3rd ed., London: Routledge, 124–25. See also the comments by P. von

Flotow and J. Schmidt. 2003. 'Die 'Doppelrolle des Geldes' bei Simmel und ihre Bedeutung für Ökonomie und Soziologie', in O. Rammstedt (ed.), *Georg Simmels Philosophie des Geldes. Aufsätze und Materialien,* Frankfurt/Main: Suhrkamp, 63.

17. See M. M. Postan. 1944. 'The Rise of a Money Economy', *Economic History Review* 14, 126–27; G. Davies, 2002. *History of Money. From Ancient Times to the Present Day,* Cardiff: University of Wales Press, 113–75. For a concise survey, see G. Ingham. 2004. *The Nature of Money,* Cambridge: Polity, 89–106.

18. An impression of this is conveyed in the volume by J. Crick and E. van Houts (eds). 2011. *A Social History of England, 900–1200,* Cambridge: Cambridge University Press; see especially the contribution by R. H. Britnell. 2011. 'Commerce and Markets', in J. Crick and E. van Houts (eds), *A Social History of England, 900–1200,* Cambridge: Cambridge University Press, 179–87.

19. This demand was expressed by C. P. Kindleberger. 1975. 'Commercial Expansion and the Industrial Revolution', *Journal of European Economic History* 4, 613–53, back in 1975.

20. It should be noted at this point that K. Polanyi's book *The Great Transformation* (1944), which also deals with English history, does not preempt the present study, although it has on various occasions been referred to in the literature as a model study on commercialization processes. After all, Polyani's treatment only begins with the onset of the Industrial Revolution, which, writing before the boom in modern economic and social history, he condemns one-sidedly as a 'Satanic mill' that 'grounds men into masses'. Furthermore, Polyani's aim was not to reconstruct commercialization as an historical process but rather to arrive at a comprehensive explanation for the collapse of the nineteenth-century liberal economic order in the interwar years. On the perception of Polyani in the historiography, see J. Tanner. 2004. 'Die ökonomische Handlungstheorie vor der 'kulturalistischen Wende'? Perspektiven und Probleme einer interdisziplinären Diskussion', in H. Berghoff and J. Vogel (eds), *Wirtschaftsgeschichte als Kulturgeschichte. Dimensionen eines Perspektivenwechsels,* Frankfurt/Main: Campus, 76 ff.

21. Such an overburdening would be inevitable, as Pomeranz, Vries, Wong and other participants in the divergence debate operate with a neoclassical definition of the market, which, for the above-mentioned reasons, is out of the question for this long-term study. Directly comparative statements would render it necessary to make blanket and misleading 'translations'.

22. S. N. Eisenstadt. 1966. *Modernization. Protest and Change,* Englewood Cliffs: Prentice Hall, 67.

23. Cf. D. Cohen and M. O'Connor. 2004. 'Introduction: Comparative History, Cross-National History, Transnational History – Definitions', in D. Cohen and M. O'Connor (eds), *Comparison and History. Europe in Cross-National Perspective,* London: Macmillan, IX-XXIV; C. Conrad. 2006. 'Vergleich und Transnationalität in der Geschichte', in A. Wirsching (ed.), *Oldenbourg Geschichte Lehrbuch: Neueste Zeit,* Munich: Oldenbourg, 317–32.

24. H.-C. Schröder. 1977. 'Die neuere englische Geschichte im Lichte einiger Modernisierungstheoreme', in R. Koselleck (ed.), *Studien zum Beginn der modernen Welt,* Stuttgart: Klett, 32–43. In the later stages of the debate about England's 'special path', this question was no longer relevant; see H. Wellenreuther. 1992. 'England und Europa. Überlegungen zum Problem des englischen Sonderwegs in der europäischen Geschichte', in N. Finzsch (ed.), *Liberalitas: Festschrift für Erich Angermann zum 65. Geburtstag,* Stuttgart: Steiner, 89–123; B. Weisbrod. 1990. 'Der englische "Sonderweg" in der neueren Geschichte', *Geschichte und Gesellschaft* 16, 233–52.

25. K. Marx and F. Engels. 2012 (1848). The *Communist Manifesto,* introduced by E. Hobsbawm, London: Verso, 38.

26. Cf. J. Habermas. 1998. 'Konzeptionen der Moderne. Ein Rückblick auf zwei Traditionen', in J. Habermas, *Die postnationale Konstellation,* Frankfurt: Suhrkamp, 226–31. J. Hirsch unfurls the argument in 1976. *Social Limits to Growth,* Cambridge, MA: Harvard University Press.

27. Cf. E. Hobsbawm and T. Ranger (eds). 1983. *The Invention of Tradition,* Cambridge: Cambridge University Press, as well as the explicit rejection of the German view of things, e.g., by C. Crouch in 1993. 'Co-operation and Competition in an Institutional Economy: the Case of Germany', in C. Crouch and D. Marquand (eds), *Ethics and Markets, Co-operation and Competition within Capitalist Economies,* Oxford: Blackwell, 98.

28. 'Commerce cures destructive prejudices, and it is an almost general rule that everywhere there are gentle mores, there is commerce and that everywhere there is commerce, there are gentle mores.' C. L. de Secondat Baron de Montesquieu. 1989. *The Spirit of the Laws,* ed. A. Cohler et al., Cambridge: Cambridge University Press, 338.

29. Cf. A. O. Hirschman. 1977. *The Passions and the Interests: Political Arguments for Capitalism before its Triumph,* Princeton: Princeton University Press, 60, as well as – as proxies for a discussion that has by now garnered considerable attention – J. G. A. Pocock. 1985. *Virtue, Commerce, and History. Essays on Political Thought and History, Chiefly in the Eighteenth Century,* Cambridge: Cambridge University Press; I. Hont and M. Ignatieff (eds). 1983. *Wealth and Virtue: The Shaping of Political Economy in the Scottish Enlightenment,* Cambridge: Cambridge University Press; N. McKendrick et al. 1982. *The Birth of a Consumer Society. The Commercialization of Eighteenth-Century England,* London: Hutchinson. For the American discussion, which has been influenced by this literature, see P. Nolte. 1997. 'Der Markt und seine Kultur – ein neues Paradigma der amerikanischen Geschichte?', *Historische Zeitschrift* 264, 329–60.

30. W. Sombart. 2001. *The Jews and Modern Capitalism,* Kitchener/Ontario: Batoche Books, 46. The essay from which this quotation originally derives, 'Die Kommerzialisierung des Wirtschaftslebens' (1910), which with some slight changes was incorporated into the execrable work *The Jews and Modern Capitalism,* did not even convince contemporaries; see F. Lenger. 1994. *Werner Sombart 1863–1914. Eine Biographie,* Munich: Beck, 193.

31. See the programmatic essay by M. Granovetter. 1985. 'Economic Action and Social Structure. The Problem of Embeddedness', *American Journal of Sociology* 91, 481–510, as well as the compilation of relevant literature in idem and R. Swedberg (eds). 2001. *The Sociology of Economic Life,* 2nd ed., Boulder, CO: Westview Press; N. Smelser and R. Swedberg (eds). 2005. *The Handbook of Economic Sociology,* 2nd ed., Princeton/NJ: Princeton University Press, and N. W. Biggart (ed.). 2002. *Readings in Economic Sociology,* Oxford: Blackwell. On the context within which this research emerged, see B. Convert and J. Heilbron. 2007. 'Where Did the New Economic Sociology Come From?', *Theory and Society* 36, 31–54. Polyani elaborates on the above-mentioned essay in his 1944 book *The Great Transformation,* New York: Rinehart; see also C. Hann and K. Hart (eds). 2009. 'Market and Society: *The Great Transformation* Today', Cambridge: Cambridge University Press. An overview of the development of the discussion can be found in H. Berghoff and J. Vogel. 2004. 'Wirtschaftsgeschichte als Kulturgeschichte. Ansätze zur Bergung transdisziplinärer Synergiepotentiale', in H. Berghoff and J. Vogel (eds). *Wirtschaftsgeschichte als Kulturgeschichte. Dimensionen eines Perspektivenwechsels,* Frankfurt/Main: Campus, 9–41, and the other contributions to the volume; also see J. Tanner. 2004. '"Kultur" in den Wirtschaftswissenschaften und kulturwissenschaftliche Interpretationen ökonomischen Handelns', in F. Jaeger and J. Rüsen (eds), *Handbuch der Kulturwissenschaften. Themen und Tendenzen,* vol. 3, Stuttgart: J.B. Metzler, 195–224. Swedberg traces the development from an economic historical perspective in 'Major Traditions of Economic Sociology', *Annual Review of Sociology* 17, 251–76.

32. See, for example, M. Bevir and F. Trentmann (eds). 2004. *Markets in Historical Contexts: Ideas and Politics in the Modern World,* Cambridge: Cambridge University Press; W. M. Reddy. 1984. *The Rise of Market Culture. The Textile Trade and French Society, 1750–1900,* Cambridge: Cambridge University Press; D. Margairaz and P. Minard. 2006. 'Le marché dans son histoire', *Revue de synthèse* 5(127), 241–52.

33. The relevant volume of K.-G. Faber and C. Meier (eds). 1978. *Historische Prozesse,* Munich:

Deutscher Taschenbuch Verlag already proved disappointing in this respect, and little of sub-stance has been written on the subject since. Tellingly, S. Jordan's *Lexikon Geschichtswissenschaft* (Stuttgart: Reclam), which appeared in 2002, contains no entry on 'processes'. On this issue, also see T. Welskopp. 2002. 'Die Theoriefähigkeit der Geschichtswissenschaft', in R. Mayntz (ed.), *Akteure – Mechanismen – Modelle. Zur Theoriefähigkeit makro-sozialer Analysen*, Frank-furt/Main: Campus, 66–72. Nor does the field of historical sociology have much more to offer than a general structuring into 'duration', 'pace', 'trajectories' and 'cycles'; see R. Aminzade. 1992. 'Historical Sociology and Time', *Sociological Method and Research* 20, 456–80. One of the few productive contributions is P. Ridder's essay 'Kinetische Analyse historischer Prozesse. Modellfall Gesundheitssystem', *Historical Social Research* 25, 49–72; also see his 'Messung sozialer Prozesse', *Soziale Welt* 17, 144–61.

34. The concept derives from P. A. David's essay, 'Clio and the Economics of QWERTY', *American Economic Review* 75, 332–37. On the recent discussion, J. Beyer. 2006. *Pfadabhängigkeit. Über institutionelle Kontinuität, anfällige Stabilität und fundamentalen Wandel*, Frankfurt/Main: Campus, 11–40.

35. On the limits of modernization theories, see T. Mergel. 1997. 'Geht es weiterhin voran? Die Modernisierungstheorie auf dem Weg zu einer Theorie der Moderne', in T. Mergel and T. Welskopp (eds), *Geschichte zwischen Kultur und Gesellschaft. Beiträge zur Theoriedebatte*, Munich: Beck, 203–32.

36. The contributions go back to 1945 at the earliest; see P. A. Hall and D. Soskice (eds). 2001. *Varieties of Capitalism. The Institutional Foundations of Comparative Advantage*, Oxford: Oxford University Press; V. Berghahn and S. Vitols (eds). 2006. *'Gibt es einen deutschen Kapitalismus?' Tradition und globale Perspektiven der sozialen Marktwirtschaft*, Frankfurt, Main: Campus. On the critique, see also C. Crouch. 2005. 'Models of Capitalism', *New Political Economy* 10, 439–56.

37. See E. M. Wood. 2002. *The Origins of Capitalism. A Longer View*, London: Verso; J. Fulcher, 2004. *Kapitalismus*, Stuttgart: Reclam. I. Wallerstein's presentation is also based on this bold (and mistaken) conclusion; see his 1983. *Historical Capitalism*, London: Verso, 13: 'Capitalism is first and foremost a historical social system. To understand its origin, … we have to look at its existing reality.'

38. Cf. W. Sombart. 1915. *Händler und Helden. Patriotische Besinnungen*, Leipzig: Duncker and Humblot, as well as the relevant passages on the disappearance of the 'heroic' due to modern 'commercialism' in idem. 1988 (1913). *Der Bourgeois. Zur Geistesgeschichte des modernen Wirt-schaftsmenschen*, Reprint, Reinbek: Rowohlt, 343 ff.; see also idem. 1969 (1916). *Der moderne Kapitalismus. Historisch-systematische Darstellung des gesamteuropäischen Wirtschaftslebens von seinen Anfängen bis zur Gegenwart*, vol. 2/2, Berlin: Duncker and Humblot, 922–23.

39. Cf. R. Biernacki. 2001. 'Labor as an Imagined Commodity', *Politics and Society* 29, 173–206, and Pollard. 1983. 'England: Der unrevolutionäre Pionier', in J. Kocka (ed.), *Europäische Arbeiterbewegungen im 19. Jahrhundert*, Göttingen: Vandenhoeck and Ruprecht, 21–22.

40. Cf. D. Sugarman, D. 1997. 'In the Spirit of Weber: Law, Modernity and the "Peculiarities of the English"', in C. Peterson (ed.), *History and European Private Law. Development of Common Methods and Principles*, Lund: Institutet for Rättshistorisk Forskning Grandat av Gustav och Carin Olin, 219–20, 251; R. Swedberg. 1998. *Max Weber and the Idea of Economic Sociology*, Princeton, NJ: Princeton University Press, 83, 105–07; D. d'Avray. 2008. 'Roman Law and Common Law: Medieval England and Germany' in Weber's *Wirtschaft und Gesellschaft*, in M.-L. Heckmann and J. Röhrkasten (eds), *Von Nowgorod bis London. Studien zu Handel, Wirt-schaft und Gesellschaft im mittelalterlichen Europa. Festschrift für Stuart Jenks zum 60. Geburts-tag*, Göttingen: Vandenhoeck and Ruprecht, 343–57.

41. W. Sombart. 1910. 'Die Kommerzialisierung des Wirtschaftslebens', *Archiv für Sozialwissen-schaft und Sozialpolitik* 30, 631.

42. See, as a proxy, R. Britnell. 1996. *The Commercialisation of English Society 1000–1500,* 2nd ed., Manchester: Manchester University Press; M. Bailey. 1998. 'Historiographical Essay: The Commercialisation of the English Economy, 1086–1500', *Journal of Medieval History* 24, 297–311; McKendrick et al., *Birth of a Consumer Society.*

43. For this reason Max Weber found Simmel's presentation of the money economy to be 'unhistorical'; see D. Frisby. 1988. 'Die Ambiguität der Moderne: Max Weber und Georg Simmel', in W. J. Mommsen and W. Schwentker (eds), *Max Weber und seine Zeitgenossen,* Göttingen: Vandenhoeck and Ruprecht, 580–94, 585 ff.

44. 'There's a lot of talk about their embeddedness without really talking about markets themselves. … I thought you could leave out the word 'market' almost entirely, and it would not take one iota away from your analysis.' Contribution by J. Hall to a discussion during a symposium on the 'New Economic Sociology'; see G. Krippner et al. 2004. 'Polanyi Symposium: a Conversation on Embeddedness', *Socio-Economic Review* 2, 128.

45. F. Nietzsche. 1997. *On the Genealogy of Morality,* ed. K. Ansell-Pearson, trans. C. Diethe, Cambridge: Cambridge University Press, 53.

46. An example of the closing of a market would be the legal banning of child labour. The terminology references F. Block. 1994. 'The Roles of the State in the Economy', in N. Smelser and R. Swedberg (eds), *The Handbook of Economic Sociology,* Princeton/NJ: Princeton University Press, 697–98.

47. According to the current state of research, the much-cited laissez-faire state appears to be a nineteenth-century development; cf. P. Harling and P. Mandler. 1993. 'From "Fiscal-Military" State to Laissez-faire State, 1760–1850', *Journal of British Studies* 32, 44–70. See also the general discussion of the role of the state in connection with the 'embedding' of markets in Block, 'Roles of the State'.

48. I subscribe to the assessment of the economic historian R. Grassby on these and other 'gurus': '[N]one of their works are reliable as histories and they now have mainly antiquarian interest as tracts for their times'. *The Idea of Capitalism before the Industrial Revolution,* Lanham/MD: Rowman and Littlefield, 76. See also the well-informed and ultimately devastating discussion of Braudel and Wallerstein in D. Ormrod. 2003. *The Rise of Commercial Empires. England and the Netherlands in the Age of Mercantilism, 1650–1770,* Cambridge: Cambridge University Press, 4–7.

49. Cf. J. Kocka. 1996. 'Annäherung und neue Distanz. Historiker und Sozialwissenschaftler seit den fünfziger Jahren', in M. Hettling and P. Nolte (eds), *Nation und Gesellschaft in Deutschland. Historische Essays,* Munich: Beck, 15–31; R. Floud and P. Thane. 2005. 'Sociology and History: Partnership, Rivalry, or Mutual Incomprehension?', in A. H. Halsey and W. G. Runciman (eds), *British Sociology. Seen from Without and Within,* Oxford: The British Academy by Oxford University Press, 57–69.

50. Cf. R. R. Davies' 1990 and 2000 studies *Domination and Conquest. The Experience of Ireland, Scotland and Wales 1100–1300,* Cambridge: Cambridge University Press and *The First English Empire. Power and Identities in the British Isles 1093–1343,* Oxford: Oxford University Press, do not answer the question, nor do S. Duffy. 2003. 'The British Perspective', in S. H. Rigby, *A Companion to Britain in the Later Middle Ages,* Oxford: Blackwell, 165–82, or K. E. Wrightson. 1989. 'Kindred Adjoining Kingdoms: An English Perspective on the Social and Economic History of Early Modern Scotland', in R. A. Houston and D. Whyte (eds), *Scottish Society 1500–1800,* Cambridge: Cambridge University Press, 245–60. On the relationship between 'English' and 'British' history more generally, see D. Cannadine. 1995. 'British History as a "New Subject"', in A. Grant and K. J. Stringer (eds), *Uniting the Kingdom? The Making of British History,* London: Routledge, 12–28, and C. Harvie. 1994. '"These Islands" und ihre Nationen: Das Dilemma "britischer" Geschichte', *Blätter für deutsche Landesgeschichte* 130, 49–63.

Chapter 1

MEDIEVAL FOUNDATIONS OF
MARKET EXCHANGE

As late as the 1970s and 1980s, the dominant opinion in economic history was still that England's early modern upturn had been preceded by a stagnating medieval economy. Significant social changes had not taken place, productivity had been low, and most of the rural population had laboured for their own subsistence.[1] These assumptions have proven to be unfounded; rather, during the High Middle Ages, the English economy experienced a considerable upswing. In the area of agriculture, efforts were made for the first time to coordinate farming and livestock breeding, regional specialization developed, and the population grew. In a parallel development, the number of both cities and their residents rose, as did the price of labour, land and capital. Against this background, the amount of money in circulation increased, and a rudimentary system of credit developed.[2] The trans-European plague epidemic of 1348/49 interrupted this development only temporarily.

One can observe similar processes at this time on the European continent. However, it is clear that the demographic and economic crises caused by the plague in the mid-fourteenth century were overcome more quickly and easily in England than in the north, south or west of Europe (with the exception of the Netherlands).[3] In England, the plague-related labour shortage led to permanent wage increases despite the fact that the collapse of the system of bonded labour towards the end of the fourteenth century added a great number of new workers to the workforce. A further indication that the crisis was successfully overcome was that landowners gave some of their former bondsmen posts and entrusted them with administrative duties, with the effect that knowledge of trade, laws and management methods were further spread.[4] The sustainability of the postpestilential upswing is attested to not least by the observation that while extraction

---

Notes from this chapter begin on page 35.

methods remained the same, coal production steadily increased into the sixteenth century due solely to the fact the additional demand for it existed.[5]

These findings give us occasion to suspect that in England, communication structures and behavioural routines were in place that enabled contemporaries to take advantage of economic changes flexibly and productively. Two observations underline this assumption and simultaneously point to possible explanations.

For one, with the exception of London, English cities – in comparison with southern Germany and northern Italy, for example – had relatively small populations of about five thousand inhabitants, a particularity that can be explained not only in terms of the relative unimportance of foreign trade at that time, but also and above all of the high level of market integration locally. Unlike in Germany, where cities were isolated 'islands' amidst the surrounding countryside that '[raised] themselves above the general barter economy', to quote the historian Georg Brodnitz from a 1914 publication, English cities were market locations engaged in brisk trade with the equally market-oriented rural areas. If they wanted to survive as 'centres of economic exchange', they had to respond to impulses from the surrounding countryside.[6]

For another, one could argue that already with the Norman Invasion in the eleventh century, a specific form of feudalism developed in England that was more encouraging of the emergence of market-supported (and therefore flexible) trade than were the comparable governance and economic structures on the European continent. In the following, this English type of feudalism shall be discussed at greater length, since it is safe to assume that it created the preconditions for the formation and establishment of processes of commercialization.[7]

Both particularities – the size of English cities and their feudal governance structures – were interrelated, and both developed in the wake of the political upheavals triggered by the Norman Invasion of 1066.

Institutions and Law

After his victory at the Battle of Hastings, William the Conqueror, Duke of Normandy, not only made England into a colony of the West Frankish Kingdom, but also into a uniformly occupied territory. In contrast to comparable invasions by the Normans elsewhere in Europe, for example in Sicily or the Kiev region, there was no cooperation with the old ruling elites. Rather, in subsequent battles of conquest, William liquidated or drove out nearly all of the four thousand to five thousand members of the Anglo-Saxon aristocracy. He divided the conquered territory up among 189 of his followers, whom he elevated to the status of lords and upon whom he imposed tax duties and military service obligations.[8]

These feudal obligations might in themselves be an extension of the Anglo-Saxon tradition; the experts are not of one mind on this point. The centralist administration of the new state, which was tailored to the King, can, however, be regarded as an innovation in terms of governance, even if on the local level, the old Anglo-Saxon administrative organization into 'shires' and 'hundreds' was preserved.[9] In all of the shires, William and his successors set up courts of law. As local office holders, the aldermen represented the King's interests, while the sheriffs and bailiffs served as the forces of order. The King's Court, established in the early thirteenth century as the central court of law, was responsible for major cases. A central tax authority, the Exchequer, received the account statements and earnings of the King's agents from all corners of the empire and audited them. In the Chancery, official state documents were issued and stored. Such writs documented, among other things, the modalities of tax collection and the changes in the distribution of land ownership.[10] Cities had a subordinate status within this centralized system. Neither military nor political competencies were granted to them by the King or his successors.[11]

The new state was stable: the emergence of dynasties, with the associated subdivision of territories into ever-smaller sovereignties observable elsewhere in Europe, did not take place here. This was surely due in part to England's literal insularity, which offered a certain measure of protection from invasion, as well as to the modest size of the territory, which made internal integration easier. Thus it was possible for the King and his travelling judges to regularly visit all parts of the country, despite the difficult conditions of travel in the Middle Ages.[12] However, there were also other small dominions in Europe, e.g., Scotland and Sicily, that did not achieve as high a degree of integration as England. This speaks in favour of regarding the early development of a unitary state and the associated monopoly of power by the King as particular stabilising factors.

Within the framework of the present study, this thoroughgoing centralism is relevant primarily because it gave the

Figure 1.1. Coin of William of Conqueror, 1068.

country a considerable push towards commercialization. Of foremost significance is the side effect that it resulted in the creation a contiguous economic and juridical area without any significant internal tariffs[13] and that free persons could, with the aid of royal justice and of professional legal experts, take action against swindlers, bankrupts, bad debtors and contract breakers. By 1362, they could even do so in the vernacular tongue, as English became the official language of justice in that year.[14] Furthermore, in a continuation of Anglo-Saxon conventions, unitary weights and measures as well as a single currency were used. The

Normans gradually replaced the old penny coins with ones of sterling silver, and thenceforth value was measured in pounds sterling.[15]

Secondly, William the Conqueror and his successors introduced a reorganization of the market for agricultural land. As this market calls for a state framework, one could presumably even say that they 'introduced' this type of market. The lords were permitted to sell the use rights to the land allotted to them to anyone they chose, or to purchase or lease land, so long as no contiguous territories resulted that might have called into question the direct dominion of the King. As is documented in the famous *Domesday Book* (1086), which William commissioned to gain and maintain an overview of the distribution of property and to avoid a concentration of acreage in the hands of individuals, the number of land-holders had grown to several thousand within twenty years of the Conquest.[16] When the King's Court placed the purchasers of land, the so-called freemen, under its jurisdiction in the course of the thirteenth century so that they could emancipate themselves from the lords by means of royal writs and then work the land as they pleased, the number of market participants increased once again.[17]

Thirdly, the institutionalization of a land market gave impetus to the capital market. Land could henceforth stand as a security, and in turn loans were entered into to purchase land. Furthermore, feudal dues and leaseholds were generally rendered in cash, and for this, as well, it was often necessary to borrow money.[18]

Fourthly, the Crown monopoly on foreign currency trading – yet another aspect of royal centralism – favoured the early and universal establishment of a credit system. That the Royal Exchanger and his functionaries rigorously confiscated coins in foreign currencies to take them to the Tower Mint to be melted down and reminted as sterling coins contributed significantly to the English peculiarity that neither deposit banks nor a system of monetary trading, which elsewhere in Europe emerged out of currency trading in the Middle Ages, were founded. Instead, in England – and at this early point in time only there – bills of exchange, bonds and other commercial papers were acknowledged in payment transactions.[19] While such papers did carry a certain amount of risk, they had the advantage that they were transferable and could be freely reproduced independently of the right of coinage. This increased the range and speed of capital circulation, reduced the loss of value through currency exchange and averted the necessity of the risk-laden transport of coins. Furthermore, it helped circumvent the church ban on interest, as bills of exchange allowed the interest on borrowings to appear as a fee or to be hidden in the exchange rate. Above all, however, in view of the notorious shortage of coins in the Middle Ages, the economy of bills of exchange increased the number of market actors and the volume of transactions. As Matthew Rowlinson notes, it also stimulated professional trading because it 'sets a price not only on the abstractions of time and place, but also on that of money itself'.[20]

That a society of owners and acquisition emerged out of the system of 'distributive feudalism' (*Verteilungsfeudalismus,* Günther Lottes) was an effect of, rather than the motivation behind, the state-building efforts of William the Conqueror and his successors. What was of primary concern to these kings was the securing of their rule and the assurance of the cooperation of the lords that this demanded.[21] The former could never, however, be entirely certain of the latter's loyalty, and this led to further measures of enforcing their sovereignty, which had commercial side effects.

The financial side of rule was comparatively unproblematic. It was possible where necessary to enforce the collection of agricultural dues and taxes directly from all tax-paying subjects so as to reduce the financial dependence of the King upon the lords.[22] With respect to military service, however, such (precautionary) measures were not so easy to implement, as the troops led by the lords could abandon the battlefield at any time. The solution to the problem consisted for the King in replacing military service requirements with shield money (also known as scutage) and, in times of war, hiring armies of mercenaries – a measure that was apparently motivated by the experience that '[o]f all demands, the demand for money is the demand whose fulfilment is the least dependent on the good will of the obligated person' (Georg Simmel).[23] This step towards the submission of the relationship of dependence between the King and his lords under the cash nexus, which already took place in the twelfth century and was then reaffirmed in the fourteenth century, was described by the medievalist K.B. McFarlane as the transition to 'bastard feudalism'.[24] The negative connotations of the term refer to the associated emergence of a purely civilian class of rentiers devoted to wealth and pompous display – in a certain sense, the forerunners of the gentry – who were bound to the King as the highest feudal lord only through an impersonal contract.

The significance of this brand of feudalism for future historical development becomes clear when one calls to mind the much-cited formula of the legal historian Sir Henry Maine 'from status to contract'. It does not do justice to the English case outlined here. Maine had coined the phrase around 1860 to describe a centuries-long process that allegedly encompassed every country on earth. Later on, ennobled by the classical social-scientific theorists, it was to become a building block of social-scientific theories of modernization. However, the specificity of feudal rule in England consisted in the fact that both poles, 'status' and 'contract', were already part of the system in the Middle Ages and opened up new courses of action.[25] It is therefore not surprising that early on, the lords saw themselves as contract partners of the King and endeavoured to have the details of their obligations to him put down in writing. The Magna Carta, an agreement with some rebellious lords signed by King John in 1215, testifies to this.

Over time, the development towards written contracts also made itself felt in relations between the lords and their tenants. The King's Court served them as a conflict mediator and notary.[26] Several of these agreements also encompassed extra-economic service and fealty obligations, e.g., marriage authorizations for villeins. However, the military duties of the tenants towards the lord could not be the subject of a contract, nor could their performance be sworn to through an oath. In the centralized system of rule tailored to the King, such agreements would have been regarded as treason. The tenants and the common folk were allowed (and indeed obligated) to serve exclusively under royal officers – a clear breach of the feudal principle of layered obligations, which continued to develop on the European continent.[27] This characteristic reveals particularly clearly that in England, the feudal era ended scarcely after it had begun.[28]

That the landowning class of the lords was allowed to settle a large number of matters itself and yet was subject to a uniform, national law underlines this finding. This law was the Common Law.[29] It even applied to the King, who, while he may have stood above his subjects, was not above the law and in extreme cases might 'violate' it. In 1649, this global understanding of the law would contribute to Charles I being executed.[30]

While Common Law, which also applied in the English communities of Wales and Ireland and significantly influenced Scottish law, had been established under the reigns of Henry II (1154–1189) and Edward I (1272–1307) with the particular needs of the monarchy in mind, in some respects it represented a continuation of ancient Anglo-Saxon law. Roman law, which generally applied on the Continent, was adopted only selectively, having not yet been modernized or adapted to English conditions and thus not demanding serious consideration as an alternative.[31] As a result, over time, a number of deviations of English from Continental law took root, which would also prove significant for the economic development of England.

In particular, one specific formal quality of English law would have lasting effects. While Roman law was laid out systematically, Common Law was based on precedence. It opened up the possibility of honouring individual cases without having to apply overriding principles so as to promote unconventional solutions, experimentation and the autonomy of individual thought and behaviour. Against a background of upheavals in which economic and political conditions were rapidly changing and the extent to which previous experience could be drawn upon was limited, a procedurally orientated kind of law that also served as social practice was extraordinarily expedient. Moreover, it provided a high level of legal certainty, since the judges tended to pay scrupulous attention to judicial precedent.[32] The structural deficits of case law – its pronounced inability to dispose of outdated decisions and the increasing murkiness of the legal situation associated with this[33] – would not, at this early stage in the development of Common Law, have been perceived as troublesome.

In terms of the content of the provisions, Common Law had implications above all for property relations. It stated that everyone – men, women and children – could own property. Even bondsmen could purchase and sell land subject to the consent of their lord.[34] Furthermore, with some kinds of property, be it in the form of land or moveable goods, certain use rights and duties were associated, which were binding even for the owner. Thus landless people had the right to graze their animals on land belonging to others, and landowners could collect fees from those wishing to enter or traverse their property. The former practice reduced the number of poor people, while the latter proved to be an effective incentive for the expansion of streets and canals and was an important precondition for the regional specialization of the production of goods and commodities in the late Middle Ages.[35]

A further characteristic of Common Law was its openness to individual arrangements in financial matters. Of primary importance here is 'merchant law' or *lex mercatoria,* which made it possible for merchants and other persons engaged in trade – Englishmen and foreigners alike – to pursue legal claims outside of the customary legal avenues. The framework conditions for trade having already been outlined in the Magna Carta in 1215, special staple courts for commercial dealings were set up in London and fifteen other port cities and market towns towards the end of the thirteenth century. Like all courts of law, they were subordinate to the King; nevertheless they practised a comparatively uncomplicated form of jurisprudence in which they dispensed with certain time-consuming procedures, such as the obligation to submit writs with the seal of the King. Instead, bills of exchange, obligations and the written agreements of the signatories (or their authorized agents) were accepted in evidence. Furthermore, consideration was paid to local customs.[36]

The *lex mercatoria* was therefore not a special body of law but rather an accelerated procedure for the settling of disputes between persons who, due to the nature of their commercial activity, could not afford to linger at the location in question. Although the jury was composed of half local and half foreign merchants, the courts privileged not the status of the merchant, as was customary elsewhere on the European continent, but rather trade dealings as such (thus *lex mercatoria,* not *ius mercatorum*).[37] Over four centuries, these accelerated procedures were an important precondition for unimpeded commercial activity; it was only in the late seventeenth century that the customs that had developed in their wake began to be codified, and it was only in 1765 that the commercial courts were integrated into the general jurisdiction of Common Law.

Like the *lex mercatoria,* the legal form of the trust also opened up the possibility for market participants to independently shape their contractual relations, and this possibility would also take on great practical significance in everyday life.[38] A landowner would entrust his land to a group of trustees, who were to administer it in his name but in the interest of a third party. At the same time, he named this third party – usually a person or group of persons who were supposed to be endowed by the trust with financial means – or he specified a particular purpose for which the funds were to be used. This gave property owners a way of de facto bequeathing their land, although this was actually forbidden until 1540 out of deference for the direct dominion of the King. Furthermore, they were able to avoid the charges that would accrue in the event of a bequest – a kind of inheritance tax – and circumvent certain provisions of the inheritance law that forbid them from leaving their property to more than one of their children. In this way, they could bequeath assets to illegitimate children or protect assets intended for a married daughter from being seized by her husband. Such regulations could endure because the group of trustees could replace members when they died.[39]

The legal form of the trust developed as far back as the fourteenth century. This is noteworthy because the trust emerged out of the transformation of a personal right into property law; that is, independently of the state and the King. It was therefore not a matter of a legal relationship of a contractual nature, nor of a corporation or a legal person that could have appointed itself a 'state within a state', as rulers on the Continent might have feared. In England, there were no fundamental problems with the recognition of trusts by the royal courts, and so they could spread more or less unimpededly.[40]

As free associations – which over time also developed on political, sociopolitical, religious and cultural terrain and were able to establish themselves on a long-term basis with their property in land, buildings and assets – trusts are seen as seeds of modern civil society in England.[41] This legal form has stood the test of time, not only in the administration of the assets that collectives and foundations such as the universities of Oxford and Cambridge have accumulated since the Middle Ages, but also in the modern financial world. For the separation of property and usufruct was, with the progressive commercialization of the economy, more and more frequently seen as a necessary framework for collective forms of enterprise outside of agriculture, which is why courts since the late seventeenth century were just as happy to accept trusts of money as trusts of land. Thus it is to some extent idle to investigate under what concrete circumstances legislators since the mid-nineteenth century agreed to codify the law of public or limited liability companies; for the issue had long since evolved on its own, and the multitudinous variations of the concrete organization of trusts served as a legal basis for corresponding agreements.[42]

Those path-breaking financial institutions that are described in greater detail below – the Bank of England, the London Stock Exchange and Lloyd's of London – also unquestionably developed within this legal form. They retained it for decades and even centuries, until some of them for a variety of reasons had themselves incorporated.[43]

Social Structure, Mobility and Social Relations

The rural social structure of the Kingdom of England differed fundamentally from that of other European societies. While on the Continent, in accordance with the general model of feudalism, property was a function of status, in England status resulted from property. The internal differentiation among aristocratic landowners also adhered to this pattern.[44] As a result, apart from the clergy, the rural social structure consisted for the most part of two social groups: landowners producing for the market (i.e., owners and tenants), on the one hand, and servants and landless farmworkers and wage labourers, on the other.

For the entire period of the Middle Ages, the numbers of landowners did not exceed twenty thousand persons. From the King at the top, there descended a hierarchy of roughly one thousand landowners from the aristocracy and the clergy, each one of whom owned less property and land than the King. According to estimates for the early fourteenth century, this small group accounted for nearly half of the total income from landownership. The other half was divided among some nineteen thousand smaller landowners. The majority of these belonged to the gentry, into the ranks of which wealthy townsmen had by this point already risen.[45] All of these owners cultivated one part of their land and leased the rest. In 1086, when the *Domesday Book* was compiled, the total number of tenants amounted to some 250,000 individuals. Initially, the majority of them were villeins. In the second half of the fourteenth century, when landowners had to compete for tenants, the number of villeins dropped, such that by around 1500 nearly all leaseholders were free 'copyhold' tenants. The process was only finally completed with the dissolution of the monasteries around 1540. And yet even the initially remaining villeins could freely engage in economic activity, for which reason some of them were able to accumulate greater wealth than were freemen. Their status merely prohibited them from taking legal action in the King's courts; they remained under the jurisdiction of their lords.[46]

The second group in the rural social structure – that of the farm and wage labourers – comprised the majority of those workers without whom the landowners and tenants could not have cultivated their land. Here, as well, there were villeins and free labourers, and the number of freemen increased greatly towards the end of the medieval era. As with the tenants, the reason for this was that the supply of labourers shrank after the Black Death of the mid-fourteenth century. The landowners were able to adjust to this because free labourers, being more highly motivated than the villeins, were considered preferable.[47] Furthermore, the monarchy made concessions to them by issuing laws and edicts that regulated and disciplined the market activity of the freemen and stigmatized self-interested behaviour.[48] To characterise the free labourers as a rural proletariat would, however, be premature. While it is true that the labourers largely belonged to the ranks of the landless, many of them – including farm hands, maidservants and stable boys – lived in the households of landowners, where their immediate needs were similarly provided for. Most of those who lived exclusively from wages were surplus labourers or the adult children of small tenant households, who had left their parents' home. These 'pure wage labourers' still constituted a minority at the end of the Middle Ages.[49]

A third group within the rural social structure, which one would anticipate based on knowledge of conditions on the Continent – namely that of free peasants cultivating their own land, with the family economy at the centre of production and consumption[50] – were, in contrast, quite rare, and their numbers grew even smaller over time. This is not due to the fact that England, as an island nation, did not require a large army but rather a navy, and therefore had no need to protect the peasantry, as previous generations of economic historians, e.g., Max Weber, have argued.[51] The decisive factors were rather that after 1066, more or less all of the land suitable for agriculture had already been divided up among the lords, and they preferred to deal with a smaller number of tenants.[52] Another determining factor was England's characteristically dense infrastructure of integrated regional markets.

This had developed since the second half of the thirteenth century, when the cash-strapped kings began in grand style to sell concessions for town and village markets to individuals, including monasteries and corporate entities – a move that in most other Continental European countries, where market law and municipal law were interconnected, would have been unthinkable. The minimum legal distance that had to be maintained between the more than one thousand new markets and the pre-existing ones, whose economic activity must not be impaired, was 6 2/3 miles. The market owners were obliged to collect consumer taxes for the King and, in exchange, were awarded monopoly rights. They derived revenue not only from the stand fees but also and above all through the collection of tolls. Hence they attempted to attract merchants from further afield, an ambition which, in view of the local and regional markets also developing elsewhere, did not signify a fundamental problem. As the transport of rural products from the surrounding villages to the towns – a distance that in many cases did not exceed twenty miles – was organized by merchants and their middlemen, even small rural producers without the time or means to bring their goods to market could integrate themselves into the economy. In this system, hardly anyone had to rely on subsistence agriculture.[53]

Without access to markets, small farmers could not have paid the taxes, annuities or penalties demanded of them by the landowners, which were to be rendered in cash. They would not have been able to purchase tools or other objects of everyday use, nor food items, upon which specialized enterprises were particularly dependent. The extent to which even small farmers thought in categories like supply and demand resulted from the willingness of at least the freemen among them to sell everything that they owned and relocate elsewhere if this seemed advantageous. And they did so even when this meant that family traditions would be broken and relatives could no longer be supported.[54]

Among the first scholars to reveal the noteworthy finding that already in the Middle Ages, England was to some extent a country without peasants was the anthropologist Alan Macfarlane in his original book *The Origins of English*

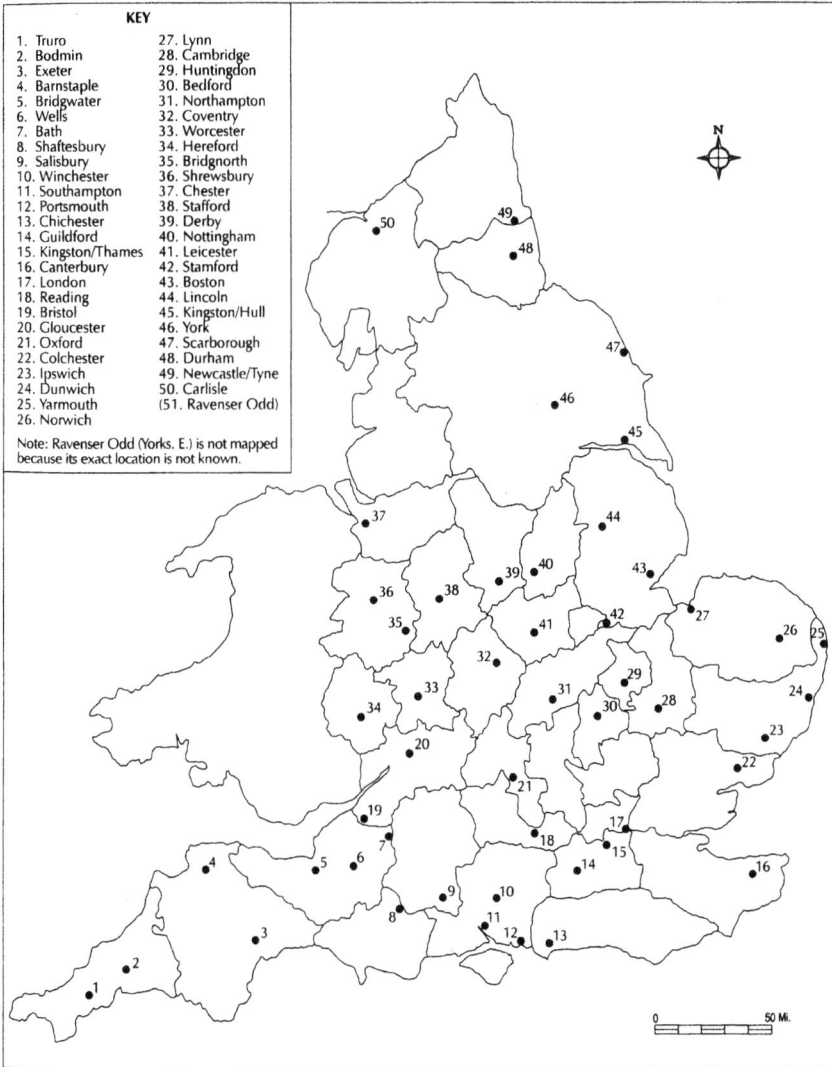

KEY

1. Truro	27. Lynn
2. Bodmin	28. Cambridge
3. Exeter	29. Huntingdon
4. Barnstaple	30. Bedford
5. Bridgwater	31. Northampton
6. Wells	32. Coventry
7. Bath	33. Worcester
8. Shaftesbury	34. Hereford
9. Salisbury	35. Bridgnorth
10. Winchester	36. Shrewsbury
11. Southampton	37. Chester
12. Portsmouth	38. Stafford
13. Chichester	39. Derby
14. Guildford	40. Nottingham
15. Kingston/Thames	41. Leicester
16. Canterbury	42. Stamford
17. London	43. Boston
18. Reading	44. Lincoln
19. Bristol	45. Kingston/Hull
20. Gloucester	46. York
21. Oxford	47. Scarborough
22. Colchester	48. Durham
23. Ipswich	49. Newcastle/Tyne
24. Dunwich	50. Carlisle
25. Yarmouth	(51. Ravenser Odd)
26. Norwich	

Note: Ravenser Odd (Yorks. E.) is not mapped because its exact location is not known.

Figure 1.2. Country towns as regional centres in England around 1300

Individualism (1978).[55] Initially this thesis met with massive criticism among medievalists and was only confirmed by a younger generation of social and economic historians. When, in these more recent studies, published since the 1990s, reference is made to 'peasants', this should not be seen as relativizing this finding. Rather, it is a concession to the traditional use of language among medievalists, which is based on a different understanding of the word. The researchers of the younger generation namely use this term to refer to land-poor subtenants, village tradesmen and both menial and casual labourers who derived additional income from supplemental agriculture work. Nevertheless, the fact remains that until the sixteenth century, the word 'peasant' was not in common use, and it was employed primarily to refer to conditions in foreign countries.[56]

Holders of use rights to common land are also classified by some medievalists as 'peasants'. This is problematic to the extent that in many parts of England around 1500, the 'common land' or 'common fields' available amounted to about one-third of all land used for agriculture[57] and hence were by no means 'no man's land' or commons in the convention sense. Rather these 'commons' were private property to which people other than the owners also enjoyed use rights. When property relations changed, as happened with increasing frequency in the sixteenth and seventeenth centuries as more and more enclosures were created, these use rights were lost without compensation to the rights holders, and those cottagers who had previously been permitted to graze their animals on the commons were deprived of their livelihoods but not of their property. Against this background, it should not be surprising that in the mental status hierarchy of sixteenth- and seventeenth-century contemporaries, the term 'peasant' no longer figured.[58]

Despite the (viewed from this perspective) relatively undifferentiated social hierarchy in the countryside, the population acquired a considerable degree of social mobility. After all, not only wage labourers but also landowners and tenants were vulnerable to economic cycles, poor harvests and other factors affecting the relationship between supply and demand on the markets: the agricultural land market, capital markets, labour markets and markets for agricultural produce. As a rule, upward mobility took place though the purchase of (additional) land, while downward mobility resulted from economic setbacks. Frequently such setbacks were the result of poor harvests, plagues and other 'acts of God', but just as frequently the cause was insufficient adaptation to changed market conditions, including the failure to transition from crop farming to livestock farming. Altogether, the opportunities and limits of adaptation depended to a large extent on one's prospects of acquiring wealth through marriage as well as access to private loans, but also on one's individual willingness to pursue an alternative career in the clergy, the military or – the most natural option in the case of freed bondsmen – the city.[59] Although many people were not themselves able to experience social mobility, contemporaries were most definitely aware of the phenomenon as such and often viewed it with suspicion. This is attested to by the sumptuary laws enacted in the late Middle Ages, which gave expression to an unease with the 'pretentions' of social climbers, as well as by aphorisms referring to insensitive behaviour on the part of parvenus, such as 'manners maketh man'.[60]

Social decline was furthermore regularly precipitated by the practice of inheritance according to the principle of primogeniture, which was introduced by William the Conqueror and adopted into Common Law. From the middle of the twelfth century, the consequences became increasingly apparent, when William's successors failed to add to the existing landmass by conquering additional terri-tory.[61] Primogeniture meant that upon the death of the owner, the inheritance was not divided among all of the children but fell to only one child – usually the oldest son, in exceptional cases also all of the daughters together.[62] The other chil-dren were left empty-handed or, if they were awarded an income, it was usually too small to enable them to start their own family. In contrast to other European countries, in which some form of primogeniture was also known and to some extent practiced, in England it was rigorously enforced, even among the social classes below that of the nobility.[63]

On the one hand, the principle of primogeniture had the effect that land ownership and wealth were bound together. On the other hand, it permanently created a sizeable number of 'second sons', a mechanism that stimulated indi-vidual acquisitive strivings among those affected.[64] Over the long term, these second sons of wealthy families formed a reservoir of well-bred young people in English society, who were suitable for leading positions within the army and navy, the clergy and the mercantile and free professions. Certainly in the Middle Ages, such opportunities were only to a limited extent available. Many of the 'disinherited' therefore lived according to knightly ideals and indulged in courtly love or roamed through the land in groups. As late as the English Civil War in the mid-seventeenth century, second sons are believed to have played a leading role in the Leveller Movement, which fought for equality before the law.[65]

It was not only among these downwardly mobile people that social and geo-graphic mobility went hand in hand. The children of menial labourers, farm-hands, subtenants and small-scale landowners – sons as well as daughters – were also highly mobile from a young age. Most of them remained within a radius of some five to ten miles from their home village, but some, especially day labour-ers, managed to cover quite a bit of distance. In general, young people tended to travel until they could afford to start a family. The proportion of those who never married was, however, extraordinarily high, especially among women. In the town of Ealing near London in 1599, for example, some 25 per cent of women aged between forty and seventy were unmarried. Some members of this early rural proletariat spent their entire lives on the road, their standard of living scarcely differing from that of vagabonds, who survived by begging and stealing.[66]

When landless people married, they tended to do so in their mid or late twenties, for women and men, respectively.[67] For the majority, this step did not involve a return to their place of origin. Instead they tended to settle where they had found work and a marriage partner. Consequently there was generally a high degree of turnover in the populations of English villages, and cross-generational family connections were weak: on the whole, they only played a role in propertied households. This was discovered by demographers in the 1960s and 1970s, who attempted in grand style to advance research on the demographic history of the late medieval and Early Modern periods through so-called family reconstitution studies. It turned out that the family names in the baptismal registers were very different from those in the marriage and burials registers and that many families that had had their children baptized in one locality had later simply disappeared, i.e., had moved on.[68]

Under these circumstances, farmworkers and servants, at least, cultivated their social relations not primarily among their relatives but rather among their neighbours, preferentially at neutral locations such as alehouses. It was to this network, if any, that one turned for credit or loans, financial support in times of crisis and consolation.[69] The system functioned on the basis of reciprocity, i.e., one must previously have 'invested', either through contributing to poor relief or by participating in the preparations for a festival, as well as by accepting the general ethical and behavioural codes. Group pressure, social control and associated conflicts were common occurrences, and the creation of outsiders was also a necessary result.[70] Nothing could be further from the truth than to view such social relations in medieval and Early Modern England as representing an intimate *Gemeinschaft* ('community'), in the sense coined by the German sociologist Ferdinand Tönnies, in contradistinction to the modern *Gesellschaft* ('society'), with its high degree of anonymity. It was rather the case that already at this time, social relations in England were shaped by *Gesellschaft* and were in this sense extraordinarily modern.[71]

Knowledge of this pattern is also necessary to explain the observation that the community network could break down under economic pressure. Already in the late sixteenth century – a time of crop failures, inflation and considerable population growth – this experience led to the enactment of state poor laws. The political elites could no longer ignore that, alongside the 'deserving' and the 'undeserving' poor, i.e., those who were unable or unwilling to work, there was also a broad stratum of labouring poor, who could not feed themselves and their families because they were unemployed, underemployed or poorly paid. Now – in addition to the old neighbourhood networks – cities, village communities and parishes were also called upon to provide support, such that poor relief, as deficient as it may have been in many cases, was more or less universally established a century later.[72] The feature that, in contrast to Continental European customs, the system was also open to nonlocals was in a certain sense an official acknowledgement that England had become a society of individuals on the move.[73]

It is only possible to understand the behaviour of both these individuals and the administrative authorities if one accepts the finding that anthropologist Alan Macfarlane first made in the late 1970s: namely, that since the waning of the Middle Ages, England, both economically and socially, possessed important attributes of a modern commercialized society:

> [T]here were already a developed market and mobility of labour, land was treated as a commodity and full private ownership was established, there was very considerable

geographical and social mobility, a complete distinction between farm and family existed, and rational accounting and the profit motive were widespread. This has generally been obscured by an over-emphasis on technology or *per capita* income.[74]

This diagnosis is consistent with the more recent medieval research finding outlined above on the special character of feudalism in England. Important bases for the market economy were already laid down in England in the eleventh century, and from that time forward the development progressed unimpededly. That economic slumps periodically limited economic growth does not contradict this overall assessment, as such crises are inherent to a market economy; they therefore need not be addressed in detail in this study.[75] The question this raises is rather that of what new structures were formed in the Early Modern period that followed the Middle Ages. Did the English market economy at this time achieve new quantitative dimensions? Did it assume a new quality?

Notes

1. That was the common ground between the opposing sides in the so-called Brenner controversy of the 1970s, which shall not be discussed here. On this, see T. H. Aston and C. H. E. Philpin (eds). 1985. *The Brenner Debate: Agrarian Class Structure and Economic Development in Pre-Industrial Europe*, Cambridge: Cambridge University Press.
2. Cf. C. Dyer. 1995. 'How Urbanized was Medieval England?', in J.-M. Duvosquel and E. Thoen (eds), *Peasants and Townsmen in Medieval Europe. Studia in honorem Adriaan Verhulst*, Gent: Snoeck-Ducajn and Zoon, 169–83; Britnell, *Commercialisation*, 102–25 and passim; idem. 2003. 'England: Towns, Trade and Industry', in S. H. Rigby (ed.), *A Companion to Britain in the Later Middle Ages*, Oxford: Oxford University Press, 47–64; S. H. Rigby. 2006. 'Introduction: Social Structure and Economic Change in Late Medieval England', in R. Horrox and W. M. Ormrod (eds), *A Social History of England, 1200–1500*, Cambridge: Cambridge University Press, 24; Bailey, 'Historiographical Essay', 298–99; M. Allen. 2004. 'The English Currency and the Commercialisation before the Black Death', in D. Wood (ed.), *Medieval Money Matters*, Oxford: Oxbow Books, 31–45.
3. Cf. S. Pamuk. 2007. 'The Black Death and the Origins of the 'Great Divergence' across Europe, 1300–1600', *European Review of Economic History* 11, 189–317; see also J. Walter and R. Schofield. 1989. 'Famine, Disease and Crisis Mortality in Early Modern Society', in J. Walter and R. Schofield (eds), *Famine, Disease and the Social Order in Early Modern Society*, Cambridge: Cambridge University Press, 68–73.
4. Cf. Britnell, *Commercialisation*, 115–17, 299; C. Dyer. 1994. *Everyday Life in Medieval England*, London: Hambledon Press, XII-XVI, 4–7, 173.
5. Cf. Bailey 'Historiographical Essay', 298–99 (with valuable evidence).
6. Quotation from G. Brodnitz. 1914. 'Die Stadtwirtschaft in England', *Jahrbücher für National-ökonomie und Statistik* 102, 36; see also 21–22. In addition, see R. Britnell. 1991. 'The Towns of England and Northern Italy in the Early Fourteenth Century', *Economic History Review* 44, 21–35; idem. 2006. 'Town Life', in Horrox and Ormrod, *A Social History of England*, 145–46.
7. The 'almost completely spontaneous course of evolution' of feudalism in England was already noted by M. Bloch. 1964. *Feudal Society*, trans. by L. A. Manyon, vol. 2, Chicago: University

of Chicago Press, 181. However, on this topic Bloch's account is unspecific and cryptic in equal measure, and therefore no further use of it will be made in this study. The same applies to his work *Seigneurie français et manoir anglais*, which was based on lecture notes.

8. Cf. H. R. Lyon. 1962. *Anglo-Saxon England and the Norman Conquest*, London: Longman, 320. For a general European perspective, see Rowley's *The Normans* as well as C. Harper-Bill and E. van Houts (eds). 2003. *A Companion to the Anglo-Norman World*, Woodbridge: The Boydell Press. In addition, see K. Heller. 1993. *Die Normannen in Osteuropa*, Berlin: Duncker and Humblot.

9. K.-F. Krieger. 2002. *Geschichte Englands von den Anfängen bis zum 15. Jahrhundert*, Munich: Beck, 89, points to the fundamental difference according to Germany, 'where much of the land was held by the aristocracy as an allod and thereby formed the basis for an autogenous aristocracy, deriving its sovereignty from no one, not even the King'.

10. Cf. J. R. Strayer. 1970. *On the Medieval Origins of the Modern State*, Princeton, NJ: Princeton University Press, 34–49.

11. Cf. Brodnitz, 'Stadtwirtschaft', 36–38.

12. See the reflections on the size of the territory and its consequences for the exercise of power in N. Elias. 1994. *The Civilizing Process: the History of Manners and State Formation and Civilization*, Oxford: Blackwell, 195 ff.

13. For details, see J. Masschaele. 2007. 'Tolls and Trade in Medieval England', in L. Armstrong et al. (eds), *Money, Markets and Trade in Late Medieval Europe. Essays in Honour of John H.A. Munro*, Leiden: Brill, 175–78.

14. Cf. S. R. Epstein. 2000. *Freedom and Growth. The Rise of States and Markets in Europe, 1300–1750*, London: Routledge, 68. On the 'legal professions', see S. Walker. 2006. 'Order and Law', in R. Horrox and W. M. Ormrod (eds), *A Social History of England 1200–1500*, Cambridge: Cambridge University Press, 99, 103.

15. This measure served to enforce the state monopoly of coinage and establish better control of foreign exchange trading; see P. Nightingale. 1983. 'The Ora, the Mark, and the Mancus: Weight-Standards and the Coinage in Eleventh-Century England (Part 1)', *Numismatic Chronicle* 143, 248–57.

16. Cf. M. Chibnall. 2003. 'Feudalism and Lordship', in C. Harper-Bill and E. van Houts (eds), *A Companion to the Anglo-Norman World*, Woodbridge: The Boydell Press, 130. On the development of the land market, see also B. L Anderson. 1986. 'Entrepreneurship, Market Process and the Industrial Revolution in England', in idem and A. J. H. Latham (eds), *The Market in History. Papers Presented at a Symposium Held 9–13 September 1984 at St George's House, Windsor Castle, under the Auspices of the Liberty Fund*, London: Croom Helm, 182.

17. Cf. D. C. North and R. P. Thomas. 1973. *The Rise of the Western World. A New Economic History*, Cambridge: Cambridge University Press, 64.

18. Cf. B. M. Campbell. 2009. 'Factor Markets in England before the Black Death', *Continuity and Change* 24, 92, 97; idem. 2006. 'The Land', in R. Horrox and W. M. Ormrod (eds). *A Social History of England, 1200–1500*, Cambridge: Cambridge University Press, 213.

19. Cf. J. H. Munro. 2000. 'English "Backwardness" and Financial Innovations in Commerce with the Low Countries, 14th to 16th Centuries', in P. Stabel et al. (eds), *International Trade in the Low Countries (14th–16th Centuries). Merchants, Organisation, Infrastructure*, Leuven-Apeldoorn: Garant, 143. This resulting backwardness in the banking sector could only begin to be offset in the 1640s, when merchants of the goldsmiths' guild exploited the weakening of the monarchy through the Civil War to establish themselves as illegal currency traders and bankers. On the uncommonness of bills of exchange on the other side of the Channel, see O. Volckart. 2009. 'Regeln, Willkür und der gute Ruf: Geldpolitik und Finanzmarkteffizienz in Deutschland, 14. bis 16. Jahrhundert', *Jahrbuch für Wirtschaftsgeschichte*, 117–18.

20. Cf. N. Jones. 1989. *God and the Moneylenders. Usury and Law in Early Modern England*, Oxford: Blackwell, 140–41. Quotation in M. Rowlinson. 1999. '"The Scotch Hate Gold":

British Identity and Paper Money, in E. Gilbert and E. Helleiner (eds), *Nation-States and Money. The Past, Present and Future of National Currencies,* London: Routledge, 49.

21. Cf. R. C. Palmer. 1985. 'The Origins of Property in England', *Law and History Review* 3, 1–50; idem. 1985. 'The Economic and Cultural Impact of the Origins of Property: 1180–1220', *Law and History Review* 3, 375–96. Quotation: G. Lottes. 1995. 'Von "tenure" zu "property". Die Entstehung des Eigentumsbegriffes aus dem Zerfall des Feudalrechts', in G. Lottes (ed.), *Der Eigentumsbegriff im englischen politischen Denken,* Bochum: Brockmeyer, 7.

22. See A. Macfarlane. 2002. *The Making of the Modern World. Visions from the West and East,* Houndmills: Palgrave, 48 (with reference to the legal historian Frederic Maitland).

23. *The Philosophy of Money,* 398. On the problem of disciplining the barons on the battlefied, see M. Mann. 1994. *Geschichte der Macht, vol. 2: Vom Römischen Reich bis zum Vorabend der Industrialisierung,* Frankfurt, Main: Campus, 234; for a more extensive account: M. Powicke. 1962. *Military Obligation in Medieval England. A Study in Liberty and Duty,* Oxford: Clarendon Press. See also H. M. Thomas. 2008. *The Norman Conquest: England after William the Conqueror,* Lanham, MD: Rowman and Littlefield, 80–83.

24. K. B. McFarlane. 1944. 'Parliament and Bastard Feudalism', *Transactions of the Royal Historical Society* 4(26), 53–79. For an overview of the state of the ensuing discussion, see M. Hicks. 1995. *Bastard Feudalism,* London: Longman; P. Coss. 2002. 'From Feudalism to Bastard Feudalism', in N. Fryde et al. (eds), *Die Gegenwart des Feudalismus,* Göttingen: Vandenhoeck and Ruprecht, 79–107. It should be noted here that the mounting of private armies only definitively ceased at the beginning of the sixteenth century, when Henry VII was able to push through a corresponding statute.

25. An explanation for Sir Henry Maine's failure to account for the English situation presumably lies in the fact that while he was an expert on Roman law (and India) who was inspired by the German legal tradition, he was relatively unversed in English Common Law; see R. Graveson. H. 1941. 'The Movement from Status to Contract', *Modern Law Review* 4, 261–72; K. Dockhorn. 1950. *Der deutsche Historismus in England. Ein Beitrag zur englischen Geistesgeschichte des 19. Jahrhunderts,* Göttingen: Vandenhoeck and Ruprecht, 177. On the reception of Maine in the social sciences, see E. Shils. 1991. 'Henry Sumner Maine in the Tradition of the Analysis of Society', in A. Diamond (ed.), *The Victorian Achievement of Sir Henry Maine. A Centennial Reappraisal,* Cambridge: Cambridge University Press, 143–78. The above-cited formulation is from H. S. Maine. 1965 (1861). *Ancient Law,* New York: Dutton, 100.

26. Cf. S. L. Waugh. 1986. 'Tenure to Contract: Lordship and Clientage in Thirteenth-Century England', *English Historical Review* 101, 811–39.

27. Cf. A. Macfarlane. 1988. 'The Cradle of Capitalism: The Case of England', in J. Baechler et al. (eds), *Europe and the Rise of Capitalism,* Oxford: Blackwell, 185–203 (in relation to the legal historian Frederic Maitland); idem, *Making of the Modern World,* 47–48. See also Krieger. 2002. *Geschichte Englands,* 89.

28. See C. W. Hollister. 1963. 'The Irony of English Feudalism', *Journal of British Studies* 11, 1–26.

29. Cf. Strayer. *On the Medieval Origins,* 47. An excellent overview of the key structural elements of Common Law can be found in H. Weber. 1988. 'Common Law', in R. Sheyhing (ed.), *Ergänzbares Lexikon des Rechts* 1(270), 29 February 1988, Neuwied: Luchterhand, 1–4.

30. Cf. A. Cromartie. 2006. *The Constitutionalist Revolution. An Essay on the History of England, 1450–1642,* Cambridge: Cambridge University Press.

31. Cf. R. C. van Caenegem. 1973. *The Birth of the English Common Law,* Cambridge: Cambridge University Press, 99–110. However, the connections to experts on Roman law were never completely severed; see J. H. Baker. 2002. *An Introduction to English Legal History,* 2nd ed., London: Butterworths, 27–29; R. Zimmermann. 1993. 'Der europäische Charakter des englischen Rechts: Historische Verbindungen zwischen Civil Law und Common Law', *Zeitschrift für europäisches Privatrecht* 1, 4–51.

32. Cf. A. L. Goodhart. 1934. 'Precedent in English and Continental Law', *Law Quarterly Review* 50, 40–65; D. Lieberman. 1995. 'Property, Commerce, and the Common Law. Attitudes to Legal Change in the Eighteenth Century', in J. Brewer and S. Staves (eds), *Early Modern Conceptions of Property*, London: Routledge, 148.

33. 'In a case-law system the initiative [for change] rests with the litigants, and it is only when the advantage to be gained in the instant case by doing something different is large enough to outweigh the loss that the well-advised litigant will take the risk and depart from the well-trodden path.' D. J. Ibbetson. 1999. *A Historical Introduction to the Law of Obligations*, Oxford: Oxford University Press, 299; see also ibid, 294–302.

34. Villeins, however, were still denied the right to appeal to the Royal Court; they remained subject to the jurisdiction of their lord. Cf. Campbell, 'The Land', 210. Also see P. Coss. 2006. 'The Age of Deference', in R. Horrox and W. M. Ormrod (eds), *A Social History of England, 1200–1500*, Cambridge: Cambridge University Press, 32–33.

35. Cf. P. Stein. and J. Shand. 1974. *Legal Values in Western Society*, Edinburgh: Edinburgh University Press, 212–14; R. Szostak. 1991. *The Role of Transportation in the Industrial Revolution: A Comparison of England and France*, Montreal: McGill-Queen's University Press, 88–90.

36. Cf. Baker, J. H. 1979. 'The Law Merchant and the Common Law before 1700', *Cambridge Law Journal* 38, 300–04, 316–22. References to the strategic significance of the *lex mercatoria* for the representation of merchants by authorized representatives can be found in P. R. Milgrom et al. 1990. 'The Role of Institutions in the Revival of Trade: The Law Merchant, Private Judges, and the Champagne Fairs', *Economics and Politics* 2, 4–6. The stipulations of the Magna Carta are cited in C. Kerr. 1929. 'The Origin and Development of the Law Merchant', *Virginia Law Review* 15, 359–60.

37. A. Cordes. 2005. points to this difference in 'The Search for a Medieval *Lex mercatoria*', in V. Piergiovanni (ed.), *From* lex mercatoria *to Commercial Law*, Berlin: Duncker and Humblot, 61.

38. The word 'trust' did not yet exist in the Middle Ages. The corresponding term was 'use'; it referred to the same subject matter. The presentation below follows F. W. Maitland. 1905. 'Trust und Korporation', *Grünhuts Zeitschrift für das Privat- und öffentliche Recht der Gegenwart* 32, 1–76; Baker, *Introduction to English Legal History*, 290–93, and D. B. Parker and A. R. Mellows. 1994. *The Modern Law of Trust*, ed. A. J. Oakley, London: Sweet and Maxwell, 1–25.

39. Even in the eighteenth and nineteenth centuries, 'trusts' proved to be a flexible legal form. They were well-suited, among other things, to alleviating the undesirable effects of the institution of 'strict settlement' that had emerged around 1660, which – much like the entailed estates (*Fideikommisse*) of Continental Europe – prevented the sale of lands out of consideration for the family of the landowners; cf. R. Harris, 2004. 'Government and the Economy, 1688–1850', in R. Floud and P. Johnson (eds), *The Cambridge Economic History of Modern Britain, vols 1: Industrialisation, 1700–1860*, Cambridge: Cambridge University Press, 229.

40. Cf. W. Hartmann. 1956. *Der Trust im englischen Recht*, Zürich: Juris-Verlag, 23–24.

41. Cf. Macfarlane, *Making of the Modern World*, 269–72.

42. Cf. R. Harris, 2000. *Industrializing English Law: Entrepreneurship and Business Organization, 1720–1844*, Cambridge: Cambridge University Press, 21–22, 147–58.

43. Cf. B. L. Anderson, 1975. 'Law, Finance and Economic Growth in England: Some Long-Term Influences', in B. M. Ratcliffe (ed.), *Great Britain and Her World 1750–1914. Essays in Honour of W. O. Henderson*, Manchester: Manchester University Press, 103ff.; M. R. Chesterman. 1984. 'Family Settlements on Trust: Landowners and the Rising Bourgeoisie', in G. R. Rubin and D. Sugarman (eds), *Law, Economy and Society, 1750–1914. Essays in the History of English Law*, Abingdon, Oxon.: Professional Books Ltd., 124–68.

44. Cf. H. Perkin. 1981. *The Origins of Modern English Society, 1780–1880*, London: Routledge 38; H.-C. Schröder, 1988. 'Der englische Adel', in A. von Reden-Dohna and R. Melville (eds), *Der Adel an der Schwelle des bürgerlichen Zeitalters 1780–1860*, Stuttgart: Steiner, 31–32.

45. Cf. Campbell, 'The Land', 201, 213.
46. Cf. ibid., 206–07, 210–11, 213, 237; Rigby, 'Introduction', 15.
47. Cf. D. Stone. 1997. 'The Productivity of Hired and Customary Labour: Evidence from Wisbech Barton in the Fourteenth Century', *Economic History Review* 50, 640–56. See also R. Britnell. 1993. 'Commerce and Capitalism in Late Medieval England: Problems of Description and Theory', *Journal of Historical Sociology* 6, 364; Campbell, 'Factor Markets', 84–86.
48. Cf. F. Rexroth. 2007. *Deviance and Power in Late Medieval London,* Cambridge: Cambridge University Press, 68–125.
49. Cf. Campbell, 'The Land', 219; N. Mayhew. 2007. 'Wages and Currency: The Case in Britain up to c. 1600', in J. Lucassen (ed.), *Wages and Currency. Global Comparisons from Antiquity to the Twentieth Century,* Berne: Peter Lang, 212–14.
50. The definition goes back to A. V. Chayanov. 1966. *The Theory of Peasant Economy,* ed. D. Thorner, Homewood, IL: Irwin. See also R. E. F. Smith (ed.). 1986. *A. V. Chayanov on the Theory of Peasant Economy,* Madison, WI: University of Madison Press.
51. Cf. M. Weber. 1927. *General Economic History,* trans. Frank Knight, New York: Greenberg Publishers, 164.
52. Cf. J. Gillingham. 1996. 'Some Observations on Social Mobility in England between the Norman Conquest and the Early Thirteenth Century', in A. Haverkamp and H. Vollrath (eds), *England and Germany in the High Middle Ages,* Oxford: Oxford University Press, 340–41, 353.
53. Cf. Masschaele, J. 1997. *Peasants, Merchants, and Markets. Inland Trade in Medieval England, 1150–1350,* New York: St. Martin's Press, 57–73. See also the older essay by R. H. Britnell. 1981. 'The Proliferation of Markets in England, 1200–1349', *Economic History Review* 34, 209–221.
54. Cf. Campbell, 'The Land', 208; P. R. Schofield. 2003. 'England: The Family and the Village Community', in Rigby, *A Companion to Britain,* 26–46.
55. *The Origins of English Individualism. The Family, Property and Social Transition,* Oxford: Blackwell. See also A. Macfarlane. 1984. 'The Myth of the Peasantry; Family and Economy in a Northern Parish', in R. M. Smith (ed.), *Land, Kinship and Life-Cycle,* Cambridge: Cambridge University Press, 333–49; idem. 1987. 'The Peasantry in England before the Industrial Revolution – a Mythical Model?', in A. Macfarlane, *The Culture of Capitalism,* Oxford: Blackwell, 1–25.
56. Cf. J. V. Beckett. 1994. 'The Peasant in England. A Case of Terminological Confusion', *Agricultural History Review* 32, 117. For a review of the literature on which the terminology used in this study is based, see Smith, R. M. 1998. 'The English Peasantry, 1250–1650', in T. Scott (ed.), *The Peasantries of Europe from the Fourteenth to the Eighteenth Centuries,* London: Macmillan, 339–71.
57. Cf. Campbell, 'The Land', 196.
58. Cf. Overton, M. 1996. *Agricultural Revolution in England. The Transformation of the Agrarian Economy 1500–1850,* Cambridge: Cambridge University Press, 42; see also 22–30, 176–77.
59. Cf. P. C. Maddern. 2006. 'Social Mobility', in R. Horrox and W. M. Ormrod (eds), *A Social History of England, 1200–1500,* Cambridge: Cambridge University Press, 113–33.
60. Cf. R. Horrox. 2006. 'Conclusion', in R. Horrox and W. M. Ormrod (eds), *A Social History of England, 1200–1500,* Cambridge: Cambridge University Press, 475–76.
61. On the dating, see Gillingham, 'Some Observations', 340–41. According to Cecil, this principle of inheritance was introduced by the Norman kings. He cites considerations of military policy as an explanation. Presumably, the expectations of the entourage of William the Conqueror and his successors also played a role. Cf. E. Cecil. 1895. *Primogeniture. A Short History of its Development in Various Countries,* London: John Murray, 1–25.
62. Cf. J. H. Baker, *Introduction to English Legal History,* 227.

63. Cf. J. Thirsk. 1976. 'The European Debate on Customs and Inheritance, 1500–1700', in J. Goody et al. (eds), *Family and Inheritance. Rural Societies in Western Europe 1200–1800*, Cambridge: Cambridge University Press, 184.

64. 'The result was insecurity and constant acquisitive striving, each generation remaking itself through acquisitive activity. … From very early on, a child is being trained to be an independent entity, for he or she will leave home and never return.' A. Macfarlane. 1992. 'On Individualism. Radcliffe-Brown Lecture in Social Anthropology', *Proceedings of the British Academy* 82, 179–80.

65. Cf. J.Thirsk. 1969. 'Younger Sons in the Seventeenth Century', *History. The Journal of the Historical Association* 54, 369.

66. Cf. Z. Razi, 1980. *Life, Marriage and Death in a Medieval Parish: Economy, Society and Demography in Halesowen, 1270–1400*, Cambridge: Cambridge University Press, 209. The example comes from B. Coward. 1988. *Social Change and Continuity in Early Modern England 1550–1750*, London: Longman, 20–21, who also cites additional relevant literature.

67. Cf. Rigby, 'Introduction', 16–17; Coward, *Social Change*, 20.

68. Cf. Coward, *Social Change* , 6. More recent studies confirm this research; cf. Dyer, *The Self-Contained Village*.

69. Cf. C. Muldrew. 1998. *The Economy of Obligation. The Culture of Credit and Social Relations in Early Modern England*, London: Macmillan, on the significance of the 'web of credit' for the formation and consolidation of community. See also P. Clark. 1983. *The English Alehouse: a Social History, 1200–1830*, London: Longman; as well as K. E. Westhauser, 1994. 'Friendship and Family in Early Modern England: the Sociability of Adam Eyre and Samuel Pepys', *Journal of Social History* 27, 517–36.

70. Cf. Schofield, 'England', 26–46; Coward, *Social Change*, 26.

71. F. Tönnies. 2001 (1887). *Community and Civil Society*, ed. J. Harris, trans. M. Hollis, Cambridge: Cambridge University Press. The best overview of the literature on this topic is T. Sokoll. 1983. 'Zur Rekonstruktion historischer Gemeinschaftsformen. Neuere sozialgeschichtliche Gemeindestudien in England', *Zeitschrift für Volkskunde* 79, 15–41; see also P. Withington and A. Shepard. 2000. 'Introduction: Communities in Early Modern England', in A. Shepard and P. Withington (eds), *Communities in Early Modern England. Networks, Place, Rhetoric*, Manchester: Manchester University Press, 1–15; C. Muldrew. 2000. 'From a 'Light Cloak' to an 'Iron Cage': Historical Changes in the Relations between Community and Individualism', in A. Shepard and P. Withington (eds), *Communities in Early Modern England. Networks, Place, Rhetoric*, Manchester: Manchester University Press, 156–77.

72. Cf. P. Slack. 1988. *Poverty and Policy in Tudor and Stuart England*, London: Longman, 122–37; idem. 1990. *The English Poor Law 1531–1782*, Basingstoke: Macmillan; S. Hindle. 2004. *On the Parish? The Micro-Politics of Poor Relief in Rural England c. 1550–1750*, Oxford: Clarendon Press. P. M. Solar and R. M. Smith emphasize the almost welfare state-like quality of the comprehensive Poor Law in 'An Old Poor Law for the New Europe? Reconciling Local Solidarity with Labour Mobility in Early Modern England', in P. A. David and M. Thomas (eds), *The Economic Future in Historical Perspective*, Oxford: Oxford University Press, 463–78.

73. Cf. E. A. Wrigley. 2004. 'City and Country in the Past: a Sharp Divide or a Continuum?', in E. A. Wrigley, *Poverty, Progress, and Population*, Cambridge: Cambridge University Press, 266.

74. A. Macfarlane. 1978. *Origins*, 195–96.

75. The current scholarly discussion among medievalists dedicated to such economic slumps and crises tends to blow them up them into fundamental problems; cf. Britnell, 'Commerce and Capitalism', 359–76; Campbell, 'Factor Markets'.

Chapter 2

GROWTH AND CONSOLIDATION
OF MARKET EXCHANGE
IN THE EARLY MODERN PERIOD

Although a broad consensus exists among British historians that the Early Modern period began roughly around 1500 and ended roughly around 1800, their use of the adjectives 'medieval' and 'modern' has tended to be rather unspecific. In this, they differ from their colleagues on the European continent. The explanation for this convention lies in the fact that in British history, one can point to no profound historical caesura dividing the Middle Ages from the Early Modern period. Furthermore, despite unmistakable signs of developmental progress, a high level of continuity existed in the economy as well as in society. Both factors placed the contemporary population of England in a privileged position in relation to the inhabitants of the European continent, at least in terms of their living conditions: they were able to live out their lives in a manner comparatively free of disruption from either severe internal crises or external threats.

To add concrete weight to this statement, one must begin by explaining that 'from time immemorial' and especially after the Black Death of the fourteenth century, England was less severely beset by famines, contagions and epidemics than were other countries. The mild, temperate climate and the abundance of water are among the general factors contributing to this. The country's insular location made it possible to temporarily stop foreign travel to protect the population from infectious diseases. Furthermore, the fact that English farmers, unlike most of their Continental brethren, did not tend to fertilise their fields with human excrement also resulted in a better state of hygiene. The diversified cultivation of grains and agricultural crops mitigated the effects of crop failures, and in times of scarcity or during food emergencies, North Sea fishing could provide the population with an important source of protein. Finally, the widespread practice of sheep farming assured a steady supply of warm clothes and soft beds.[1]

A further circumstance that privileged late medieval and Early Modern England with respect to the European continent was the relative absence of warfare on its own soil. Since 1066, no foreign power had invaded the island. Although the Spanish Armada did get as far as the coast in 1588, the invasion had to be called off due to stormy weather and was ultimately crushed. While the Wars of the Roses (1455–85), fought between supporters of two noble houses rivalling for the English throne, and the English Civil War (1642–46, 1648) cost hundreds if not thousands of lives, their impact on the everyday lives of the population was highly localized. The Thirty Years War (1618–48), which devastated huge swathes of the European continent, left England unscathed. And although the English Crown was at war for seventy-three of the 125 years between the Glorious Revolution of 1689 and the end of the Napoleonic Wars in 1815, these military conflicts took place either at sea or on foreign soil.

As a consequence of these fortunate circumstances, the infrastructure that had been developing since the Middle Ages was spared; in civilian life, wealth and experience could accumulate, and security and confidence prevailed in private matters and economic investments.

Impulses towards Commercialization: Population Growth, Agrarian Revolution and Urbanization

Between the middle of the sixteenth and the early nineteenth century, the English population grew by 280 per cent, a rate of growth that is to a large extent attributable to a decline in the age of marriage and the concomitant rise in fertility (births per marriage). By way of comparison: in France, the Netherlands, Germany, Spain and what was later to become Italy, populations increased during the same period by only 50 to 80 per cent.[2]

In and of itself, population growth was already an important instigator of the process of commercialization in general. The concentration of settlement structures eased access to markets, made it easier to compare prices and multiplied relationships of exchange. For the sellers, it lowered transport and information costs, improved economies of scale, favoured specialization, encouraged the hiring of new workers and increased profits. Tellingly, the number of merchants, tradesmen, middlemen and other commercial agents grew at a rate even faster than that of the population as a whole, as Ray B. Westerfield, the historian of this professional group, has found.[3] In practice, the law of diminishing returns in agriculture, which in the early Middle Ages had seemed insurmountable and regularly led to widespread food shortages, had less of an impact on the way the English lived.[4]

Indirectly, population growth was beneficial to broader processes of commercialization because it spurred urbanization. Around 1700, London, with some 575,000 inhabitants, overtook Paris as Europe's largest city. Approximately one-third of England's urban and 5 per cent of its general population lived there. And yet urbanization was making recognizable headway in the provinces, as well. While in 1600 only two provincial cities – Norwich and Bristol – could count more than ten thousand inhabitants, by 1714 that number had risen to six, with another eighteen cities having populations of between five thousand and ten thousand inhabitants. Venerable cities like York, Exeter, Chester and Worcester lost population, while new stars arose: provincial cities like Durham, Stamford and Salisbury; spa towns such as Bath, Tunbridge Wells, Harrogate and Hampstead; port cities and manufacturing centres like Liverpool, Manchester, Birmingham, Nottingham, Leicester and Leeds. The urban geography of modern England was taking shape.[5] Between the beginning of the eighteenth century and the beginning of the nineteenth century, the percentage of the English population living in cities increased from around 17 to 27.5 per cent.[6] In the second half of the eighteenth century, this increase accounted for 70 per cent of all the urban population growth in Europe, although England made up only 8 per cent of the European population.[7] According to the 1811 census, 12 per cent of the English population was living in large cities with over one hundred thousand inhabitants, a figure that would not be reached in the German Empire until 1890. Ten of those 12 per cent were living in London alone.[8]

In the conduct of their daily lives, city dwellers were highly dependent on markets, first and foremost because they were unable to produce their own food, but also because their demand for consumer goods tended to be more differentiated than that of the rural population. Paradoxically, one effect of the increase in market integration was a diminution in the importance of urban (weekly) farmers' markets and (annual) trade fairs. The number of cities with regularly scheduled markets dropped continually – by 28 per cent, for example, between 1690 and 1720. Instead, the network of wholesale and retail establishments became denser. According to a survey by the contemporary tax authorities, in 1759 there were 141,700 mercantile establishments in England and Wales, 21,603 of them in London.[9]

Behind this development was a process of improved communications and increased specialization and rationalization in trade. Within wholesale trading, there was a noticeable move towards pre-ordering and organized product presentations in public houses. Meanwhile, retail trade shifted to fixed-location shops (figure 2.1). In contrast to the outdoor markets, these shops were open seven days a week and were not dependent upon weather conditions. Above all, they offered a wider range of goods than did the market stalls and were usually also attached to a warehouse so that consumers could receive their purchases immediately. Fur-

THE WEST PROSPECT OF THE CHURCH OF S.T. ETHELBURGH.

To Sir Robert Godschall Kn.t
Alderman of the Ward of Bishopsgate
London.

This Plate is Humbly Inscribed by the Proprietors, Robert Wilkinson and William Henry Toms.

Figure 2.1. Shops and stalls along the wall of the Church of St. Ethelburga, Bishopsgate, London, 1737.

thermore, the sales were no longer made by the producers themselves but rather by apparently objective vendors.[10]

The parallel developments of population growth and urbanization also contributed to this market consolidation, as they enabled the lower classes to grow. While the quality of life of low-income and poor people did remain low, it was nevertheless possible to keep food crises, which might have delayed or reversed the expansion of these classes, from spreading beyond a localized area.[11] The explanation for this development, which refuted the predictions of the population theorist Robert Malthus, lies first and foremost in a significant rise in agricultural productivity, which more than compensated for the loss of manpower to the cities. In the seventeenth century in particular, the positive effects of this development made themselves felt. This had already begun around 1540, when a long phase of price rises set in, encouraging both landowners and tenants to invest. Additional land purchases, the consolidation of land into enclosures,[12] forest clearance, wetlands drainage and the building of roads and streets augmented the amount of usable land. Furthermore the shift in emphasis to pasturing and systematic livestock breeding, the more intensive use of horses as draught animals, the cultivation of new field crops such as clover and swede turnips, the standardization of crop rotation and finally the construction of storage facilities all contributed to making more intensive cultivation possible. The increase in production was so great that around 1650, England advanced to become an agricultural exporter, despite a growth in domestic demand.[13] By around 1750, the amount of grain being exported was sufficient to have fed a quarter of the English population.[14]

However, one should not overestimate the role of improved agricultural methods in making this production increase possible. In Ireland, the Netherlands and some regions of France, for example, similar modernization techniques were adopted without generating an upswing as steady and sustained as that in England.[15] Rather, the explanation for the development in England lies additionally and above all in the fact that many of the fundamental preconditions for a capitalist agriculture were in place there even before the onset of the agrarian revolution and that they persisted, independent of economic incentives.

The most important of these preconditions was the circumstance that the aristocracy and the gentry – i.e., the dominant social class – owned between 70 and 75 per cent of arable land and derived their income either from their own agricultural activity or from leaseholds granted to other producers. This stimulated interest in profitable cultivation methods on the part of landowners and tenants alike. Furthermore, due to the custom of inheritance via primogeniture, the farms were not divided up. To the contrary, the close connection between land ownership, social prestige and political power (suffrage) strengthened the tendency to large-scale land ownership. Where additional land purchases and strategic marriage alliances were added to the mix, economies of scale in land cultivation could develop. Finally the absence of a self-sufficient peasantry played a role. For it was only through the use of wage labourers willing to produce better results in exchange for higher wages that the remarkable 75 per cent rise in labour productivity over the course of the seventeenth and eighteenth centuries could be achieved.[16]

How remarkable this was becomes evident when one bears in mind that the productivity of English farming in the mid-nineteenth century, when the other European countries had begun to catch up, was still half again as great as that of France and twice as great as that of Germany, Sweden and the European part of Russia. Measured in terms of the number of calories per worker, productivity levels in England were twice as high as in France and three times that of the other three regions.[17]

Reciprocal Effects between Commerce and Industry

Most broadly defined, the Early Modern period encompassed the three centuries between 1500 and 1800. The spread and proliferation of markets over such a long period of time is difficult to quantify, and this can only be done on the basis of estimates. This task becomes even more challenging when – as in this study – the focus of interest lies less in the amounts and prices of the goods exchanged at the markets than in the social relationships that developed in the process of economic exchange. A makeshift and yet still useful indicator of the level of market integration in the Early Modern period is the development in the proportion of the population not engaged in agriculture, as is shown in table 2.1.

The category 'nonagricultural population' encompasses those people resident in cities with more than five thousand inhabitants – including London, the statistics for which are once again shown separately in table 2.1 – as well as the rural population not engaged in agriculture. The table shows that this category's share of the general population, which for its part was also experiencing considerable growth, increased from 23.7 per cent in 1520 to 63.7 per cent in 1800. The agricultural historian Mark Overton, from whom the table derives, regards this change in size as an indirect indicator of the long-term growth of that segment of the population that had to procure its daily food supplies in part or entirely through the market. However, he reminds us that this indicator suggests merely a minimum of the general market activity in the food sector, as other factors not captured in the table also need to be taken into account: the regional specialization of agriculture, the products of which had to be transported over considerable distances before they reached consumers; the disproportionate consumption of Londoners, which according to estimates was twice as great as that of provincial townspeople; and finally the transactions (transport, warehousing, distribution),

Table 2.1. The Nonagricultural Population in England, 1520–1800 (as a Percentage of the General Population)

Year	General population (absolute)	Population of cities with more than 5,000 inhabitants	London	Rural nonagricultural population	Nonagricultural population in total
1520	2,400,000	5.25	2.25	18.5	23.7
1600	4,110,000	8.25	5.00	22.0	30.2
1670	5,140,000	13.5	9.5	26.0	39.5
1700	5,060,000	17.0	11.5	28.0	45.0
1750	5,770,000	21.0	11.5	33.0	54.0
1800	8,660,000	27.50	11.0	36.3	63.7

Source: M. Overton. 1996. *Agricultural Revolution in England. The Transformation of the Agrarian Economy 1500–1850,* Cambridge: Cambridge University Press, 75 (population figures for 1520, 1601, 1661, 1701, 1751) and 138.

Figure 2.2. 'The Cries of London', circa 1740. The cards were part of a children's game. Engravings by M. Lauron from late sixteenth-century drawings.

indirectly stimulated by both factors – regional specialization and urbanization – that took place partly on regional and partly on national markets.[18]

The transactions necessitated by increasing market integration must also be taken into account if the trends reflected in the table are to serve as a source of information on the development of the employment structure. It would in any event be mistaken to equate the 'nonagricultural population' exclusively with those engaged in commerce and industry, as the category also included a substantial number of people, in both rural and urban areas, who provided services that straddled the boundary between agriculture and commerce. These service providers included not only the domestic servants and employees of landed estates and their related businesses, but also and above all the host of middlemen – traders and brokers, agents and sales representatives, commission merchants and warehousemen, bankers and lawyers, sellers and money-lenders, carters and deliverymen, hawkers and market criers – who organized the exchange between city and countryside (figure 2.2).[19]

Thus, although table 2.1 does not directly chart the increase in those engaged in commerce and industry, the growth of the 'nonagricultural' segment of the population, from 23.7 per cent to 63.7 per cent in the period between 1520 and 1800, points to a significant intensification of the exchange of commercial (and agricultural) goods between the city and the countryside. The question thus arises of what judicial, infrastructural and other preconditions favoured the development of such relationships of exchange.

In the following chapter sections on the commercialization of artisanal and industrial production, special emphasis is placed on the web of relationships between cities and the countryside. To understand their in some ways very different developments, the individual branches of centralized commercial production in large-scale facilities, urban trades and decentralized production in the countryside (proto-industry) will be treated separately. In these chapter sections, qualitative aspects of the interrelationships between the commercial economy, on the one hand, and broader social and cultural development, on the other, will be analysed.

Centralized Production

In the eighteenth century, the number of centralized large-scale production facilities remained quite small. These emerged chiefly in those branches of industry where greater technical requirements and, concomitantly, higher capital demands ruled out decentralized alternatives. In concrete terms, this meant areas in which raw materials had to be smelted or otherwise combined in a complex production process necessitating a certain division of labour, e.g., the production of metals, glass, soap or beer; large-scale building projects and shipyards; paper manufacturing and milling, both of which were dependent on energy generated by windmills or watermills; and, finally, the mining of coal and other minerals. A few of these production sites, such as mills, could be found all over the country, the majority in just a few scattered locations. With the exception of mining, they rarely employed a workforce of more than five, as demand was still too small and too irregular to warrant greater dimensions, a circumstance that also inhibited the foundation of joint stock companies in the manufacturing sector.[20]

That some of the above-named branches had nevertheless experienced a noticeable upswing since the sixteenth century is largely explained in terms of the impetus they received from an extraordinary rise in the extraction of bituminous coal. Some experts suggest that the amount of coal produced underwent a fifteen- to twentyfold increase between 1500 and 1800; others regard these estimates as exaggerated. Nevertheless, in view of the facts that the rate of growth exceeded population growth, that the initial values were already relatively high and that there was a general scarcity of wood, the development does indeed signify a leap forward in energy production.[21]

An explanation can be found in the qualitative features of bituminous coal. Foremost of these is the fact that the burning of bituminous coal generates temperatures considerably higher than in the case of wood or charcoal. The English glass industry profited from this, as it was now able to produce the clear glass required for higher-quality window glass and optical instruments, with the result that England became the European market leader in this area. Iron foundries likewise received sustained impulses for development, as did smelting of all kinds and – indirectly – the entire metal-working industry; building construction (brickworks); book and newspaper printing (cast matrices); and some manufacturers of consumer goods (tin tableware, ceramics, lead glass).[22] The historian E. A. Wrigley postulated that the technical challenges associated with the bituminous coal mining, especially the necessity to pump groundwater out of the shafts, even inspired Thomas Savary and Thomas Newcomen to develop the first steam engine in the early eighteenth century.[23] In agriculture, tracts of productive land were preserved as the rate of deforestation decreased,[24] and for the cities, a more appropriate household fuel was produced. There were particular advantages for those contemporaries who could afford to build brick houses and install transparent-glass windows. The brick houses were comparatively fire resistant, and brighter interiors contributed to improved hygiene.[25]

As bituminous coal is a mass-produced commodity, the increase in production since the sixteenth century furthermore had positive effects for the transport industry. Following the expansion of coastal shipping ('the river round England') during the Middle Ages, now, in the interest of coal transport, the rivers in the interior were made navigable for larger and larger barges. In addition, canals were dug and interconnected so that a nationwide network of waterways developed.

Tellingly, in the late seventeenth century, half of the English merchant fleet was engaged in coal transport.[26] To make further transport on land possible, hundreds of turnpike societies were founded, which invested in the building of roads and also paid for their maintenance. Each of these societies had a local catchment area, and they financed themselves through the collection of tolls, for which reason it made sense for them to orient their building activities towards concrete local needs. When necessary, they promoted private bills in Parliament to expropriate uncooperative owners.[27]

The upswing in coal mining in England had begun some two hundred years earlier than in the rest of Europe, and in the early nineteenth century, English coal production was still seven times greater than the combined output of all the Continental European countries.[28] The building of canals and roads hereby contributed considerably to England becoming the country with the best infrastructure in the world, even before the age of the railroad. In this respect, it surpassed not only the Holy Roman Empire with its plethora of small states, where customs borders lengthened travel and transport times and through roads did not exist, but also France, the country with the world's second-best infrastructure, where ramrod straight roads were laid out with the needs of the State and the military in mind, but to a certain extent bypassing local developments.[29]

A cultural historical consequence of this advanced infrastructure was the extraordinary pull that the political and cultural capital of London developed in the seventeenth and eighteenth centuries with respect to the residents of the provinces. According to E. A. Wrigley, already at this time, at least 16 per cent of the English population spent at least a brief period of their lives in London[30] – a phenomenon that is due not least to the fact that streets and roads now led from nearly every far-flung village to the capital via a network of increasingly busy arterial highways (figure 2.3). Already in 1637, a regular schedule of carriages transported passengers and goods 272 times per week from London to the provinces; by the beginning of the eighteenth century, the corresponding figure had risen to 600.[31]

Urban Trades

In the case of England, it is problematic to speak of 'urban trades' in the Early Modern period, as social and economic historians of the German-speaking countries commonly do, for this expression presupposes a certain insularity of the urban economy with respect to the surrounding region, and, concomitantly, the equation of 'urban' with 'guild' trades. Since the late Middle Ages, neither of these conditions had existed on the island.

With few exceptions, English cities were not surrounded by walls, and so it was generally difficult to keep the output of rural craftsmen, i.e., producers who

Figure 2.3. The English turnpike road network, 1770.

were not members of guilds, out of urban markets. One explanation for this is that city walls were not needed because English towns and cities generally speaking did not possess royal privileges, the enjoyment of which could be denied to strangers. Another has to do with the absence of threats of war. While many central European cities were reinforcing their fortifications during the Thirty Years' War, in England they were being torn down, even in places such as East Anglia, where some had remained standing since Anglo-Saxon times. The interest in free market access as well as in introducing more fresh air and ventilation outweighed any monopoly interests on the part of the crafts.[32]

These monopoly interests could also no longer be enforced due to the institutional instability of the guilds. Albeit more slowly and later than elsewhere in Europe, craft guilds had been forming in English cities since the thirteenth century to regulate access to the trades and to codify quality standards. Such federations existed in the majority of professions, and in many cases their statutes were given legal weight by the Crown. In 1393, Edward III even tried to make guild membership mandatory within all trades.[33] And yet already at this time, many guilds, including those of weavers, tailors and goldsmiths, fell under the influence of capital-rich merchants, many of whom has risen up from their own ranks. To evade their control, craftsmen withdrew from the guilds, which in turn lost their economic function. Frequently they were obliged to relinquish the use of their trade names, as for example in London, where, with reference to the right of members to furnish themselves – and, according to some sources, their employees as well – with the distinctive dress (or 'livery') of their trade, they began to refer to themselves as 'livery companies'. Although craft guilds continued to exist in numerous trades, the tendency for them to dissolve gained momentum over the course of the fifteenth century. Most guilds turned into professional organizations of rich merchants, whose task was limited primarily to the organization of ostentatious ceremonies at festivals and on public occasions.[34]

As the sixteenth century drew to a close, the remaining craft guilds experienced a further weakening as a result of state economic policy. On the face of things, this policy appeared to be friendly to craftsmen. Elizabeth I, attempting to siphon off municipal finances, took measures to stem the expansion of trade over the country. In this connection, she issued a Statute of Artificers in 1563 that set the wages and working conditions of all occupational groups, and prescribed a seven-year apprenticeship for tradesmen – masters as well as journeymen. This was a long-standing demand on the part of the trades. However, in a departure from previous practice, the statute simultaneously demanded that access to vocational training be made easier and that the children of the poor also be taken on as apprentices. The trades were thereby set on a course of transformation. Elizabeth furthermore stripped the guilds of their jurisdiction in professional and commercial matters, handing it over to justices of the peace, who were directly subordinate to the Crown. Whether everyday working life was changed by this is unlikely, since the traditional perception of the hierarchical relationship between master and servant continued to serve as the foundation for decision-making by both legislatures and the courts well into the nineteenth century.[35] However, the authority and assertiveness of the guilds had become weakened from within, and journeymen and apprentices could henceforth remove themselves from their jurisdiction: their opponent in disputes over contracts and concrete working conditions was no longer a corporation but rather their master as an employer.[36]

For the Stuarts who succeeded the Tudors, cities and the crafts were also primarily sources of income. In the revolutionary seventeenth century, the guilds could in any event not be relied upon to support the monarchy. Politically power-less and weakened by the differentiation between craftsmen and merchants, they finally lost their internal coherence. How far they had fallen can be measured by the fact that in some cities, a tendency towards supra-professional associations developed.[37]

What significance did the demise of the craft guilds have for English market society? Firstly, it should be noted that in a process that unfolded over centuries, more or less complete freedom of enterprise was established – an important precondition for migrants from the countryside to find work in the cities and therefore also for a successful urbanization.

Secondly, the tradesmen adapted themselves to the new conditions. Where professional and economic success was no longer dependent on the backing of the guild, the term 'master' mutated into a synonym for 'employer', and old stipulations such as the requirement to produce a masterpiece according to the rules of the guild sank into oblivion. Instead, a premium was placed on market-appropriate behaviour. That a tailor, for example, faced with a good demand situation, would choose to farm out work to casual workers and would launch fashion trends at the right place and the right time was what mattered.[38]

The shift in mentality among master craftsmen thereby set in motion marked a fundamental difference to the Continental European countries. This touches on a third consequence of the development outlined here. On the Continent, freedom of enterprise was not generally introduced until the end of the eight-eenth (France) or over the course of the nineteenth century (Central and Eastern Europe), and when this did happen, the move was more or less abrupt and initi-ated 'from above'. In Germany and other Central European countries, these legis-lative decisions, which were often perceived as arbitrary, led to the special interests of the guilds continually reforming themselves far into the twentieth century, until finally all national special regulations were superseded by the more recent EU legislation.[39] In contrast, the creeping development in England, which con-temporaries could only attribute to anonymous market forces, early on effected a tendency towards the individualization of master craftsmen. Significantly, already in the seventeenth and eighteenth centuries, they engaged themselves profession-ally, if at all, no longer with reference to their role as guild members but simply as employers, and politically they presented themselves as subjects of the Crown and as citizens.[40] Thus England became, in the opinion of one German historian, not only a 'land without peasants' but also 'without artisans'.[41]

Fourthly, the gradual demise of the guilds likewise affected the dependently employed among the classic guild professions, i.e., the journeymen. In the course of this development they evolved into free wage labourers who exchanged their manpower for money and saw themselves as vulnerable to the fluctuations of supply and demand on the labour market. As wage labourers, they were hired by contractors, who could be masters or merchants, and they worked either in the traditional manner in a workshop or on their own premises: in attics, cellars or their flats. Not infrequently their wives and children were co-employed as unpaid workers, so that the border between regular and 'sweated' trades, i.e., those characterized by highly exploitative urban domestic industry, became blurred.

The loss of status which the journeymen suffered in the course of their proletarianization was, however, not as pronounced as among the masters. While the journeymen did lose some of the protective functions of the guilds (restricting access to work to only qualified workers, providing sickness benefits and corporative sociability), the skills they acquired during their apprenticeship – of which they were proud and which they regarded as a personal possession – were still recognized, as the Statute of Artificers was only abolished in 1814. Thus, skilled artisans saw themselves as standing above unskilled ones. Added to this was the advantage that with the demise of the guilds, their employment relationship was finally free of the affronts that continued to be experienced in Central Europe on a daily basis deep into the nineteenth century. Thus no English journeyman (or, for the most part, apprentice) was still obliged by guild regulations to live in the household of the master or have to forego monetary wages. None had to argue with the master and his wife about his right to have his own key. And none was prevented from starting his own family or striking out on his own.[42]

Paradoxically, the early erosion of the guild tradition was the precondition for English journeymen artisans already in the Early Modern period to wistfully bemoan the lost golden age of their craft, when wages had allegedly still been fair and the conditions of labour contracts bearable. Such nostalgic myths were cultivated not least by the free journeymen's associations and mutual aid funds, which had been forming since the sixteenth century. As these associations – whose mission it was to cultivate sociability and provide mutual support in cases of illness, bereavement and seasonal or cyclical unemployment – were thoroughly prepared to finance strikes in conflict situations, they are regarded by historians of the labour movement as the forerunners of English labour unions.[43] Only few sources provide information about their activities, as they often were of an informal character and had to hide their existence to avoid political persecution. And yet for the time period from 1717 to 1800 alone, there is evidence of 333 separate labour disputes, most of which were carried out by members of the classical artisanal trades.[44] Some of these tradesmen, such as tailors, were so well organized that the journeymen not only decided which of their colleagues should be sent to a particular employer, but even whether the latter should be allowed to receive workers at all.[45]

Not despite but rather precisely because of the early demise of the guilds, the craft tradition provided urban journeymen artisans with a basis for the acquisition of market power. When one considers that in unregulated labour markets, a power gap between employers and employees exists, as the latter are existentially dependent on the sale of their labour and might, in certain circumstances, have to sell it at any price; and when one further considers the sustained support of this asymmetry by labour laws and the labour courts, one can say that the English unions of the eighteenth century – as 'price cartels with the power to fix labour supply quotas' (Götz Briefs) – contributed importantly to the functioning of labour markets.[46] At least in the classical artisanal trades, the price of labour as a commodity was henceforward negotiable. Not least for this reason were wages in English cities in the Early Modern period considerably higher than in the Netherlands and many times higher than in other European countries.[47]

Rural Proto-industry

This production system was based on merchants, capital-rich artisans and other investors 'putting out' raw materials to producers living in scattered locations in the countryside to be processed by the latters' families in their own homes or workshops. The contractors then arranged for the finished or half-finished products to be collected or delivered to a central warehouse, where they were either finished or distributed. This 'putting out system' is also referred to by historians as proto-industry. It existed (and continues to exist today) in many countries of the world and served among the agricultural population as supplemental seasonal work. In England, where the children of agricultural producers were sent away from home at an early age, this practice had been known since the fourteenth century.[48] Reliable statistical data on its long-term development are lacking; however, it is certain that the majority of work subcontracted in this manner was within the textile industry, especially in wool weaving, the production levels of which are estimated to have quintupled between 1485 and 1714. Towards the end of that period, a large number of new sectors were added to the textile industry, such as the manufacturing of knitted fabrics and cotton processing, as well as leatherworking, woodworking and various metalworking crafts.[49]

In Early Modern England, these rural production sites were characterized by their use of simple tools, which for the most part had been in use since the Middle Ages, as well as a pronounced division of labour.[50] Most of the tasks were performed by unskilled and poorly paid workers, including women and children. Proper journeymen and apprentices, as were employed at dye works or in textile printing, were the exception. The rules and conventions of the trades were therefore rarely adhered to, particularly as many of the rural trades were new specializations of older ones, to which the Statute of Artificers of 1563 did not apply.

The regions with a high concentration of proto-industrial production included the main centres of wool manufacturing: East Anglia, the West Country, the Southwest and West Riding in Yorkshire. Woollen cloth was also produced in small pockets of Shropshire, Westmorland and the Weald of Kent, as well as in parts of Surrey, Berkshire and Hampshire. Textile regions with an emphasis on linen and fustian developed in Lancashire. In the Vale of Trent as well as in the vicinity of Nottingham, Derby and Leicester, a specialization in knitted fabrics emerged. A rural small-ironware industry was concentrated in the West Midlands, especially in Birmingham.

There can be no doubt that from the late Middle Ages to the early nineteenth century, a growing share of the wares that ended up on the market had been manufactured in a decentralized manner in the countryside. It would be risky, however, to make any further generalizations about English proto-industry. As far as its conditions of emergence are concerned, reference is occasionally made to the widespread pastoral economy in the north, west and Midlands regions of England and to the spare labour capacity associated with it. However, this precondition was neither necessary nor sufficient, as concentrated pockets of domestic industry also developed in cereal-growing regions. Furthermore, the effects of nonagricultural income on workers' choice of partner, age at marriage and family size varied considerably. In many cases, whole families laboured together, while some contractors only hired young women for piecework. Finally, no generalizations can be made about the longer-term development of the proto-industrial regions. A few temporarily successful ones fell off over time, while others surged steadily ahead before undergoing a boom in the seventeenth or eighteenth centuries. In some branches of the textile industry, especially linen and cotton manufacturing, a transition from decentralized to centralized production in steam-driven factories was successfully achieved in the early nineteenth century.

The heterogeneity of proto-industry in England is a reason why British historians have remained conspicuously reserved with respect to far-reaching theories and models that attempt to elevate the phenomenon to a precursor of modern industrial capitalism and why few have risked making general statements about the household structure or reproductive behaviour of producers. Such interpretations were discussed particularly the 1970s and 1980s, and the succeeding wave of empirical research brought together historians from all over Europe.[51] In the reservations of the British towards the concept of proto-industrialization, a general scepticism towards theory can be detected; and yet, one must concede that the contrast, so appealing to historians of the European continent, between 'proto-industrial', on the one hand, and 'traditional', 'peasant' or even 'feudal' methods of production, on the other, does sidestep the historical evidence for England. Furthermore, English proto-industry can hardly be separated from other factors of economic development such as the Agrarian Revolution, urbanization or population growth, so that the broader economic effects of artisanal production in the countryside were less obvious than elsewhere in Europe.[52]

The general scepticism with regard to the concept of proto-industrialization does not mean that British historians have not thoroughly studied the matter. However, they had different points of interest from their Continental European colleagues. While the latter kept their focus on the producers and the production process, the Britons more closely examined the sale and consumption of proto-industrially produced products.[53] In particular, two connections emerged from these studies that are of particular interest in the framework of the history of commercialization.

The first relates to the demand for proto-industrially produced goods. Here, more recent research has substantiated the thesis already posited in the 1970s and 1980s that in England in the course of the seventeenth and eighteenth centuries, a 'consumer revolution' took place that changed the lives not only of the aristocracy, the gentry and other wealthy people, but also of agricultural labourers, servants and workers.[54] The increased demand had its origin in economic policy initiatives on the part of the Crown, and for this reason it already became apparent in the first half of the seventeenth century. It then increased after 1650 under the impact of a massive rise in income and the emergence of closely meshed credit relations in cities, villages and neighbourhoods, which also helped to compensate for the problem of the dearth of coins.[55] Everyone now purchased provisions via the market, and the lower classes also acquired a great number of goods that they had never previously owned. These included sugar, tea and tobacco, as well as silk and cotton fabrics from North and South America, the Caribbean and the Far East; but also domestically produced textiles and other, largely proto-industrially manufactured products such as glass, housewares, furniture and haberdashery. The British manufacturers of these consumer goods drew inspiration for their designs in part from the foreign imports.[56]

The shops and second-hand markets that emerged in London and the provincial cities brought these products to the people. Shopkeepers advertised their wares in the local newspapers; contemporaries became accustomed to shopping and to window shopping.[57] Consumers invested a particularly large amount of time and money in acquiring fashionable clothing, whether these were purchased new or second hand; for carefully selected clothing opened up new forms of symbolic communication and provided people with an opportunity to help define their own place in the fluid social structure.[58] Clothing and wigs were furthermore an investment, as in times of need they could be exchanged for cash on the second-hand market. Significantly, in the second half of the seventeenth century, they made up at least 70 to 80 per cent of goods pledged at pawnbrokers. In view of the pronounced shortage of coins, they were often accepted as currency, although their gradual divergence over time from current fashions was accompanied by a certain drop in value.[59]

A second research interest that British historians associate with proto-industry relates to the figure of the contractor-merchant, who brought the consumer goods manufactured in the countryside to market, be it foreign or domestic (figure 2.4). In the Continental European discussion about proto-industry, merchants and middlemen are generally characterized as exploiters of cheap labour: although they did not have to invest in production facilities, they made huge profits so

Figure 2.4. A London cloth merchant inspecting goods delivered, 1690. Oil painting by Egbert van Heemskerck the Elder. The office was likely located in Blackwell Hall or in a room at the Royal Exchange.

long as market conditions were favourable, and in bad economic times or when there were conflicts they simply let workers go.[60] British historians, on the other hand, also saw the contribution of the merchant-contractors to the densification of the communications network and to the integration of the emerging market society.[61]

In this connection, they have emphasized that the investments in proto-industry and the search for distribution channels for industrial products created new opportunities for those who were displaced as a result of the Agricultural Revolution. That these employment opportunities could also be found in the countryside protected the growing cities from overpopulation and at the same time turned the rural population engaged in industry into consumers of the products of urban manufacturing. In this manner, so the argument, rural industry and the urban economy stimulated one another's ongoing development.[62]

Furthermore, British historians argue that merchants and middlemen were directly useful to the growing cities because at a time when banking was still underdeveloped, they took over important financing tasks in the area of city planning. In contrast to the equally wealthy shop owners, merchants and middlemen either held liquid assets or could easily gain access to them thanks to their numerous connections.[63] Since in the area of city planning, few impulses emanated from the Crown or from the cities themselves, merchants – and here I am referring especially to the numerically larger group of those who served the domestic market – contributed significantly to the creation of what today would be referred to as 'urbanity'.[64] This included the continued demolition of older neighbourhoods, a practice that had begun in the seventeenth century, and the building of newer, in some cases suburban, ones for workers and the newly arising 'middling sort' (to which the merchants themselves also belonged). They furthermore cofinanced the construction of municipal buildings, such as hospitals, poorhouses, courthouses and theatres, and helped to bankroll diverse measures within the framework of urban improvement, such as the provision of water pumps, wastewater removal and street lighting. Finally, their efforts contributed to the realization of grander, 'coach-worthy' cities with broad, paved streets and generous squares; pedestrian zones free of road traffic, such as pavements, promenades and public gardens; and covered markets and rows of shops.[65] For the social and cultural historian, these initiatives are relevant because the development towards a consumer society was supported by changes in the public space. Those who were attempting to rise in the social hierarchy could use the city as a stage for their self-representation.

Concentration of Powers: The Financial Revolution of the Eighteenth Century

Having increased continually in the century between Elizabeth I's accession to the throne (1558) and the restoration of the monarchy under Charles II (1660), only to enter a phase of uneven development in the following decades, the volume of exports of goods overseas once again experienced an appreciable rise between 1697 and 1815. Under the Navigation Acts (1651), which gave English ships a monopoly over the transport of English goods, exports grew at an even faster pace than either the population or the gross national product. And yet the share of trade with (northern) European countries, which had been carried out since the Middle Ages, was on the decline. Most of the exports and re-exports (as raw materials from abroad were often processed and shipped out again as finished products) were now going to North and South America, as well as to the Caribbean, Africa and the Far East. It was above all in those regions of the world that the slave trade – a precondition for the promising cotton industry – was taking place. The British merchants and shipowners were protected and defended in their commercial activities by the Royal Navy, which had been expanded under Cromwell. To some extent, the navy, through its military activities, can even be said to have helped forge a path for them across the oceans. This reflects how the trading system was embedded within a web of imperial relations, which not only connected individual market participants but rather – as shall be shown in the following – also the credit system and the State.

With the exception of the East India, South Sea, Hudson's Bay, Royal African and Levant Companies, the London-based merchants associations did not play a noteworthy role in this connection, especially since, after 1688, Parliament showed little inclination to extend the trade monopoly granted by the Crown. Rather, it was individual merchants and the informal communities of middlemen in the port and trade cities who had control over the management of British over-seas trade. It was also they who, at the numerous links in the network – from the production of wares, to their transport over the oceans, to their storage and sale in foreign locations – put up their own capital, obtained more from investors, guaranteed loans and issued and took receipt of payments.[66]

The risks involved in such transactions were considerable and difficult for individual participants to assess. To better manage them, some merchants special-ized in insurance, others in international banking. This differentiation enabled London to draw level with Amsterdam in the course of the eighteenth century as an international financial centre. As a side effect, credit became cheaper and easier to obtain. Legislators supported this development by letting bankers do as they saw fit and by punishing fraudsters.[67]

From 1694, the still relatively undifferentiated banking system was flanked by a privately owned joint-stock company called the Bank of England. The found-ing of the bank took place under conditions in which the Crown, due to the extraordinary expenditures for the wars with France that had begun in 1689, was to a very great extent dependent on credit, and the situation was only set to exacerbate. Still amounting to only ten thousand in 1689, the number of soldiers in the British Army would increase to seventy-six thousand by 1697 and ultimately to ninety-three thousand by the war's end in 1713; this figure corresponded to approximately 7 per cent of the adult male population of Eng-land. Added to this were the expenses for forty thousand sailors. On average, the cost of the wars amounted to around £5.5 million annually for the time period between 1689 and 1697, rising to £7 million between 1702 and 1713.[68] In the mid-1690s, the Bank of England took over responsibility for the management of the government's debts and above all made arrangements for the settlement of temporary and as yet unsecured debts. The tax revenues of the State served as collateral – subject, since the Glorious Revolution, to the consent of Parliament. When this consent was granted, which was generally the case, the debts incurred by the King were converted into a national debt, and the war expenses could be distributed over a longer time span.[69]

Initially, the representatives of the government and of the bank attempted to privatize the national debt – in part through the sale of special trade rights to the dubious South Sea Company, which was founded in 1711 to spur trade with Latin America. However, after it emerged that this transaction created a huge speculative bubble, the bursting of which in 1720 drove hundreds of business-people and an unknown number of small-scale investors into ruin, no further actions of this nature were undertaken.[70] The acceptance of discredited state treasury bills as a capital payment then became routine, and in this manner the privilege of the Bank of England as the government's bank was renewed numerous times over the course of the eighteenth century.

In addition, since the beginning of the eighteenth century, the banknotes issued by the bank to the Treasury were recognized as a general means of payment and, with respect to the bank's solvency vis-à-vis its depositors, were regarded as the equivalent of precious metal reserves. Following the bursting of the South Sea Bubble, this contributed to restoring (or, in many cases, generating for the first time) trust in securities as financial instruments; for people in the seventeenth and early eighteenth centuries preferred 'tangible' coins and precious metals, and were sceptical of promissory notes.[71]

Just as important was the effect on economic policy. As the Bank of England, in its role as the government's bank, advanced to the lender of last resort, it could expand the issuing of discount loans to meet the high-level and short-term debts of London's merchants and other business people. That meant that, primarily through government borrowing, the breakthrough of the City of London as an international financial centre opened up a market for government bonds and placed the already existing market for shares and securities on a new institutional basis.[72] Within just a few years, foreign investors were briskly trading on these markets. Already around the middle of the eighteenth century, 77 per cent of those doing business in the City (and bringing in their own international connections) hailed from other European countries. Similar developments were also seen in Leeds, Manchester and other provincial trade cities.[73]

Above all, it was Dutch investors who were attracted to the City. They supplied a majority of the foreign capital, and the province of Holland provided a loan guarantee of £300,000.[74] The system of credit creation through public borrowing that was established in England had originally been conceived of in the Netherlands and had already been implemented in the Dutch provinces; and without a doubt, the English financial experts had drawn inspiration from the other side of the Channel. What was missing from the model, however, and what drew the Dutch to London, was the flexible connection and reliable mutual support that existed between private and state credit markets in England. For due to the fragmentary character of the United Netherlands – a loose federation of autonomous cities and polities without a central government – a national debt financed by taxes could not be created.[75]

Through the intermediary of the Bank of England, the Crown became a player in international trade. However, the fiscal means that it required for its military exploits could only be obtained at a high price, as Parliament mercilessly exploited the Crown's dependence upon its agreement to strengthen its own position, insisting, amongst other things, that future wars could only be waged with its consent. The Crown was additionally dependent on the continuity of the economic upswing if it was to be able to regularly service the loans. For this, sufficient tax yields were needed. Meanwhile, the commercial interests concentrated in the City of London also insisted upon the reliability of the repayments, and therefore it is hard to say what the driving force behind the development was. In any event, viewed over the longer term, it was more important that the institutions of debt management were linked to a transparent process of parliamentary ratification of the budgets, for it was upon this that the legitimacy of the British State was based.[76]

Against the background of this Financial Revolution (P. G. M. Dickson), following so closely on the heels of the Glorious Revolution, it should come as no surprise that nearly all of the major wars that the Crown financed through public funds were waged not only in the national defence but also and above all to further enhance the British presence on world markets, to conquer new territories and markets overseas and to secure its existing staging posts in Africa, Asia and America. This applies to most of the conflicts subsequent to the above-mentioned war with France (1689–97): that is, the War of the Spanish Succession (1702–13); the War of Jenkins' Ear, waged against Spain in the Caribbean and southern North America (1739–42); the War of the Austrian Succession (1739–48); and the Seven Years' War (1756–63). Of all these, only the American War of Independence (1775–83) ended in defeat; and yet for the commercial interests, it also served its purpose, since the American markets stood wide open for British products. Likewise viewed from the long-term perspective, the United States remained part of Britain's 'invisible empire': the 'empire of commerce'.

Each of these wars was more expensive than the last, and by the end, military expenditures had increased fivefold. Of total government expenditures, their share regularly amounted to between 61 and 75 per cent (1688–1783); of national income, between 9 and 14 per cent (1710–80).[77] The sharp increase in the national debt led, in the eighteenth century, to Britain becoming the most highly taxed country in Europe. Between the Glorious Revolution and the end of the Napoleonic Wars (which marked the end of the long eighteenth century), total tax revenues increased tenfold, and per capita tax revenues 4.5-fold. Parallel to tax increases, moves continued to convert the tax system from a direct land tax to indirect excise taxes, the earliest of which had already been introduced at the time of the Civil War. Indirect taxes made up 50 per cent of total tax yields at the beginning of the eighteenth century, a share that rose to 75 per cent by the century's end. Thus, anyone purchasing candles, beer, salt, coal or soap regularly paid into the national treasury.[78]

Whether contemporaries felt disadvantaged by this development – which ultimately signified a redistribution of the tax burden from the landed interests to the general population, especially the middling sort, with its strong appetite for consumer goods – is doubtful, seeing as protests remained weak. It is, moreover, a characteristic of indirect taxes to be hidden within the price of goods, and, given the general rise in income in the eighteenth century, this must have happened very easily indeed. In addition, the fact that badges of status such as houses, glass windows, coaches, riding horses and male servants continued to be subject to direct taxation must have mitigated the discontent of the less wealthy population. The Exchequer ultimately accommodated the moneyed interests – the ranks of whom by the end of the eighteenth century also included many a manufacturer – by entirely exempting from taxation most raw materials, as well as certain commercially industrially produced key products (such as cotton and wool goods, furniture, housewares, glass and paper).[79] Among those who massively and ultimately successfully protested against the high tax burden were the inhabitants of the British colonies in North America.[80]

Although the coalition between moneyed interests and the Crown and/or the State were of central significance for the future of the British financial system, economic historians view this development very critically because it came at the expense of future generations. For one, the latter had to help pay for the national debt. For another, in some cases the investment opportunities opened up overseas presumably diverted funds that would otherwise have been invested in commercial enterprises at home and contributed to making the industrialization of Great Britain a slower process than one would have expected in view of its precursory proto-industrial stage, a point to which we shall return later.[81]

However, contemporaries did not have to worry about such things, as they had no conception of the possible alternatives. Furthermore, the sums consumed by the wars could be seen as investments in the future to the extent that the costs accrued by Britain's military opponents and commercial competitors – the Spanish, French and Americans – were much higher. Finally, the wars had been legitimized by Parliament, so that those who advocated for them could claim the support of a broad consensus. Even the landowners, not all of whom were so enamoured of risk-taking that they were inclined to make their existence as rentiers more exciting by engaging in commerce, allowed themselves to be drawn into the alliance of the future after some of their demands, such as for the prospecting rights to any coal and mineral deposits on their land, were met.[82] One of the indisputable results of the Financial Revolution in the eighteenth century, which took place against a backdrop of wars, consisted in the fact that aristocratic landowners, merchants and the numerically still small group of factory owners entered into an informal alliance for the imperialistic expansion of Great Britain. This alliance was additionally strengthened through marital connections and a common fondness for gentry culture. In the following two centuries, it would also remain the basis of the system of 'gentlemanly capitalism' (P. J. Cain and A. G. Hopkins), which had its roots in the City of London.[83]

Indirectly, the culture of the general population was also determined in part by the development outlined here. Paradoxically, the connecting link was the modernization of the state apparatus in the wake of the Financial Revolution. The argument becomes tenable when one calls to mind a few connections:

To execute the new state duties reliably and efficiently, other central agencies were also set up alongside the Treasury, such as the Navy Office, the Post Office and the Board of Trade. All together, they employed some twelve thousand officials in 1720, most of them tax collectors. In comparison, the Prussian bureaucracy at this time numbered only about three thousand civil servants, 250 of whom held managerial positions.[84] The older research finding that, in terms of state administration, Early Modern England was underdeveloped in comparison with other European states with a more strongly absolutist bent is thus unsustainable, especially seeing as the officials displayed traits that one commonly associates with modern civil servants: they were offered full-time and permanent positions, received a salary and were eligible for a state pension. Their ascent up the bureaucratic ladder took place within the framework of an established hierarchy, with length of service and on-the-job performance also being taken into account. They were expected to embody integrity, devotion to the office and loyalty. Finally – and this is especially noteworthy – over time, they set aside their self-conception as 'the King's servants' and understood themselves as 'the State's servants'.[85]

For the population at large, the modernization of the state apparatus was felt less clearly, as it primarily affected the central authorities based in London. Neither the financial means nor the energy were available to correspondingly improve the administrative structure in the provinces. Furthermore, Parliament stood in the way of thoroughgoing measures, since it understood itself as a national institution for the assertion of local interests. At the lower levels, the English State thus had to rely, as before, on the ultimately medieval institutions of the lord lieutenant with his deputies and the sheriff, but above all on the justices of the peace. These were amateurs acting in a voluntary capacity who were charged with a variety of tasks, from the overseeing of public morals to the suppression of uprisings; for that reason, however, they were also permanently out of their depth.[86]

In this context, contemporaries of the eighteenth century, who, after the Glorious Revolution, developed an understanding of themselves as freeborn Englishmen, enjoyed great freedom in terms of how they organized their reciprocal social relations. This state of affairs found expression above all in popular culture, which reached a level of animation and innovation that had never before existed in Europe and which, as shall be explained below, allowed itself to be integrated in many ways into the process of commercialization.[87] This effect was surely not the worst trade-off for the high taxes that were demanded of the population.

Notes

1. Cf. A. Macfarlane. 1997. *The Savage Wars of Peace. England, Japan and the Malthusian Trap,* Oxford: Blackwell, 41–42, 75, 79, 170–74, 271, 388–89.
2. Cf. E. A. Wrigley. 1987. 'Urban Growth and Agricultural Change: England and the Continent in the Early Modern Period', in idem, *People,* 189; J. A. Goldstone. 1986. 'The Demographic Revolution in England: a Re-Examination', *Population Studies* 40, 5–33.
3. Cf. Westerfield, Middlemen, 414–15.
4. The more recent social and economic history of the Middle Ages emphasizes this; see J. Hatcher and M. Bailey. 2001. *Modelling the Middle Ages. The History and Theory of England's Economic Development,* Oxford: Oxford University Press, 121–73.
5. Figures from P. Borsay. 2002. 'Urban Life and Culture', in H. T. Dickinson (ed.), *A Companion to Eighteenth-Century Britain,* Oxford: Blackwell, 196–208; Coward, *Social Change,* 77–78. See also E. A. Wrigley. 1987. 'A Simple Model of London's Importance in Changing English Society and Economy, 1650–1750', in idem, *People,* esp. 190.
6. For both periods, the comparative figures for France are 11 per cent; cf. idem, 'Simple Model', 170, 184.
7. Figures from idem. 2004. 'The Divergence of England: the Growth of the English Economy in the Seventeenth and Eighteenth Centuries', in idem, *Poverty,* 49.
8. Cf. A. F. Weber. 1967. *The Growth of Cities in the Nineteenth Century. A Study in Statistics,* New York: Macmillan Co. 1899, Reprint of 3rd ed. Ithaca, NY: Cornell University Press, 46–47, 90. See also J. G. Williamson. 1990. *Coping with City Growth during the British Industrial Revolution,* Cambridge: Cambridge University Press, 4 (with additional European comparative data).
9. Figures from J. Hoppit. 2000. *A Land of Liberty? England 1689–1727,* Oxford: Oxford University Press, 331; J. Brewer. 1990. *The Sinews of Power. War, Money and the English State 1688–1783,* Cambridge, MA: Harvard University Press, 184. For different figures, which however point in a similar direction, see Westerfield, *Middlemen,* 334–35.
10. Cf. R. Britnell. 2006. 'Markets, Shops, Inns, Taverns and Private Houses in Medieval English Trade', in B. Blondé et al. (eds), *Buyers and Sellers. Retail Circuits in Medieval and Early Modern Europe,* Turnhout: Brepols Publishers, 109–24; D. Keene. 2006. 'Sites of Desire: Shops, Selds and Wardrobes in London and other English Cities', in B. Blondé, P. et al., *Buyers and Sellers,* 125–54; V. Harding. 2006. 'Shops, Markets and Retailers in London's Cheapside, c. 1500–1700', in B. Blondé et al., *Buyers and Sellers,* 155–170; Westerfield, Middlemen, 340–49; D. Davis, 1966. *A History of Shopping,* London: Routledge.
11. According to Macfarlane, from 1560, at least, for some 90 per cent of the English population, starvation was no longer a personal experience; see *Savage Wars of Peace,* 66.
12. Contemporary observers and historians alike long dated the enclosures to the second half of the eighteenth century, when Parliament passed the corresponding legislation. More recent research, however, has laid more stress on developments before 1750 and relativized the overall significance of enclosure. Cf. J. R. Wordie. 1983. 'The Chronology of English Enclosure, 1500–1914', *Economic History Review* 36, 501–02. For that reason, there will be no detailed treatment of the subject here.

13. Cf. J. Thirsk. 1983. 'Introduction', in J. Thirsk (ed.), *The Agrarian History of England and Wales, 1640–1750*, vol. 5, Cambridge: Cambridge University Press, XXIII; see also E. L. Jones. 1965. 'Agriculture and Economic Growth in England, 1660–1750: Agricultural Change', *Journal of Economic History* 25, 1–18; Overton, *Agricultural Revolution*.

14. Cf. P. Deane. 1996. 'The British Industrial Revolution', in M. Teich and R. Porter (eds), *The Industrial Revolution in National Context. Europe and the USA*, Cambridge: Cambridge University Press, 28.

15. For comparisons with individual countries, see J. Simpson. 2004. 'European Farmers and the British "Agricultural Revolution"', in L. Prados de la Escosura (ed.), *Exceptionalism and Industrialisation. Britain and Its European Rivals, 1688–1815*, Cambridge: Cambridge University Press, 69–85.

16. The percentage is mentioned in Wrigley, 'Urban Growth', 189.

17. Cf. G. Clark. 1991. 'Labour Productivity in English Agriculture, 1300–1860', in B. M. S. Campbell and M. Overton (eds), *Land, Labour and Livestock: Historical Studies in European Agricultural Productivity*, Manchester: Manchester University Press, 212–13.

18. Meat and other perishable commodities were traded at regional markets, and grain on the national market; cf. ibid, 136–47.

19. For details, see Westerfield, *Middlemen*; L. Weatherill. 1986. 'The Business of Middlemen in the English Pottery Trade Before 1780', *Business History* 28, 11–76. See also D. E. C. Eversley. 1967. 'The Home Market and Economic Growth in England, 1750–1780', in E. L. Jones and G. E. Mingay (eds), *Land, Labour and Population in the Industrial Revolution*, London: Hodder and Stroughton, 206–59.

20. Cf. D. C. Coleman. 1975. *Industry in Tudor and Stuart England*, London: Macmillan, 35–39. The only joint stock companies in existence in 1568 were a state mining enterprise and an armaments manufacturer.

21. Cf. Ibid, 46–47; B. Thomas. 1986. 'Was there an Energy Crisis in Great Britain in the Seventeenth Century?', *Explorations in Economic History* 2, 134–52.

22. Cf. J. U. Nef. 1994 (1932). 'The Substitution of Coal for Wood', in R. A. Church (ed.), *The Coal and Iron Industries*, Oxford: Blackwell, 66–101; A. Macfarlane and G. Martin. 2003. *The Glass Bathyscaphe. How Glass Changed the World*, London: Profile Books, 24–26.

23. Cf. E. A. Wrigley. 1987. 'The Process of Modernization and the Industrial Revolution in England', in idem, *People*, 65.

24. The rule of thumb is that a tonne of coal freed up one hectare of land for cultivation and livestock, which otherwise would have had to be used for forestry; see E. A. Wrigley. 2004. 'The Quest for the Industrial Revolution', in idem, *Poverty*, 39.

25. Cf. Macfarlane, *Savage Wars of Peace*, 218, 221, 224; E. L. Jones and M. E. Falkus. 1979. 'Urban Improvement and the English Economy in the Seventeenth and Eighteenth Centuries', *Research in Economic History* 4, 198–203.

26. Cf. E. A. Wrigley. 1987. 'The Supply of Raw Materials in the Industrial Revolution', in idem, *People*, 81.

27. Cf. Szostak, *Role of Transportation*, 85, 89–90; W. Albert. 1972. *The Turnpike Road System in England 1663–1840*, Cambridge: Cambridge University Press.

28. Cf. Wrigley, 'The Quest for the Industrial Revolution', 33.

29. This is the general result of Szostak, *Role of Transportation*.

30. Cf. Wrigley, 'Simple Model'.

31. Cf. Coward, *Social Change*, 81.

32. Cf. B. Brodt. 2003. 'Authority – Loyalty – Autonomy, or the Archaeology of Power. English Provincial Capitals Reconsidered', in A. Fahrmeir and E. Rembold (eds), *Representations of British Cities. The Transformation of Urban Space 1700–2000*, Berlin: Philo, 21–23. On the legal position of the cities, see Brodnitz, 'Die Stadtwirtschaft in England'.

33. Cf. N. Ramsay. 1991. 'Introduction', in J. Blair and N. Ramsay (eds), *English Medieval Industries. Craftsman, Techniques, Products,* London: The Hambledon Press, XX-XXV; Britnell, 'England: Towns, Trade and Industry', 58–60. Britnell mentions the belated development of guilds in England in 'Town Life', 168.

34. Cf. G. Unwin. 1904. *Industrial Organization in the Sixteenth and Seventeenth Centuries,* Oxford: Clarendon Press, chaps. 2 and 3; S. L. Thrupp. 1965. 'The Gilds', in *Cambridge Economic History of Europe,* ed. M. M. Postan et al., vol. 3, Cambridge: Cambridge University Press, 243. On the livery companies, see R. B. Dobson and D. M. Smith (eds). 2006. *The Merchant Taylors of York. A History of the Craft and Company from the Fourteenth to the Twentieth Centuries,* York: Borthwick Publications; A. Fahrmeir 2003. *Ehrbare Spekulanten. Stadtverfassung, Wirtschaft und Politik in der City of London, 1688–1900,* Munich: Oldenbourg, 52–65.

35. J. Steinfeld documents this in detail in his 1991 book *The Invention of Free Labor. The Employment Relation in English and American Law and Culture, 1350-1870,* Chapel Hill, NC: University of North Carolina Press, 15–54. See also W. Steinmetz. 2002. *Begegnungen vor Gericht. Eine Sozial- und Kulturgeschichte des englischen Arbeitsrechts (1850–1925),* Munich: Oldenbourg; and P. Johnson. 2010. *Making the Market. Victorian Origins of Corporate Capitalism,* Cambridge: Cambridge University Press, 75–82.

36. For more details, see D. Woodward. 1980. 'The Background of the Statute of Artificers: The Genesis of Labour Policy, 1558–63', *Economic History Review* 33, 32–44; M. Schulte Beerbühl. 1991. *Vom Gesellenverein zur Gewerkschaft. Entwicklung, Struktur und Politik der Londoner Gesellenorganisationen 1550–1825,* Göttingen: Vandenhoeck and Ruprecht, 67–82. The interpretation follows that in Coleman, *Industry in Tudor and Stuart England,* 22.

37. Cf. Schulte Beerbühl, *Gesellenverein.* On the negative influence of the civil war, see B. Lemire. 1997. *Dress, Culture and Commerce. The English Clothing Trade before the Factory, 1660–1800,* Houndmills: Macmillan, 44 (taking the example of the tailors' guilds).

38. See Schulte Beerbühl, *Gesellenverein.* See also J. Humphries. 2003. 'English Apprenticeship: A Neglected Factor in the First Industrial Revolution', in P. A. David and M. Thomas (eds), *The Economic Future in Historical Perspective,* Oxford: Oxford University Press, 73–102.

39. See J. Ehmer. 1998. 'Traditionelles Denken und neue Fragestellungen zur Geschichte von Handwerk und Zunft', in F. Lenger (ed.), *Handwerk, Hausindustrie und die Historische Schule der Nationalökonomie. Wissenschafts- und gewerbegeschichtliche Perspektiven,* Bielefeld: Verlag für Regionalgeschichte, 36–37, 54; S. C. Ogilvie. 1997. *State Corporatism and Proto-Industry: the Württemberg Black Forest, 1580–1797,* Cambridge: Cambridge University Press, 72–79, 413–37; U. Pfister. 1998. 'Craft Guilds and Proto-Industrialization in Europe, 16th to 18th Centuries', in S. R. Epstein et al. (eds), *Guilds, Economy and Society,* Sevilla: Secretariado de publicaciones de la Universidad de Sevilla, 11–24; W. Reininghaus. 1990. *Gewerbe in der frühen Neuzeit,* Munich: Oldenbourg, 71–63, 71–72, 79–80; H.-G. Haupt (ed.). 2002. *Das Ende der Zünfte. Ein europäischer Vergleich,* Göttingen: Vandenhoeck and Ruprecht; D. Georges. 1990. *1810/11–1993: Handwerk und Interessenpolitik. Von der Zunft zur modernen Verbandsorganisation,* Frankfurt, Main: Peter Lang.

40. This occurred regardless of whether they survived as independent entrepreneurs and employers or sank into the proletariat as impoverished master artisans who worked alone. Cf. G. Lottes. 1979. *Politische Aufklärung und plebejisches Publikum. Zur Theorie und Praxis des englischen Radikalismus im späten 18. Jahrhundert,* Munich: Oldenbourg, 114–39 and passim.

41. This was already the conclusion of H. Levy's clear-sighted 1920 *Soziologische Studien über das englische Volk,* in which the author noted '[the] absence of a particular economic interest movement such as that of the [German] *Mittelstand,* as the expression of a stratum of traditional-minded corporative-guild artisans that has not yet entered into the capitalist social scheme'. Jena: Gustav Fischer, 26.

42. These were still hotly debated points of conflict among German artisans in the mid-nineteenth century; see J. Ehmer. 1991. *Heiratsverhalten, Sozialstruktur, ökonomischer Wandel. England und Mitteleuropa in der Formationsperiode des Kapitalismus,* Göttingen: Vandenhoeck and Ruprecht, 185–203; J. Kocka. 1990. *Arbeitsverhältnisse und Arbeiterexistenzen. Grundlagen der Klassenbildung im 19. Jahrhundert,* Bonn: Dietz, 329–34; C. Eisenberg. 1986. *Deutsche und englische Gewerkschaften. Entstehung und Entwicklung bis 1878 im Vergleich,* Göttingen: Vandenhoeck and Ruprecht, 54–66. Schulte Beerbühl, *Gesellenverein,* 36–38, dates the freer conditions in England to the late Middle Ages.
43. Cf. Schulte Beerbühl, Gesellenverein; M. Chase. 2000. *Early Trade Unionism. Fraternity, Skill and the Politics of Labour,* Aldershot: Ashgate.
44. Cf. C. R. Dobson, 1982. *Masters and Journeymen. A Prehistory of Industrial Relations 1717– 1800,* London: Croom Helm, 22, 24. If one includes Scotland and Ireland, the total number of such disputes was 383.
45. Cf. Eisenberg, *Deutsche und englische Gewerkschaften,* 86–97.
46. G. Briefs. 1952. *Zwischen Kapitalismus und Syndikalismus. Die Gewerkschaften am Scheidewege,* Bern: Francke, 103. The argumentation is based on C. Offe and K. Hinrichs. 1984. 'Sozial-ökonomie des Arbeitsmarktes: primäres und sekundäres Machtgefälle', in C. Offe, *"Arbeitsge-sellschaft": Strukturprobleme und Zukunftsperspektiven,* Frankfurt, Main: Campus, 48-51.
47. Cf. R. C. Allen. 2001. 'The Great Divergence in European Wages and Prices from the Middle Ages to the First World War', *Explorations in Economic History* 38, 411–47; idem. 2009. *The British Industrial Revolution in Global Perspective,* Cambridge: Cambridge University Press, 25–56.
48. Because children left home early, *Hausindustrie* (household industry), the typical term used for Continental Europe, appears inappropriate for England; see Anderson, 'Entrepreneurship', 175.
49. Figures from R. Millward. 1981. 'The Emergence of Wage Labor in Early Modern England', *Explorations in Economic History* 18, 22. See also B. M. S. Campbell. 2003. 'England: Land and People', in S. H. Rigby (ed.), *A Companion to Britain in the Later Middle Ages,* Oxford: Blackwell, 16.
50. The discussion that follows is based, unless otherwise indicated, on P. Hudson's overview 'Proto-Industrialisierung in England', in M. Cerman and S. C. Ogilvie (eds), *Proto-Industri-alisierung in Europa. Industrielle Produktion vor dem Fabrikszeitalter,* Wien: Verlag für Gesell-schaftskritik, 61–78 and her 1989 edited volume *Regions and Industries. A Perspective on the Industrial Revolution in Britain,* Cambridge: Cambridge University Press.
51. As one example out of an extensive literature, see F. Mendels. 1972. 'Proto-Industrialization: the First Phase of the Industrialization Process', *Journal of Economic History* 31, 241–261; see also P. Kriedte et al. 1977. *Industrialisierung vor der Industrialisierung. Gewerbliche Warenpro-duktion auf dem Land in der Formationsperiode des Kapitalismus,* Göttingen: Vandenhoeck and Ruprecht. The essay collections that have appeared in the meantime include K. Ditt and S. Pollard (eds). 1992. *Von der Heimarbeit in die Fabrik. Industrialisierung und Arbeiterschaft in Leinen- und Baumwollregionen Westeuropas während des 18. und 19. Jahrhunderts,* Paderborn: Schöningh; Cerman, M. and S. C. Ogilvie (eds). 1994. *Protoindustrialisierung in Europa. Industrielle Produktion vor dem Fabrikzeitalter,* Wien: Verlag für Gesellschaftskritik; D. Ebeling and W. Mager (eds). 1997. *Protoindustrie in der Region. Europäische Gewerbelandschaften vom 16. bis zum 19. Jahrhundert,* Bielefeld: Verlag für Regionalgeschichte.
52. Cf. D. C. Coleman. 1983. 'Proto-Industrialization: A Concept Too Many', *Economic History Review* 36, 425–48; R. A. Houston and K. D. M. Snell. 1984. 'Proto-Industrialization, Cot-tage Industry, Social Change and the Industrial Revolution', *Historical Journal* 27, 473–92.
53. Early examples of this trend are Eversley, 'Home Market'; R. Samuel. 1977. 'Workshop of the World: Steam Power and Hand Technology in Mid-Victorian Britain', *History Workshop* 3, 6–72; N. McKendrick. 1974. 'Home Demand and Economic Growth: A New View of the

Role of Women and Children in the Industrial Revolution', in N. McKendrick (ed.), *Historical Perspectives: Studies in English Thought and Society*, London: Europa Publications, 152–210; idem. 1982. 'The Consumer Revolution of Eighteenth-Century England', in N. McKendrick et al., *Birth of a Consumer Society*, 9–33.

54. One of the first to espouse this interpretation was Thirsk in the 1978 *Economic Policy and Projects: the Development of a Consumer Society in Early-Modern England*, Oxford: Oxford University Press, 179. N. McKendrick et al. then published *Birth of Consumer Society* a few years later. A wealth of evidence for the integration of workers into consumption can be found in B. Lemire's 2005 book *The Business of Everyday Life. Gender, Practice and Social Politics in England, c. 1600–1900*, Manchester: Manchester University Press.

55. For that reason, consumption in England can be estimated as a good deal higher than the figures offered by contemporary statisticians, on whose work historians have largely based their estimates. Cf. Lemire, *Business of Everyday Life*, 16–55; Muldrew, *Economy of Obligation*, 90, as well as below, 78.

56. Cf. L. Weatherill. 1989. Consumer Behaviour and Material Culture in Britain, 1660–1760, London: Routledge; M. Berg. 2005. *Luxury and Pleasure in Eighteenth-Century Britain*, Oxford: Oxford University Press; Lemire, *Business of Everyday Life;* J. Styles. 2007. *The Dress of the People. Everyday Fashion in Eighteenth-Century England*, New Haven: Yale University Press.

57. See above, 43–44; see also Davis, *History of Shopping;* R. M. Berger. 1980. 'The Development of Retail Trade in Provincial England, c. 1550–1700', *Journal of Economic History* 60, 123–28; J. Stobart. 2005. 'Leisure and Shopping in the Small Towns of Georgian England', *Journal of Urban History* 31, 479–503.; J. Benson and L. Ugolini (eds). 2002. *A Nation of Shopkeepers: Retailing in Britain, 1550–2000*, London: I. B. Tauris; N. Cox and K. Dannehl. 2007. *Perceptions of Retailing in Early Modern England*, Aldershot: Ashgate. On the second hand markets, see B. Lemire. 1988. 'Consumerism in Preindustrial and Early Industrial England: The Trade in Second Hand Clothes', *Journal of British Studies* 27, 1–24; idem, *Busines of Everyday Life*, 82–109.

58. Cf. N. McKendrick. 1982. 'The Commercialization of Fashion', in N. McKendrick et al., *The Birth of a Consumer Society. The Commercialization of Eighteenth-Century England*, London: Hutchinson, 34–99; D. Kuchta. 2002. *The Three-Piece Suit and Modern Masculinity: England 1550–1850*, Berkeley: University of California Press; see also P. J. Corfield. 1989. 'Dress for Deference and Dissent: Hats and the Decline of Hat Honour', in *Costume* 23, 64–79.

59. Cf. Lemire, *Business of Everyday Life*, 82–109, percentages on 92, 94.

60. This interpretation is formulated with veritably classic one-sidedness in Kriedte et al., *Industrialisierung vor der Industrialisierung*, 249–50. This image of the merchant has also entered literary texts and the social sciences; see D. Slater and F. Tonkiss. 2001. *Market Society. Markets and Modern Social Theory*, Cambridge: Polity, 11, 16.

61. Cf. J. M. Price, 1989. 'What Did Merchants Do? Reflections on British Oversea Trade, 1660–1790', *Journal of Economic History* 49, 267–84. See also Westerfield, *Middlemen*, 111–45.

62. Cf. E. A. Wrigley. 2004. '"The Great Commerce of Every Civilized Society": Urban Growth in Early Modern Europe', in idem, *Poverty, Progress, and Population*, esp. 281–84.

63. Cf. R. Grassby. 1970. 'English Merchant Capitalism in the Late Seventeenth Century. The Composition of Business Fortunes', *Past and Present* 46, 106; R. G. Wilson. 1971. *Gentlemen Merchants. The Merchant Community in Leeds, 1700–1830*, Manchester: Manchester University Press, 149.

64. Cf. P. J. Corfield. 1982. *The Impact of English Towns 1700–1800*, Oxford: Oxford University Press, 131; Wilson, *Gentlemen Merchants*, 86, 194–206.

65. Cf. Corfield, *Impact*, 168–85; Jones and Falkus, 'Urban Improvement'; P. Borsay. 1989. *The English Urban Renaissance: Culture and Society in the Provincial Town, 1660–1770*, Oxford:

Oxford University Press; idem. 2003. 'The Rise, Fall and Rise of Polite Urban Space in England 1700–2000', in A. Fahrmeir and E. Rembold (eds), *Representations of British Cities. The Transformation of Urban Space 1700–2000,* Berlin: Philo, 32–34; J. Stobart. 1998. 'Shopping Streets as Social Space: Consumerism, Improvement and Leisure in an Eighteenth-Century Country Town', *Urban History* 25, 3–21.

66. On this, see Hancock, *Citizens of the World.*

67. For a detailed account, see L. Neal. 1990. *The Rise of Financial Capitalism. International Capital Markets in the Age of Reason,* Cambridge: Cambridge University Press.

68. Cf. Brewer, *Sinews of Power,* 30–31.

69. P. G. M. Dickson. 1967. *The Financial Revolution in England: A Study in the Development of Public Credit, 1688–1756,* London: Macmillan, remains a fundamental work. See also M. C. Lovell. 1957. 'The Role of the Bank of England as Lender of Last Resort in the Crises of the Eighteenth Century', *Explorations in Entrepreneurial History* 10, 14–15; H. V. Bowen. 1995. 'The Bank of England during the Long Eighteenth Century, 1694–1820', in R. Roberts and D. Kynaston (eds), *The Bank of England. Money, Power and Influence 1694–1994,* Oxford: Clarendon Press, 1–18.

70. For a brief summary of this period of 'bubble economics', see Hoppit, *Land of Liberty,* 334–38.

71. On this problem, see J. J. Baker. 2005. *Securing the Commonwealth. Debt, Speculation, and Writing in the Making of Early America,* Baltimore: The Johns Hopkins University Press. Baker, however, studies the North American case; whether reservations were equally marked in England, with its long tradition of bills of exchange, remains to be explored. On the social basis of those damaged by the Bubble, see J. Hoppit. 1986. 'Financial Crises in Eighteenth-Century England', *Economic History Review* 39, 48.

72. In 1853 British government bonds still represented 70 per cent of the securities traded at the London Stock Exchange.

73. Cf. Chapman, *Merchant Enterprise,* 29–30. See also Schulte Beerbühl, *Deutsche Kaufleute.*

74. Cf. M. 't Hart. 1991. '"The Devil or the Dutch": Holland's Impact on the Financial Revolution in England, 1643–1694', *Parliaments, Estates and Representation* 11, 50. See also C. Wilson. 1966. *Anglo-Dutch Commerce and Finance in the Eighteenth Century,* Cambridge: Cambridge University Press, 70–79.

75. Cf. t' Hart, '"The Devil or the Dutch"'; L. Neal. 2004. 'The Monetary, Financial and Political Architecture of Europe, 1648–1815', in Prados de la Escosura, *Exceptionalism and Industrialisation,* 173–90. For the broader context of these developments, see D. Ormrod. 2003. *The Rise of Commercial Empires. England and the Netherlands in the Age of Mercantilism, 1650–1770,* Cambridge: Cambridge University Press.

76. Cf. R. C. Michie. 1999. *The London Stock Exchange: A History,* Oxford: Oxford University Press, 15–36.

77. Figures from Brewer, *Sinews of Power,* 38–41. Cf. also P. Mathias and P. K. O'Brien. 1976. 'Taxation in Britain and France, 1715–1810. A Comparison of the Social and Economic Incidence of Taxes Collected for the Central Government', *Journal of European Economic History* 5, 601–50.

78. An income tax was introduced in 1799.

79. Cf. P. K. O'Brien, 1988. 'The Political Economy of British Taxation, 1660–1815', *Economic History Review* 41, 10–11, 26–27; some of the figures come from E. Hellmuth. 2002. 'The British State', in H. T. Dickinson (ed.), *A Companion to Eighteenth-Century Britain,* Oxford: Blackwell, 21. On tax protests and the varied means of tax evasion, see W. J. Ashworth. 2003. *Customs and Excise. Trade, Production, and Consumption in England, 1640–1845,* Oxford: Oxford University Press.

80. Cf. T. H. Breen. 1988. '"Baubles of Britain": The American and Consumer Revolutions of the Eighteenth Century', *Past and Present* 119, 73–104.
81. On this effect, see J. G. Williamson. 1984. 'Why Was British Growth so Slow During the Industrial Revolution?', *Journal of Economic History* 44, 687–712; P. Deane. 1996. 'The British Industrial Revolution', in M. Teich and R. Porter (eds), *The Industrial Revolution in National Context. Europe and the USA,* Cambridge: Cambridge University Press, 23–24; O'Brien, 'Inseparable Connections'; idem. 1994. 'Central Government and the Economy, 1688–1815', in R. Floud and D. McCloskey (eds), *The Economic History of Britain since 1700, vol. 1: 1700–1860,* 2nd ed., Cambridge: Cambridge University Press, 215–15.
82. Cf. Deane, 'British Industrial Revolution', 21.
83. Cf. P. J. Cain and A. G. Hopkins. 1986. 'Gentlemanly Capitalism and British Expansion Overseas, I: The Old Colonial System 1688–1850', *Economic History Review* 39, 507–08, and Cain and Hopkins. 1993. *British Imperialism. Innovations and Expansion, 1688–1914,* vol. 1, London: Longman.
84. Figures from J. Brewer. 1994. 'The Eighteenth-Century British State. Contexts and Issues', in L. Stone (ed.), *An Imperial State at War. Britain from 1689–1815,* London: Routledge, 58–59.
85. Cf. Hellmuth, 'The British State', 22; B. Coward. 1997. *Stuart England, 1603–1714. The Formation of the British State,* London: Longman, 317. See also the explicitly comparative studies in J. Brewer and E. Hellmuth (eds). 1999. *Rethinking Leviathan: The Eighteenth-Century State in Britain and Germany,* Oxford: Oxford University Press, especially Brewer and Hellmuth's introduction and Ertman's essay 'Explaining Variations in Early Modern State Structure. The Cases of England and the German Territorial States'.
86. Cf. J. Innes. 1994. 'The Domestic Face of the Military-Fiscal State. Government and Society in Eighteenth-Century Britain', in L. Stone (ed.), *An Imperial State at War. Britain from 1689 to 1815,* London: Routledge, 96–127; Hoppit, *Land of Liberty,* 457–91, esp. 464–70.
87. Cf. J. M. Golby and A. W. Purdue. 1984. *The Civilisation of the Crowd. Popular Culture in England 1750–1900,* London: Batsford Academia and Educational Ltd., as well as the classic essays by E. P. Thompson collected in the 1991 volume *Customs in Common. Studies in Traditional Popular Culture,* New York: The New Press. See also T. Harris (ed.). 1995. *Popular Culture in England, c. 1500–1850,* London: Macmillan. For insights into the mechanisms of social discipline on the European continent, see G. Lottes. 1984. 'Popular Culture and the Early Modern State in 16th Century Germany', in S. L. Kaplan (ed.), *Understanding Popular Culture. Europe from the Middle Ages to the Nineteenth Century,* Berlin: Mouton, 147–88, and S. Ogilvie. 1999. 'The German State: A Non-Prussian View', in J. Brewer and E. Hellmuth (eds), *Rethinking Leviathan: The Eighteenth-Century State in Britain and Germany,* Oxford: Oxford University Press, 167–202.

Chapter 3

THE EMBEDDEDNESS OF MARKET EXCHANGE

❧❦❧

By around 1800, market relations in England had become so universal that hardly anyone, apart from infants or the institutionally incarcerated, could entirely elude the opportunities and importunities associated with them. Everyone – man or woman, city-dweller or villager, wage earner or self-employed person – had at some point in the context of their professional or personal lives to engage with the interplay of supply and demand, be it through the purchasing of goods or services, the selling of their labour, or investing, speculating or either borrowing or lending money. The market mechanism had infiltrated everywhere, for every household was a unit of consumption and not infrequently of production, as well. Already in the Middle Ages, barter had become the exception, and by this point was still commonly practiced only among the inhabitants of remote villages. And yet even the rural population could not survive entirely without money, as they still had to purchase equipment, pay market fees and remit taxes to the King. Additionally, charitable donations, alms and gifts were given in monetary form.[1]

Like all market actors, those in Early Modern England were therefore confronted with the specific capacity of markets to systematically create uncertainty; and indeed contemporaries experienced this uncertainty to a special degree. For one thing, the general increase in economic activity was accompanied by a large number of new and inexperienced enterprises, many of which brought new and fashionable items onto the market. In so doing, they ran considerable risks, as was reflected in the great number of bankruptcies.[2] For another, in addition to the pre-existing ties with other European nations, additional trade relations were established with more distant continents, and this also increased the level of uncertainty in market exchange. Although the countries of Europe remained the primary consumers of English lead, tin, coal, herring, leather, grain, salt and malt, more and more exports were shipped to continents further afield, especially Asia and Africa. In the opposite direction, as a result of growing wealth, the import of foodstuffs, raw materials and finished goods from overseas increased significantly. Cod from Newfoundland, skins and furs from New England and tobacco from Maryland were introduced, as were sugar and dyes from the Caribbean Islands, cheap calico from India and tea and porcelain from China. The Chinese porcelain in particular served as both a luxury good in itself and a source of designs and patterns for indigenous proto-industrial mass production.[3] As prior to 1800, these developments on either side of the ocean stood in no systematic relation to one another,[4] the mechanisms of pricing must have remained a mystery even to wholesale merchants and their staffs of professionals. Many importers saw storms at sea and unpredictable events in foreign countries as the most important factors determining the success or failure of their ventures. A further experience was that market relations in the seventeenth and eighteenth centuries – be they in the context of international or regional trade – were conducted along supply chains so long that even the good character of one's business partner could serve as no guarantee. Was a particular bill of exchange that one accepted in fact backed by assets? Would the revenues upon which one's business partner was basing his calculations really materialize?

Those seeking advice on such matters could turn to the pool of commercial literature, which already by the seventeenth century had grown to a considerable size. However, the bulk of these writings consisted of pamphlets and short occasional pieces, often no longer than two or three pages in length, most having been published anonymously by authors responding to legislative initiatives or other current questions and topics. Before Adam Smith, with *The Wealth of Nations* (1776), founded a canon of academic literature on economic questions that was thoroughly ambivalent in its assessment of the market mechanism, not even the most prolific of these authors managed to establish themselves as authorities on the subject. Tellingly, educated gentlemen who were well versed in the literature of the day complained about the 'boundless chaos of matter, relating to commerce'.[5] Opinions on the risks and benefits of the national debt diverged widely; and when confronted with the unanticipated effects of mass behaviour – as when the South Sea Bubble burst in 1720, triggering London's first stock-market crash and propelling numerous business people and an unknown number of small investors into bankruptcy – even the experts were baffled and left the prerogative of interpretation to writers and journalists.[6]

This inability to comprehend economic affairs is reflected in the use of the term 'market' in the early eighteenth century. Originally used to refer to the time and location at which trading took place, as well as for the acts of buying and selling, the word 'market' came increasingly to be employed as an abstract noun.[7] Yet this usage was imprecise, and the way market competition functioned remained a mystery. Apparently some contemporaries managed, by way of sporting analogies, to conjure up an image of market competition as 'a race to get limited supplies or a race to be rid of excess supplies'.[8] In general, however, the abstract noun 'market' signified nothing more than interaction or exchange, for which reason the word was also commonly used as verb. It is significant that to learn more about the situation, even those who, by virtue of their profession, were involved with trade and money matters set out 'for the market' to gain some old-fashioned hands-on experience.

Not all marketplaces were, in terms of their architecture, so deliberately planned as the London Stock Exchange (figures 3.1 and 3.2), which was designed as if to compel the 'intersection of social circles' (Georg Simmel)[9] and, like a sports field covered with markers, at once spurred and regulated their movements. With other markets, such as those for food and clothing, the geometrically defined space of the area upon which the activity took place was often not recognizable to visitors because of the way in which the trading often overflowed into the adjoining streets and alleys.[10] And yet, wherever this interaction occurred, it effected what in modern market sociology is referred to as the 'embedding' of market exchange in the context of lived experience.

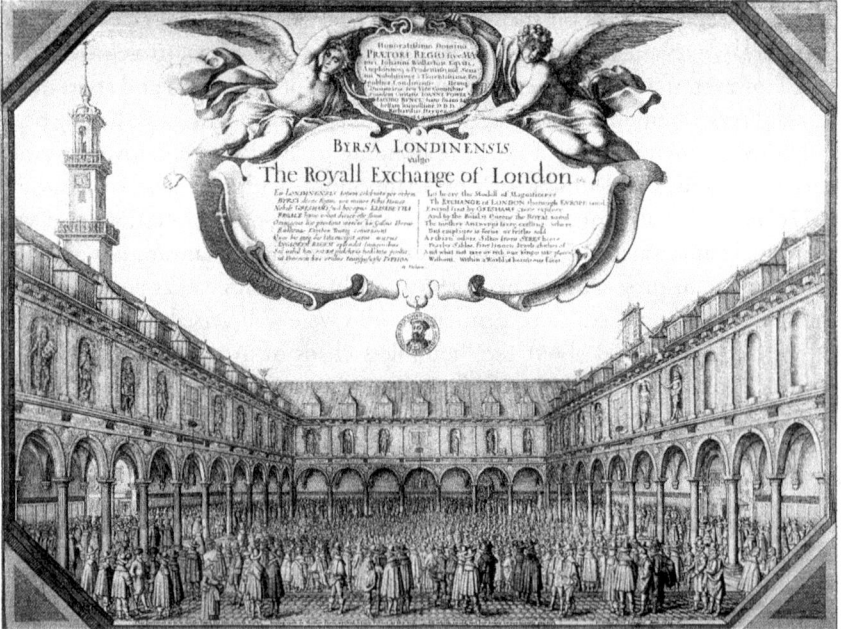

Figure 3.1. Interior courtyard of the Royal Exchange, 1644. Copperplate engraving by Wenceslas Hollar.

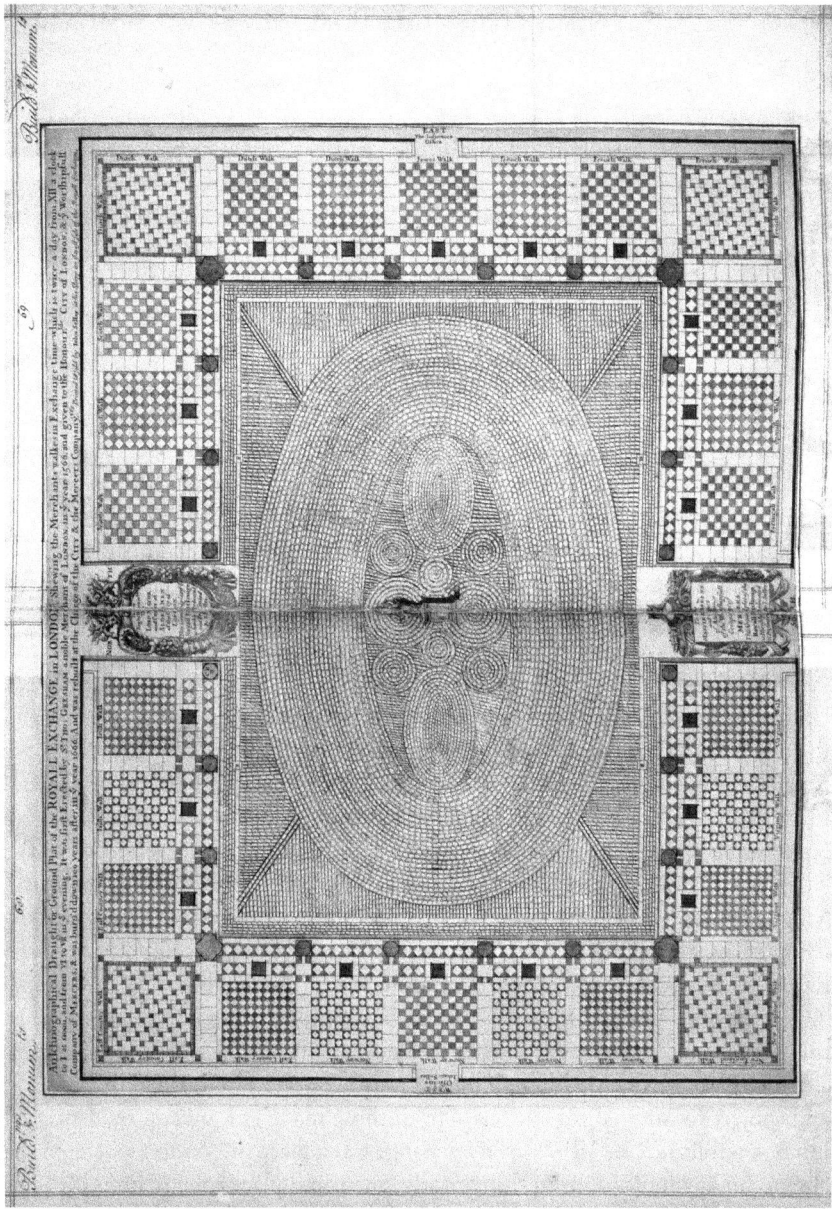

Figure 3.2. Floor mosaic in the rebuilt Royal Exchange. Drawing by John Seller, 1669.

Generating Trust

The Royal Exchange in London was regarded as the most important marketplace for monetary transactions and the trade in colonial goods. Located in the heart of the City between Cornhill and Threadneedle Street, this centre of international trade was built in 1565 by the merchant and royal advisor Thomas Gresham; it was furnished with the attribute 'royal' by Elizabeth I. After the Great Fire destroyed the Royal Exchange in 1666, it was rebuilt according to the old plans but on a larger scale. Other English cities also erected building complexes following this format, but the one in London was the largest and the most heavily frequented.[11]

The Royal Exchange consisted primarily of galleried arcades, some of which were named after the region with which the trade taking place there was conducted (e.g., the 'Italian Walk' or the 'Dutch Walk'), as well as an interior courtyard large enough to accommodate eighty-five hundred people. In the arcades, luxury goods from overseas could be purchased as well as commercial literature, newspapers, price lists and advertising brochures. Insurance companies maintained offices and financial newspapers their desks there, while elsewhere in the building, lawyers, notaries, scribes and copyists all plied their respective trades. Most of those who gathered at 'exchange time' were merchants, bankers and investors (including a small number of women) who wanted to trade stocks. Under the arcades in the interior courtyard of the Royal Exchange, but also in the numerous 'coffee houses' in Exchange Alley and the adjoining streets, people sought out business contacts and negotiated over prices and conditions. Here, information about investment projects, earnings potentials, scandals and the reputations of individual market participants spread at lightning speed, in the latter case at times in the form of written lists.[12] Although the 'market cross', which in medieval cities had stood as a permanent reminder of both royal authority and Christian morality, survived – absent the once obligatory pillory[13] – as a motif in the floor mosaic (figure 3.2), criteria for 'honourable' and 'dishonourable' behaviour developed, as well as for the appropriate responses to them. In this connection, a distinction was made between business dealings conducted in a marketplace – which, although public, was delineated from the outside world and subject to internal regulations – from those made in a private residence, an inn or a public house.[14] The Royal Exchange was a place in London where, in the absence of any indications to the contrary, one could place trust in one's business partners and indeed was ultimately obliged to do so: 'He that gives no trust, and takes no trust, either by wholesale or by retail … is not yet born', wrote Daniel Defoe in 1725 in *The Complete English Tradesman*, 'or if there ever were any such, they are all dead'.[15]

During the establishment phase of the Royal Exchange, the scope of stock trading was still quite limited; in 1689, for example, only fifteen large joint-stock companies existed.[16] However, under the impact of the Financial Revolution, it experienced a considerable upswing from the end of the seventeenth century onwards. Now, professional 'brokers' began to purchase and sell stocks and other securities on behalf of those who lacked the necessary time or specialized knowledge to do so themselves or who preferred to remain anonymous. 'Jobbers' working on their own account established themselves as middlemen, expediting the buying and selling of stocks and making it possible for the trading to continue even when there were momentarily no takers. Towards the end of the seventeenth century, the aspiration arose within the ranks of the brokers and jobbers to establish a monopoly over direct market access for themselves and their ilk, with the aim of developing and enforcing appropriate professional rules and conventions. In 1801 the London Stock Exchange was formally founded and was awarded the legal status of a trust.[17]

After the bursting of the South Sea Bubble in 1720, a number of insurance companies specializing in maritime insurance, the so-called underwriters, formed a loose association in Lloyd's Coffee House so as to be able to present themselves as a serious alternative to certain colleagues who sold insurance as a wager.[18] In 1771 these underwriters formed a trust and acquired their own premises, and Lloyd's of London was born.[19] In so doing, they followed in the footsteps of the Bank of England, an institution that gave those with capital to invest the opportunity to do so, not just in private enterprises but also in wars led by the Crown. These investors had quit the Royal Exchange in 1694, and the Bank had, as previously mentioned, also taken the form of a trust.

In this manner, financial transactions became relatively independent of the personal morals of the business partners. At the same time, however, they became more bureaucratic, abstract, and anonymous than other dealings. As an openly traded currency, reputation dwindled in importance, at least in the City of London. The task of generating trust was left to experts, whose actions could be measured in terms of their personal success. This is a prime example of the mechanism that the sociologist Niklas Luhmann called the 'reduction of social complexity': 'provisionally, one trusts that the other will successfully master ambiguous circumstances …; and indeed, on the basis of such trust the other in fact has a better chance of being successful'.[20]

However, this development initially found acceptance only among the new professions within the financial world. Among the general population, the move to decouple economic interests from personal sympathies and emotions would not have been recognized as a confidence-building measure. Instead, it aroused suspicion, especially as few contemporaries understood how the new institutions functioned and what concrete interests the actors were pursuing. In particular, 'stock jobbers' were regarded as corrupt and dangerous for the whole economy.[21] Therefore, in the business practice of 'ordinary' people – and these were the majority of actors in the development of a market society in England – the value placed on reputation, backed by face-to-face contact, remained just as high in the eighteenth century as it had been in the preceding ones.

With the growth in the demand for credit and the lengthening of credit chains, this factor presumably even gained in importance. For in contrast to the situation in the Continental European countries, the English Crown was generally unwilling to respond to the general shortage of coins by putting more money into circulation, and did so only in exceptional circumstances.[22] Correspondingly, in the year 1745, one-third – in some sectors up to four-fifths – of all commercial transactions in England were conducted on credit.[23] In this situation, virtually everyone was ultimately both a creditor and a debtor to someone, being directly connected through numerous loan agreements (generally oral covenants, bonds or contracts) with the other people in his or her social environment and indirectly connected to everyone else their contacts did business with. This was no different in the countryside than in the cities; it even transpired that landowners borrowed money from their labourers to remain solvent until the next round of leasehold payments was due. Conversely, landowners lent money to their workers in the hope that the latter would someday repay the amount, be it in kind or through their labour.[24] Although as a general rule, a maturity date was agreed upon and defaulters could even be sent to prison, most creditors were reserved when it came to collecting on debts, especially when the debtor showed a willingness to pay and rendered at least symbolic payments; for creditors who pressed their debtors too hard signalized their own lack of sufficient cash flow – something that could damage their reputation within the community.

This orientation towards the expectations of the community also determined the way in which financial relationships were configured within the broader population. Thus, the desire to satisfy the expectations of one's fellows through one's own behaviour marked the actions of the members of the innumerable local associations and societies that had been proliferating since the end of the seventeenth century.[25] This desire was especially commanding among members of so-called friendly societies (also called 'benefit clubs' or 'box clubs'). In these self-governing mutual aid societies, professional colleagues, neighbours or members of faith communities came together to support one another in the event of illness, unemployment or death. And they did so not only out of concern for their own reputation but rather as a show of solidarity, a good upon which any individual member might himself someday have to rely.

To this must be added the fact that against the background of the high level of geographic mobility in English society, local mutual aid societies served many important functions when it came to the social integration of migrants. Friendly societies were characterized by a certain measure of openness to strangers; indeed, their boards took this function for the community seriously, especially as the close relations among the members allowed for a high degree of social control.[26] It was not least in this respect that local benevolent funds distinguished themselves from for-profit providers of life, fire and other types of insurance, whose clients did not know one another and frequently even sold their policies on to third parties.[27]

By the time the first of these commercial insurance companies entered the market in the early eighteenth century, the friendly societies could already look back on centuries of tradition: The oldest association of this kind for which documentation exists was established in 1555.[28] With the Friendly Societies Act (or Rose's Act) of 1793, which obliged such associations to register with the government, legislators attempted to get an overview of the scope of such benevolent funds and to regulate their activities. For by this time, the societies were facing a barrage of criticism for a variety of reasons: theologians and fundamentalists were bothered by the fact that most of their business transactions took place in pubs, so that the benevolent purpose at times took a back seat to the sociability that went on there. Furthermore, in the wake of the French Revolution, employers and local authorities feared that the money would be diverted to fund labour unrest and political conspiracies. Representatives of the emerging insurance industry, which saw the societies as unwanted competition, accused them of financial mismanagement and being incapable of calculating risk.

This latter accusation might well have been justified. Nevertheless, the number of contemporaries who insured themselves through local benevolent funds and in so doing took advantage of the opportunity to get to know their fellow members greatly exceeded the customer base of the commercial companies. According to official statistics, in 1803 there were just short of ten thousand registered friendly societies in England and Wales, with a combined membership of over seven hundred thousand individuals. And this figure represents merely the tip of the iceberg, as most of the funds avoided registering and thereby having their existence publicly acknowledged. For the larger cities, it has been estimated that in 1800, between 40 and 50 per cent of the working population had insured themselves against risk in this manner.[29]

Against this background, it is not surprising that manuals for merchants, economic treatises and morally uplifting literature and plays, in which contemporaries were admonished to behave reputably, were orientated towards an imagined community.[30] Whether one should also view such admonishments in a religious context, as Max Weber suggests in his classic essay *The Protestant Ethic and the Spirit of Capitalism* (1904/05)[31] is, in contrast, questionable. In any event, historians and sociologists who have analysed a large number of such writings have been able in only a few cases to find evidence for the connection that Weber alleges between business and/or professional success, on the one hand, and the search for signs of divine favour, on the other. Furthermore, such examples grew increasingly few and far between over the course of the seventeenth and eighteenth centuries.[32] The analysis of personal diaries and letters has proven equally fruitless for scholars. For here, as well, contemporaries distinguished between behaviours relating to one's dealings with other people and those directed towards one's relationship with God. For the latter, they resorted to prayers and sermons.[33]

Thus, little speaks in favour of interpreting more into Weber's primary source, the 'Advice to a Young Tradesman' (1748) by the polymath Benjamin Franklin – an American who lived for twenty-five years in London – than that which he concretely advises: namely, that in an environment in which one is equally dependent on pecuniary and moral credit, one should always fulfil one's business obligations and be mindful of safeguarding one's reputation.[34]

> Remember that credit is money. If a man lets his money lie in my hands after it is due, he gives me the interest, or so much as I can make of it during that time. …
>
> Remember this saying, *The good paymaster is lord of another man's purse.* He that is known to pay punctually and exactly to the time he promises, may at any time, and on any occasion, raise all the money his friends can spare. This is sometimes of great use … therefore never keep borrowed money an hour beyond the time you promised, lest a disappointment shut[s] your friends' purse for ever.
>
> The most trifling actions that affect a man's credit are to be regarded. The sound of your hammer at five in the morning, or eight at night, heard by a creditor, makes him easy six months longer; but if he sees you at a billiard-table, or hears your voice at a tavern, when you should be at work, he sends for his money the next day …
>
> It shows, besides, that you are mindful of what you owe; it makes you appear a careful as well as an honest man, and that still increases your credit.[35]

From today's vantage point, Max Weber's interpretation of the connection between the 'Protestant ethic' and the 'spirit of capitalism' is nothing more than an amusing intellectual game, as it does not stand up to source criticism. Weber read Franklin's 'Advice to a Young Tradesman' in a translation that was both incomplete and embedded in a misleading interpretation; furthermore, he admixed statements on the functioning of markets with his personal notions of a rational 'life conduct' (*Lebensführung*).[36] In view of the sustained fascination with his thesis in the social sciences, but also of the great significance that the history of religion would later acquire within the historiography of the Early Modern era, it would seem advisable at this point to add two further objections from the English perspective.

The first objection relates to Weber's claim that in England, the Puritans had a particular predisposition towards the modern work and professional ethic. With regard to this statement, it should be noted that the Puritans were but one of many Protestant sects existing both within and outside of the Anglican state church, and that all of these sects combined – including Presbyterians, Independents, Baptists and Quakers – made up less than 10 per cent of England's population (1715). If one accepts Weber's argument, then one must, in view of the well-advanced commercialization of the economy and society, ask oneself why so few Englishmen and women should have developed a 'Protestant ethic'. The question proves to be moot, however, as advice similar to that of Benjamin Franklin with regard to responsible behaviour in one's business and professional dealings can also be found in the broader mainstream of the Anglican state church.[37]

The second objection relates to the fundamental criticism that in England, the market society arose many centuries before Puritanism and indeed even before the Reformation. It seems more plausible to argue, along with the economic historian Richard Henry Tawney, a contemporary of Weber's who proposed the idea in 1922, that instead of the 'spirit of capitalism' arising out of the 'Protestant ethic', religious thought might equally have been shaped by the worldly framework in which it was 'embedded', and that religion was concomitantly functionalized for relational economic activity.[38] To the extent that this was realized, one can say that English market society itself successfully created an important basis of mutual trust, which it had already been able to tap into in the Early Modern period.

Facts, News and Periodicity

It was not only the 'soft' information on both the general and payment behaviours of one's business partners that mattered. Contemporaries in the seventeenth and eighteenth centuries were at least as interested in the 'hard' facts of market activity, for it was only with the benefit of this knowledge that they could do business rationally. This interest had both an individual and a societal dimension.

Individual merchants as well as some industrial producers made an effort to keep systematic records of their earnings and expenses, up to and including doing double-entry bookkeeping. However, one should not overestimate the value of such self-reported market data for the seventeenth and eighteenth centuries, as Werner Sombart does in his classic study *Der moderne Kapitalismus* (1916).[39] For one thing, most entrepreneurs made do with sporadic record keeping. For another, in the context of the time, bookkeeping, be it single or double-entry, served primarily as a demonstration of orderly conditions and a methodical approach and less as a retrospective appraisal of 'right' and 'wrong' economic decisions. In this sense, it could really only provide new insights extending beyond immediate experiential knowledge among quite large enterprises with an internal division of labour.[40]

In contrast, merchants had a virtually existential interest in the underlying data on economic life in England, the British Isles more broadly, and the world in general.[41] The 'political arithmetic' performed in this context lent a societal dimension to the general interest in information. The fields of observation covered by this new science included population development, frequency of births and causes of death; moreover, efforts were made to document epidemics and other expressions of 'divine management'. In addition, information on disturbances of the peace, economically relevant judicial decisions, domestic political developments, and the progress of wars – including between third countries – was collected and shared.[42]

The interest in data and facts intensified over the course of the seventeenth century and led to the addition of brochures and publications on these topics to the selection of the printed matter (e.g., lists of prices, exchange rates and auction dates) sold and distributed at the Royal Exchange in London. The demand for such information increased sharply around the turn of the eighteenth century with the Financial Revolution, not least as a consequence of London's increasingly close connections with the other financial centres of Paris and Amsterdam. Now, economic information in the form of brochures and newspapers was made available to a broader audience. Less surprisingly, the opinion that societal development was not just a God-given process but could be influenced by people themselves, including through smart policies, became mainstream.[43]

The commissions established by Parliament after the Glorious Revolution and the surveys that they were instructed to carry out concerning the number of armed units, the size of the naval fleet, and the growth in the national debt also constituted an important data base for those interested in economics. In the five-year period between 1715 and 1719 alone, the House of Commons published 286 'accounts and papers', the majority of which provided military and fiscal information. Around 1750, when the pessimists among the political observers were predicting a state bankruptcy based on the size of the national debt, the production of such reports increased even further, as the optimists strove to counter-argue on the basis of facts. At this time, enormous advances were being made in the accuracy and reliability of parliamentary reports, and an elaborate culture of financial reporting developed in Whitehall and Westminster.[44]

The limits of such surveys were obvious, however. The data were gathered unsystematically, because the personnel lacked the means to cover the whole country. Furthermore, there were reservations about a general census, especially if it was to include information on property ownership. Such 'snooping' on the part of the State was irreconcilable with English freedom, so it was argued. Above all, however, the statistics were not processed. They included only absolute figures, not even percentages, and it was uncommon to provide any form of graphic representation. At the very most, the figures were organized into tables.[45] To an even greater extent than today, the information provided in the pamphlets, newspapers, and printed materials had to be interpreted.

Coffee houses became popular venues for such discussions. The first one of its kind, the Pasqua Rosée, was established in 1652 in London's financial district; to be more precise, in St. Michael's Alley, Cornhill, directly adjacent to the Royal Exchange. It was founded by merchants from the Levant Company, the chartered company that conducted trade with the Ottoman Empire. Having learned to enjoy drinking coffee in Constantinople, Smyrna and Aleppo, these 'Turkey Merchants' wanted to continue the practice upon their return. Against the political background of Cromwell's protectorate, the restoration of the monarchy, and then the Financial Revolution, the coffee house and its successor establishments grew into places in which deals were made and political news was exchanged. The numerous foreigners and out-of-towners who took up temporary residence in these gathering places also contributed to this development: 'You have all manner of news there: you have a good Fire, which you may sit by as long as you please: you have a Dish or Coffee: you meet your Friends for the transaction of Business', wrote a visitor from the Continent in his travelogue in 1719, 'and all for a penny, if you don't care to spend more'.[46]

At the beginning of the eighteenth century, there were between four hundred and five hundred coffee houses in London, with some even springing up in the provinces.[47] Citing the free access, the informal atmosphere and above all the fact that newspapers were made available to customers and that news could be exchanged there, intellectuals in the nineteenth and twentieth centuries associated these places with the emergence of a bourgeois public sphere.[48] Particularly noteworthy in this connection is Jürgen Habermas and his 1962 study *The Structural Transformation of the Public Sphere*, which is still regarded as a standard work and has recently enjoyed a belated reception in the English-speaking world.[49] In the coffee houses, Habermas argued, strangers could meet on neutral territory as social equals. They could freely exchange ideas and opinions on political and ethical questions of the day in a manner that anticipated participatory democracy. Habermas presents the coffee houses as a precursor to the European salons and discussion clubs of the early nineteenth century, which set the new principle of a well-read public against the model of courtly culture and declared the city, as market for cultural goods, to be the basis of a pan-European movement towards Enlightenment.[50]

Habermas developed his interpretation of the coffee houses against the background of the search for models for the construction of a modern democracy in Europe after the Second World War. In the intervening decades, the emphasis in cultural-historical research has shifted, and some corrections have been made; for example, we have been reminded that, in contrast to those on the European continent, English coffee houses cannot be credited with having cultivated an elegant, educated sociability.[51] In failing to recognize this deficit – the explanation for which lies in the commercial function of the coffee houses – Habermas misunderstood the character of the 'moral weeklies' such as *The Tatler* (1709–11), *The Spectator* (1711/12, 1714) and *The Guardian* (1713), which he drew upon as source material. These publications, and in particular their attempt to put spoken dialogue onto paper, by no means depict the real way in which the patrons of coffee houses interacted with one another. Rather, the publishers Joseph Addison and

Richard Steele were attempting to speak to those who, as a rule, never set foot in such establishments. These included workers interested in current events, whom they viewed as potential readers. This population preferred to gather in brandy houses, of which about eight thousand existed in the working-class neighbourhoods of London alone (both within and outside of the City), thereby far outnumbering the coffee houses.[52] In addition, if not formally banned from entering them, ladies from the burgeoning middle class were generally not allowed into the male-dominated coffee houses, in which cursing was frequently heard and sexual lewdness and even attacks on waitresses and owners took place.[53] Based on this reading of the sources, what Habermas – and, in his wake, many others – understood as a new, cultivated form of social exchange appears as a new genre of journalism, the proliferation of which was due not least to the bad reputation of this type of establishment.[54]

Furthermore, earlier researchers failed to note that over time, some of these coffee houses – which initially had indeed been just as open to a male middle-class clientele as to aristocrats, courtiers, politicians and other prominent members of society – succumbed to the tendency to become more exclusive. This was initially true above all of the 'polite' coffee houses that were located in the genteel West End. Beginning in the 1730s, these establishments gradually evolved into exclusive gentlemen's clubs, i.e., they demanded a high entrance fee and used a balloting system to decide upon the admission of new members. Rather than enlightened conversation, what these clubs offered their members – alongside excellent food – were card games, high-stakes gambling and other diversions. A few of these early gentlemen's clubs, including White's, Brooks's and Boodle's, still exist today.[55]

Some of the coffee houses that became more exclusive were located in London's financial district. Here, brokers, jobbers and other professionals among the patrons followed the lead of the founders of the Stock Exchange and attempted to expel crooked competitors as well as the broader lay public from their ranks. In these cases, as well, membership fees were a tried and tested means of creating exclusivity. And yet the technical jargon that predominated in these establishments alone would have sufficed to frighten off lay people. Indeed, outsiders would have been able to make little sense of the cryptic information they received here, as Thomas Mortimer – a sharp critic of stock trading – made clear in his book *Every Man His Own Broker,* of which fourteen editions were published between 1761 and 1807:

> Tickets – Tickets – South Sea Stocks for the opening – Navy Bills – Bank Stock for the rescounters – Long Annuities – (here the waiter calls) Chance – Chance – Chance *Mr Chance not here Sir, he is over at his Office* – Here Tickets for August – Omnium Gatherum for September – Scrip for the third payment – 3 per Cent. consolidated, gentlemen … Here Bank Circulation, who buys Bank Circulation – Tickets for the drawing, gentlemen – Well, what have you to do in Tickets for the drawing, Mr. Mul-

berry. – I am a seller of five hundred, Sir – and I am a buyer, Sir, but at what price? – Why, as you are a friend, Mr. Point-royal, I shall give you the turn, you shall have them at 14. ... Well, you shall have them, put 'em down.[56]

The general public therefore did not mourn the loss of the coffee houses as they gradually disappeared. Merchants, too, who by the late eighteenth century had long since been meeting in functionally equipped offices, no longer needed them (figure 3.3). The decline of the coffee houses accelerated around 1815, when financial traders, due to the opportunity presented to them by the booming real estate market, moved to other parts of the city, and the clerks and poor people who remained did not provide enough revenue to sustain the owners' livelihoods.[57]

A further contribution to the demise of coffee houses was made by the private reading of newspapers at home, a development that was encouraged by changed political and infrastructural conditions. Already in 1695, the precensorship of published materials was lifted, removing any remaining legal obstacles to the mass distribution of printed matter.[58] A short time later, the numbering of houses expedited postal deliveries, and since the leadership of the General Post Office was divided equally between Whigs and Tories, fears that postal items would be confiscated dissipated.[59]

Figure 3.3. Insurance office of Lloyd's of London, circa 1800. Drawing by Angus Charles Pugin and Thomas Rowlandson, 1809.

Above all, however, the concept of a protective 'private sphere' as a counterpart and corrective to the 'public sphere' took shape.[60] It expressed itself in the new insularity of private residences, in the functional differentiation of the rooms within houses, and in the new custom of drinking tea – a by-product of the success of the East India Company – as an underlying activity for private conversation. Already in the early eighteenth century, the English relied more heavily on the private, individualized reading of books, brochures[61] and above all newspapers and journals to satisfy their craving for facts than on public discussions of news in coffee houses. These publications were numerous and by no means read only by educated people. The 65 per cent of the adult male population that was literate also included members of the lower classes, some of whom would have acquired this skill in Sunday school, others through self-instruction.[62]

The spectrum of news became noticeably broader, especially as it soon also began to take account of local events. While in 1700, all newspapers were printed in London, newspaper publishers began to spread out into the provinces, beginning with the *Norwich Post* in 1701. In 1760, the thirty-five provincial newspapers together attained a weekly circulation of two hundred thousand, a figure that would double by 1800. By that time, every larger town and city had at least one local newspaper, which was generally also read in the surrounding villages.[63] Estimates based on the revenues from the stamp tax, which was also imposed on newspapers, place readership at 2.5 million in 1713, 7.3 million in 1750 and 16 million in 1801.[64] By way of comparison: German-language *Intelligenzblätter* reached an estimated 300,000 to 350,000 readers in 1750 and just under a million in 1800.[65]

As a result of this growth, newspaper publishers changed their mode of operation: As of around 1720, they no longer waited for reports to reach their editorial offices, but sent reporters out in search of news.[66] The intention behind this change was certainly to increase profits further by filling current issues at shorter intervals. However, it was also driven by the conviction that the public had already grown accustomed to the periodical publication schedule and that these expectations should not be disappointed. This pressure of expectations had been growing since the seventeenth century; for even at that early stage, the Royal Exchange was not the only place where printed news was reaching the market promptly at 'exchange time'. Soon one could rely on it to be available elsewhere in London, as well. For example, between 1711 and 1713, the above-mentioned literary magazines *The Tatler* and *The Spectator* appeared six times a week, and those who could afford it had the opportunity to fork over the hefty sum of £6.00 for just six issues of economic newspapers that were published either weekly or fortnightly.[67] For the second half of the eighteenth century, table 3.1 illustrates an increase in the number of dailies among the larger-circulation London publications.

The appetite of the English for news and facts, which had been generated by market activity, had a broad effect on the country's culture and mentality that

Table 3.1. Publishing Frequency of London Newspapers, 1746–1790

Year	Fortnightly or thrice monthly	Weekly	Daily	Total
1746	6	6	6	18
1770	10	4	5	19
1783	7	?	9	?
1790	?	2	14	?

Source: B. Harris. 1996. *Politics and the Rise of the Press: Britain and France, 1620-1800,* London: Macmillan, 10.

itself impacted back upon market activity. For one, the perception of temporality changed. Especially the daily newspapers conveyed an impression of constant novelty, change and movement. It is true that there was news worthy of reporting that did not conform to the daily rhythm. However, had dailies not continually provided new and changing information, they would not have been able to survive as commercial enterprises. In the context of the Glorious Revolution and of postrevolutionary developments, a few English newspapers might thus have been politically reactionary and – just as with literature in general – sworn to the cultural authority of tradition;[68] however, they were never conservative in the sense of 'persistent'. This was impeded by the marketing strategy of periodicity, which 'chopped up' complex processes and secular developments, presenting them as a series of discontinuous facts – and in extreme cases, as 'naked' stock market data and sporting results – thereby creating the impression of permanent change. Through this mechanism, people's perceptions were steered to the present, and ties to traditions were loosened – at the price of being bound to the publication of the next issue.[69]

This mechanism of the permanent creation of novelty and transiency and, with it, the sense of 'timelessness' became even more effective when the principle of periodicity, so advantageous for the press in Early Modern England, also began to make inroads into other aspects of society – a development to which the press itself contributed significantly. Alongside the areas of trade and finance, these aspects included the entertainment business and the cultural industries in the broadest sense. While the press was not the only authority to express an interest in cultural events being staged and their future being secured, it was, in general, the first to do so. Already in the eighteenth century, with the assistance of the press, sports – originally a sociable pastime of prominent gentlemen – acquired a fixed match schedule, which competed with the traditional holidays determined by the church, the harvest cycle and local customs, and which furthermore reserved certain days of the week for certain disciplines – Mondays for cricket and pugilism, Tuesdays for football, Wednesday for horseracing, etc. – so that they would not compete with one another.[70] The press also had a hand in determining the accelerating cycles of fashion in clothing, furniture and other goods that replaced established conventions. If in the early eighteenth century, sartorial fashions had changed every ten to twelve years, by the end of the century they were changing annually; in higher circles, even monthly.[71] In musical life, the concert season took shape, if initially only for the aristocracy and the rich. For their benefit, the *Spectator* and *Gentleman's Magazine* announced events featuring Handel, Haydn and other composers brought over from the Continent, later either extolling them as a 'divine experience' or panning them entirely.

This interplay between the media and cultural events, which was manufactured over time via the principle of periodicity, supplied an inexhaustible stream of topics of conversation and initiated processes of opinion making. From an early stage, these discourses invited the participation of sections of the population, including many women, who did not tend to read the newspaper every day. Therefore, in the following chapter section, the socialization effects of the culture industry will be analysed more closely, and the surges in its development pinpointed. However, it should already be noted here that, viewed from a Continental European perspective, the structuring of temporality wrought by the press was specific to England in the late seventeenth and eighteenth centuries. For on the other side of the Channel, periodicals typically appeared at intervals of weeks or months throughout the eighteenth century.[72] Moreover, there, in contrast to England, the principle of periodicity came into effect largely in noncommercial contexts. It fused with the temporal rhythms of parade marches, the religious calendar and secular custom.[73]

The question of whether the experience of 'timeless' modernity could develop in this context just as much as in the commercial society of England cannot be answered here. However, the habit of Continental European historians to treat the development of cultural modernism as a phenomenon of the twentieth century[74] rests on the assumption that this was not the case.

Games, Speculation and the Culture of Commerce

The generation of trust by the media and their provision of an incessant flow of information made it easier for contemporaries in the seventeenth and eighteenth centuries to adjust to the demands of the modern market society. They made a further contribution to this process themselves through their pronounced ability to appropriate the changes in the world of experience through play. This form of habituation to market society is so important because games allow the participants to unconsciously negotiate the principles of order and behaviour of a society by investing these principles with new meaning and lending them sensory expression. The creative potential thereby released goes far beyond that of gestures and rituals, as in games, subjectively crafted styles, imaginative behaviours and emotions arose with which individuals could, if necessary, distance themselves from the social practice of their environment. The players have the possibility to emotionally idealize their everyday life or to defamiliarize it; they can exaggerate, distort and recode meanings. To the extent that this reshaping emancipates itself from the world of experience, games gain momentum, function according to their own rules, can be understood on their own terms and, in this manner, even shape their environment.[75]

The idea that in games, the organizing principles of a particular society are processed and expressed was clarified by the French sociologist Roger Caillois with the aid of a classification scheme.[76] He distinguishes among four categories of games: *agon* (competition), *alea* (chance), *mimicry* (mimesis), and *ilinx* (vertigo). The first two categories produce a decision. Thus in *agon,* the victor is determined in a competition, while *alea* distributes the winnings at random. In the third and fourth categories, what is at stake is the achievement of certain changes in one's social and psychological state that take one out of the 'real' world. *Mimicry* games transform the players with the aid of masks, costumes, imitation or imagination and thereby create illusion and fascination through the successful creation of deceptions. Through *ilinx* games, e.g., rapid spinning, high speeds, sounds, mass experiences or calculated risks are converted into exhilaration, ecstasy or suspense; at times, they can become addictive. This categorization is, however, highly artificial, as Caillois himself concedes; for in reality, due to their collective societal reference, the four categories often occur together.

This was also true of England, where the Old English verb 'plegian', from which the modern word 'to play' would later derive, already carried the meanings of 'to ply a trade', 'to deal with' or 'to employ', therefore producing the same connotations as the vocabulary of market trading.[77] By the end of the Middle Ages at the latest, all four categories of games can be identified. Thus, references to many examples of sporting *agon* can be found in governmental ordinances, in which a distinction was made between useful (or at least less morally unobjectionable) disciplines such as horseracing, archery, fishing, skittles (bowling) and tennis, on the one hand, and those – including animal fighting and competitive dancing or drinking – that were useless as they were accompanied by randomization (*alea*), on the other. The sources also refer to football and cricket matches.[78] With regard to theatre (*mimicry*) in the sixteenth century, little needs to be said – not only because the literature on Shakespeare and the society of his day fills entire libraries, but also because there is no doubt about the commercial character of the business of theatre, nor about the profit motive of those who ran it.[79] Exhilarating experiences (*ilinx*) were also already widespread in late medieval England. These arose out of religious enthusiasm, excessive alcohol consumption and the generalized penchant for gambling among the population. The official prohibitions that were issued under Cromwell's protectorate had little effect, especially as the majority of popular card games and wagers took place in private.[80] Already under Elizabeth I, governments undermined their own anti-gambling policies by holding lotteries to improve their finances.[81]

The games of the later seventeenth and eighteenth centuries continued this tradition (figure 3.4). What was new, however, was that they took place in an urban context and in a thoroughly commercialized environment, in which older cultural frameworks such as courtly society, relationships of patronage and seasonal festivals declined in importance. Instead, the games developed in closer cooperation with the press, the publishing industry, advertising agencies and the food service industry (coffee houses, pubs) and together with them formed the basis for professionally organized cultural industries. Musicians, painters, art dealers, poets, playwrights, actors and impresarios; professional athletes and coaches; critics, paid hacks and advertising experts; the managers of entertainment venues, pleasure gardens and events of all kinds – these and other distinct professions emerged, some of which were also open to women, and the numbers of those employed in the cultural sector increased substantially.[82] For some of these new professions, including those of publisher and writer, but also of engraver and commercial artist, the underlying conditions for the safeguarding of their economic interests were even legally defined through the copyright legislation of the early eighteenth century, as lawmakers regarded the proceeds from their work as worthy of protection, both on economic grounds as well as with regard to the ability to stimulate creativity. In addition, these groups profited from the growing social sensitivity to the notion of intellectual property and the criminal nature of plagiarism.[83] Furthermore, genteel destinations such as Bath, Buxton, Scarborough and, somewhat later, Cheltenham, the prosperity of which was dependent on the permanent provision of a broad spectrum of 'leisure and pleasure' activities, proved to be especially beneficial for the development of games of all kinds.

As a consequence of the commercialization and professionalization of the cultural industries, new games proliferated, and words such as 'divert', 'divertise' and 'divertisement', which had become fashionable in the 1640s and 1650s, entered the common parlance.[84] Above all, however, a functional differentiation was made among the various categories of games. In tradition-steeped Drury Lane, London's iconic theatre street, the old buildings were renovated, greatly expanded and in some cases replaced over the course of the eighteenth century – a development that would soon unfold in a similar manner in other parts of the city, as well as in the provinces. Audience capacities were considerably enlarged, repertoires made more varied, and special venues for variety theatre opened their doors.[85] Italian opera, which enjoyed its heyday in the first three decades of the eighteenth century, united drama and music in a new form of performing art that fascinated the King and upscale audiences and made London the musical capital of Europe. As opera gained more fans in the less genteel world, a desire was clearly

The fragmentary text visible in the left margin appears to be:

ontispiece.
its name,
ame,
grass)
the Pass.

Stage,
age,
way,
lay.
ox,
Box,
mes at Seven
en.

ll,
ick
nickt.
e come,
home;

ne win;

name;

wit;
r,

ace

Hearts.
they cut)
att.
Enough,
uff.
4,
ommand.

THE COMPLEAT GAMESTER:

Figure 3.4. Frontispiece of Charles Cotton's *The Compleat Gamester*, London 1674. In this book, games of chance are described. Illustration are provided of billiards, backgammon, dice-throwing, cock fights and card games.

expressed for English-language compositions. After the death of Henry Purcell in 1695, Georg Friedrich Handel rendered a great service to the nationalization of the concert business with his 'English' operas (and oratorios). Not least because he filled this niche, he was celebrated a national hero.[86]

Furthermore, in the second half of the eighteenth century, an active and regular concert business arose, the promoters within which struggled to outdo one another by engaging the premiere composers from the European continent. Thus, Wolfgang Amadeus Mozart came to London in 1764, and Joseph Haydn wrote several of his most famous symphonies there in the early 1790s, including his 'Drumroll' Symphony. However, the brightest star in the classical firmament in the eighteenth century was Georg Friedrich Handel, who was able to skilfully meet and help shape current tastes. His fame among London audiences was based on his 'Water Music', which he composed for King George I of England and which was first performed in 1717. In 1749, his 'Fireworks Music' was performed before an audience of twelve thousand in the Vauxhall Gardens; and in 1784, twenty-five years after his death, a legendary memorial concert with over a thousand performers laid the template for a multiyear series of follow-up events.[87] Other Handel concerts took place before mixed audiences in the smaller pleasure gardens that were founded at this time in London, and a short time later – some also under the trademark of Vauxhall – in the provinces, as well. Yet other concerts filled the standard programme at dancing clubs and masked balls. On such occasions, those who belonged to 'society' or who wanted to bathe in its reflected glory presented the latest fashions, so that ever-new opportunities for *mimicry* games arose.

The greatest upswing was experienced by the *ilinx* games, however, which included equal numbers of sporting competitions and games of chance. The popular sports of the eighteenth century included horseracing, which had been regulated and supervised since approximately 1752 by the Jockey Club, a gentleman's club located in the equestrian centre of Newmarket. In addition, there were cricket tournaments, boxing ('pugilism') and cock fighting. For the latter two disciplines, special arenas were built, which were commercially run. For all three of the aforementioned sports, written rules were also laid down in the second half of the eighteenth century, and governing bodies were established. In cricket, the gentlemen furthermore developed a code of conduct. The motivation behind these measures was to prevent corruption, as the (for the most part professional) athletes, coaches and referees not infrequently gathered amongst themselves and 'fixed' the winner. Such shady dealings negatively impacted the brisk bookmaking operations surrounding the sporting events, which for many contemporary sporting enthusiasts constituted the real thrill of the experience. The horse dealer Richard Tattersall – who had been staging betting opportunities professionally since 1777, thereby almost single-handedly adding bookmaking to the cultural industries – also had an interest in competitions unfolding in an orderly manner;

for his business success was based on the image of his establishment as the 'Turf Exchange' or the 'Lloyd's of Gambling'.[88]

Bets on sporting events were made out of a variety of motives. Some gentlemen, whether of noble origin or not, gambled away their wealth so that, having lost it, they might display the demonstrative disdain for money that was customary in courtly society and in similar circles, thereby dispelling any doubts as to the social stratum to which they belonged. 'Being a gambler gives a man a position in society', noted Baron de Montesquieu in 1714: 'It is a title which takes the place of birth, wealth and probity. It promotes anyone who bears it into the best society without further examination.'[89] Most contemporaries, however, risked only modest sums. They valued sports betting especially because it afforded them the possibility to subject their powers of judgement to a probability calculation that, while crude, could literally pay off. This was a form of betting that befitted modern commercial society and had very little in common with the chivalric code of honour of the class-conscious aristocracy.[90]

Altogether, the social spectrum of those who engaged in betting extends from the very top to the very bottom. Which social groups were over- or underrepresented is hard to say, alone because bets on sports were increasingly being made outside of the racing tracks and boxing arenas; for newspaper reporting – particularly, increasingly specialized publications such as *Sporting Life* (1792) and *Racing Calendar* (1793) – allowed contemporary betting fans the possibility to track the performance of a boxer, a cricket team, a horse or a fighting cock from a distance.[91]

Together with the regulation and organization of competitions, this possibility to thoughtfully weigh the odds contributed greatly to the fact that sports betting took on the character of a speculative but also relatively low-risk investment. To some business-minded contemporaries, it must have appeared more attractive than trading in maritime insurance, subscribing to war bonds or purchasing shares in questionable South Sea ventures.[92] And there is yet another reason for us to view sports betting as a surrogate economic activity: in 1720, after the bursting of the South Sea Bubble, Parliament decided to legally discriminate against all existing joint stock companies that had not been granted a Royal Charter; the privilege of limited liability was denied, and the foundation of new joint stock companies was entirely forbidden. This so-called Bubble Act remained in force until 1825 and led to investors experimenting with alternative forms of corporate organization or to search for entirely new investment possibilities.[93]

Conversely, some forms of shareholding were viewed less as investments than as wagers. For as everybody knew: 'Stock-Jobbing is a Play; a Box and Dice may be less dangerous, the Nature of them are alike, a Hazard' (Daniel Defoe).[94] Unsurprisingly, there were professional stock brokers who placed bets on the winning numbers in the state lottery without having purchased regular tickets, thereby initiating a form of side betting that was lucrative, at least for themselves.[95] The trade in life-insurance policies, which was popular among both insurance agents and policy-holders, were a wager and an investment at the same time. With this 'betting on lives', it was even possible, with the consent of the insurance company, to change the name of the person or persons insured so that the new owner could improve his chances in a targeted manner if the latter signed a policy on a frail or critically ill person. The companies tolerated this practice, as in the event of a claim, the amount they paid out was less than the sum of the premiums. Lawmakers did not intervene until the passage of the Gambling Law in 1774.[96]

Furthermore, due to the fickleness and unpredictability of public tastes, but also and above all to their existential dependence on the benevolent coopera- tion of the media, the cultural industries were exposed to a high degree of risk.[97] Therefore, some investments in book and newspaper projects, theatrical produc- tions, operas and concerts, in the collection of prize money for horse races and boxing matches, and the construction of event venues might have been regarded as a kind of game, as well. As a rule, such shares were purchased via 'subscription societies', some of which were well funded indeed.[98] The subscription for large concert events cost between fifty and eighty guineas, a guinea corresponding to roughly a week's wages for a skilled artisan. In 1791 a subscription for a box at the King's Theatre in London cost 150 guineas – a price that would double over the next two decades.[99] Although most of these commercial cultural subscription societies also sold less expensive shares, thereby enabling participants to diversify their capital contributions to a certain extent,[100] they were ultimately speculative enterprises. One can therefore assume that under different underlying legal con- ditions, many of them would from the outset have been founded as joint stock companies, as was the case with the Royal Academy of Music, an opera venture founded in 1719 with Handel as its musical director.'[101]

This is not to say that the financiers behind commercial cultural and sports offerings in the eighteenth century developed no genuine preferences or passions; ultimately most of them were at the same time also consumers of their own events. What should be noted, however, is that they were able to skilfully fuse these preferences with extra-cultural considerations. A thoroughly welcome eco- nomic side effect of financing via subscription societies consisted in the fact that by this means, the savings and other liquid assets of well-heeled contemporaries could be drawn into the cultural economy. Furthermore, some societies, espe- cially those in the music sector, took account of the desires of their honourable membership for socially exclusive, perhaps even hand-picked audiences, and for the cultural reinforcement of certain political messages.[102]

Such secondary aims would, however, be disappointed over time, as the devel- opment of the cultural industry was subject to a particular dynamic. For one, the extraordinary upswing in the sector contributed to the fact that the prices for good talent (and especially for exclusive contracts with the stars of the day) skyrocketed. For another, in the course of the institutionalization and differentiation of the offerings, the necessity arose for a cooperation with the organizers of larger events, the owners of the performance venues or sporting arenas and the star composers of the day, all of whom had an express interest in garnering large audience numbers. Both developments frustrated the desire of subscribers for social exclusivity.[103] However, those subscription societies with a majority middle-class membership, and which often saw themselves as an alternative to the so-called 'client economy', i.e., to the cultural offerings for the common people within the framework of aristocratic patronage, thoroughly embraced such developments. Such cooperations frequently led to a stabilization of social relations beyond the particular concrete project, so that over time, these subscription societies evolved into enduring cultural associations.[104]

The ever-present multidimensionality of the cultural industries and the speculative games associated with it doubtless contributed to the fact that the social exchange to which they gave rise was generally regarded as benign and, apart from the comments of a few moralizing clerics and the still-small circle of social reformers,[105] attracted no noteworthy criticism. At the most, visitors from the European continent expressed indignation over the fact that many English concertgoers were far more concerned with the business of seeing and being seen and with paying reverence to star composers than with the musical offerings as such; that horse races were essentially about making money, even in places where horse racing and horse breeding converged; and that wholly undisciplined theatre, opera and concert audiences tended to chat, eat, drink and stroll about during the performances.[106]

In England (as in Scotland), in contrast, the great Enlightenment figures of the age had only benevolent things to say about games, speculation and the cultural industry – and not only because their way of thinking was generally characterized by a pragmatic and practical orientation. It was moreover because they valued the virtues brought to bear at such occasions – 'competition', 'disposition of action' and 'love of adversity' – in and of themselves. Therefore, in their writings on the preconditions for a civil society, they always referred positively to 'a class of pursuits which are distinguished by the name of amusement' (Adam Ferguson). How such pursuits were to be classified by contemporaries, whether as 'business' or 'play', was ultimately of no import, as in their view, 'business or play may amuse them alike'.[107]

Thus there is much that speaks in favour of viewing the cultural sector and the vast array of games that it placed on a new commercial foundation as the real-life basis for that which the English Enlightenment tended to embellish with terms like 'doux commerce' or 'moeurs douces' (Montesquieu).[108] Indeed, contemporary thinkers saw the cultural industries as important impetuses for the formation of modern civil society. Their admiration for this branch was only heightened by the fact that – in light of the refining influence it manifestly had on the morals of even crude, profit-seeking individuals – it represented a sector of modern market society in which the paradox of 'private vices' and 'public benefits' (Berhard Mandeville) quite obviously worked.[109] Even if on certain occasions, e.g., major concerts, peers, the gentry and other rich people remained largely among themselves, there were always other events that attracted broader audiences that also included members of the middle classes. One could even have imagined that in the future, the circle of participants might include segments of the 'labouring poor'.[110]

Commercial games were also a potentially integrating force as a division between high and popular culture could not take shape. One reason for this was the fact that after the Glorious Revolution, the King and the Court lost the ability to shape culture, and it was difficult for the Royal Society and other cultural institutions modelled after the French Royal Academy of Arts to evolve into authorities with the ability to define tastes.[111] A further – and over the long term doubtless more important – reason can be found in the fact that the enterprising public relations branch systematically fought against such tendencies. For example, when advertisements explicitly targeted wealthy gentlemen and thereby indicated that the King, the upper nobility and other high-ranking figures would be in attendance, the social classes 'below' this intended elite were also involved. A variety of professions made their living from this, including newspaper publishers, fashion entrepreneurs and others with commercial interests in the milieu of the cultural industries, which here also served as a motor for social mobility and societal development.[112]

However, one type of gamer did not take root in this context or at least failed to do so in the public perception: that of the self-absorbed and daydreaming flâneur. The reason for this is quite transparent: The flâneur is a 'solitaire', as the sociologist Zygmunt Bauman emphasized, not a player: '[H]e can squeeze all the allurements of the game to the last drop, unrestricted by the selfish or jealous team-mates and the forever watchful, forever cavilling umpire. … He may disregard other players' moves, that potential limit to his own choice. In the dramas he imagines as he wanders, he is the sole mover, scriptwriter, director'.[113] In England, the fashion-conscious 'dandy', whose daily life was essentially focussed on his own person, did develop certain similarities with the flâneur. And yet even he – who was in any event more a figure of the early nineteenth than of the eighteenth century – was never sufficient unto himself, but rather craved recognition from others.[114]

The same is true for the imaginary figure of the 'spectator', whom journalists like Addison and Steele had invented as far back as the early eighteenth century.[115] In this case, too, the distance to society was only a pretence, since the newspaper owners and journalists behind the *Spectator* and its successor publications were self-interested co-shapers of the commercial cultural industry. These professional observers also wanted to 'play', and the better they succeeded at this, the more effectively they supported their contemporaries in the playful development of a commercial mentality.

Notes

1. Cf. P. Nightingale. 2004. 'Money and Credit in the Economy of Late Medieval England', in D. Wood (ed.), *Medieval Money Matters*, Oxford: Oxbow Books, 54–55; I. K. Ben-Amos. 2008. *The Culture of Giving. Informal Support and Gift-Exchange in Early Modern England,* Cambridge: Cambridge University Press, 352–65.
2. Cf. J. Hoppit. 1987. *Risk and Failure in English Business 1700–1800,* Cambridge: Cambridge University Press, 55, 72, 176–78.
3. Cf. Schulte Beerbühl, *Deutsche Kaufleute in London,* 65–74; M. Berg. 2007. 'Cargoes: The Trade in Luxuries from Asia to Europe', in D. Cannadine (ed.), *Empire, the Sea and Global History. Britain's Maritime World, c. 1763–c.1840,* Houndmills: Palgrave Macmillan, 60–71; J. Walvin, 1997. *Fruits of Empire. Exotic Produce and British Taste, 1660–1800,* Houndmills: Macmillan Press. For a general account, see K. Pomeranz and S. Topic. 1999. *The World that Trade Created. Society, Culture and the World Economy, 1400 to the Present,* Armonk, NY: M.E. Sharpe.
4. Cf. J. Osterhammel. 2000. *Die Verwandlung der Welt. Eine Geschichte des 19.* Jahrhunderts, Munich: Beck, 1037.
5. [M. Postlethwayt], *A Dissertation on the Plan, Use, and Importance, of the Universal Diction-ary of Trade and Commerce,* 1749, quoted in J. Hoppit. 2006. 'The Contexts and Contours of British Economic Literature, 1660–1760', *Historical Journal* 49, 103. In this essay, Hoppit indirectly corrects the thesis, proposed by Joyce Appleby in her study *Economic Thought and Ideology in Seventeenth-Century England* that there was anything like a dominant opinion on individual questions. According to Hoppit, such smoothly reconstructed statements are only of interest for the history of economics as a discipline, but played no role in everyday English life. On this problem, see also M. Blaug. 1997. *Economic Theory in Retrospect,* 5th ed., Cambridge: Cambridge University Press, 10–32. On even Adam Smith's quite limited understanding of the market mechanism, see S. Rashid. 1992. 'Adam Smith and the Market Mechanism', *History of Political Economy* 24, 129–52.
6. Cf. S. Stratmann. 2000. *Myths of Speculation. The South Sea Bubble and 18th-Century English Literature,* Munich: Fink, and J. Hoppit. 1990. 'Attitudes to Credit in Britain, 1680–1790', *Historical Journal* 33, 305–22. See also idem. 2002. 'The Myths of the South Sea Bubble', *Transactions of the Royal Historical Society* 6(12), 141–65, showing how lastingly contemporary myth-making distorted even the historiography of the South Sea Bubble.
7. Cf. N. Davis. 1952. 'The Proximate Etymology of Market', *Modern Language Review* 47, 152–55; R. Swedberg. 1994. 'Markets as Social Structures', in N. J. Smelser and R. Swedberg (eds), *The Handbook of Economic Sociology,* Princeton, NJ: Princeton University Press, 255. See also the explanation of the problem in J.-C. Agnew. 1988. *Worlds Apart: The Market and the Theater in Anglo-American Thought, 1550–1750,* Cambridge: Cambridge University Press, 40–43, and the incorporation of social historical reality in A. Hann. 2004. 'Modernity and the Marketplace', in S. Pinches, M. Whalley and D. Postles (eds), *The Market Place and the Place of the Market,* Leicester: Friends of the Centre for English Local History, 67–88.
8. G. J. Stigler. 1957. 'Perfect Competition, Historically Contemplated', *Journal of Political Economy* 65, 1–2. This analogy between the market and sport may also have been suggested by the fact that in the Middle Ages, marketplaces were frequently also used as sporting grounds;

see Hann, 'Modernity and the Market Place', 75–76, 86; J. Schmiechen and K. Carls. 1999. *The British Market Hall. A Social and Architectural History*, New Haven: Yale University Press, 14.

9. G. Simmel. 1983(1908). *Soziologie. Untersuchungen über die Formen der Vergesellschaftung*, 6ᵗʰ ed., Berlin: Duncker and Humblot, 305–44. This chapter of his *Soziologie* however makes no mention of the market.

10. Cf. T. R. Slater. 2009. 'Social, Cultural and Political Space in English Medieval Market Places', in S. Ehrich and J. Oberste (eds), *Städtische Räume im Mittelalter*, Regensburg: Schnell and Steiner, 227–40.

11. Cf. N. Glaisyer. 2006. *The Culture of Commerce in England, 1660–1720*, Woodbrige, Suffolk: Royal Historical Society and The Boydell Press, 41, as well as the essays and illustrations in A. Saunders (ed.). 1997. *The Royal Exchange*, London: The Typographical Society. On the successor institutions in other cities, see Westerfield, *Middlemen*, 349.

12. On the international connections within this system of information, see L. Neal and S. Quinn. 2001. 'Networks of Information, Markets and Institutions in the Rise of London as a Financial Centre, 1660–1720', *Financial History Review* 8, 7–26.

13. Cf. J. Davis. 2009. 'The Cross and the Pillory: Symbolic Structures of Commercial Space in Medieval English Towns', in S. Ehrich and J. Oberste (eds), *Städtische Räume im Mittelalter*, Regensburg: Schnell and Steiner, 241–259.

14. Cf. ibid, 245.

15. Defoe, *Complete English Tradesman*, 326.

16. Cf. Michie, *London Stock Exchange*, 15.

17. For a detailed account, see ibid, 15–36.

18. On this, see 93–94.

19. The loose form of organization may be attributed to the fact that the Bubble Act of 1720 had furnished the London Assurance and Royal Exchange Assurance, which had bribed the King, with a monopoly leaving other enterprises with no other option than to act through individuals. This organizational form persists today, so that one is not insured 'by Lloyd's' but 'through Lloyd's'. For an extensive account, see R. Flower and M. Wynn Jones. 1974. *Lloyd's of London. An Illustrated History*, London: Lloyd's of London Press, 40, 44, 54, 57.

20. N. Luhmann. 1979. *Trust and Power*, Chichester: Wiley, 25–26.

21. Cf. Michie, *London Stock Exchange*, 23–24; M. Ellis. 2004. *The Coffee-House. A Cultural History*, London: Weidenfeld and Nicolson, 174–77.

22. Cf. Nightingale, 'Money and Credit', 53. On what follows, see Muldrew, *Economy of Obligation*, 329 and passim; J. Hoppit. 1986. 'The Use and Abuse of Credit in Eighteenth-Century England', in N. McKendrick and R. B. Outhwaite (eds), *Business Life and Public Policy. Essays in Honour of D. C. Coleman*, Cambridge: Cambridge University Press, 64–78; idem, 'Attitudes'; B. L. Anderson. 1970. 'Money and the Structure of Credit in the Eighteenth Century', *Business History* 12(2), 86–89; J. Brewer. 1982. 'Commercialization and Politics', in N. McKendrick et al., *Birth of a Consumer Society*, 203–07.

23. Cf. Westerfield, *Middlemen*, 385.

24. The examples come from R. Biernacki. 2004. *New Evidence on Schemas of Action in the Protestant Ethic*. Havens Centre for the Study of Social Structure and Social Change, University of Wisconsin, Madison (http://www.havenscenter.org/VSP/readings2sort/rtf/biernacki2.rtf, last accessed 3 October 2006), 38–39; see also Muldrew, *Economy of Obligation*, 153.

25. See Brewer's discussion of 'credit, clubs and independence' in the essay 'Commercialization and Politics'.

26. Cf. E. Kowalski Wallace. 2000. 'The Needs of Strangers: Friendly Societies and Insurance Societies in Late Eighteenth-Century England', *Eighteenth-Century Life* 24, 53–72; S. Cordery. 2003. *British Friendly Societies, 1750–1914*, Basingstoke: Palgrave Macmillan; as well as the

older standard work by P. H. J. H. Gosden. 1961. *The Friendly Societies in England, 1815–75,* Manchester, UK: Manchester University Press.

27. Cf. G. Clark. 1997. 'Life Insurance in the Society and Culture of London, 1700–75', *Urban History* 24(1), 21–25.

28. Kowalski Wallace, 'Needs of Strangers', 69.

29. Figures from P. Clark, 2000. *British Clubs and Societies 1580–1800. The Origins of an Associational World,* Oxford: Oxford University Press, 350. According to G. Clark, the figure for the customers of commercial life insurance in the early eighteenth century is 12,000; see G. Clark. 1997. 'Life Insurance in the Society and Culture of London, 1700–75', *Urban History* 24(1), 18. For additional data, see M. Gorsky. 1998. 'The Growth and Distribution of English Friendly Societies in the Early Nineteenth Century', *Economic History Review* 51, 489–511.

30. Cf. Muldrew, *Economy of Obligation,* chapters 5 and 6; idem. 1998. 'Zur Anthropologie des Kapitalismus: Kredit, Vertrauen, Tausch und die Geschichte des Marktes in England 1500–1750', *Historische Anthropologie* 6, 167–99; see also M. C. Finn. 2003. *The Character of Credit. Personal Debt in English Culture, 1740–1914,* Cambridge: Cambridge University Press, 25–105.

31. 1958. *The Protestant Ethic and the Spirit of Capitalism,* trans. T. Parsons with a foreword by R. H. Tawney, New York: Charles Scribner's Sons.

32. Cf. E. A. Rothenberg. 2006. '"The Diligent Hand Maketh Rich": Commercial Advice for Retailers in Late Seventeenth- and Early Eighteenth-Century England', in J. Benson and L. Ugolini (eds), *Cultures of Selling. Perspectives on Consumption and Society since 1700,* Aldershot: Ashgate, 233. One of the most comprehensive advice manuals of the period, Defoe's *Complete English Tradesman,* tellingly dispenses almost entirely with references to religion.

33. As two examples among many, see J. Cohen. 2002. *Protestantism and Capitalism. The Mechanisms of Influence,* New York: Aldine de Gruyter; Biernacki, *New Evidence* (based on an analysis of 40 autobiographical texts).

34. The interpretation advocated here presents Franklin's 'Advice to a Young Tradesman' as a prime example of the observation discussed in recent economic sociology that performative acts by market participants are apparently indispensable for the realization of relations of exchange. This relationship is elucidated in J. Beckert. 2002. 'Vertrauen und die performative Konstruktion von Märkten', *Zeitschrift für Soziologie* 31, 27–43.

35. Quotation from Weber. 1958. *Protestant Ethic,* 48–49.

36. On the misunderstandings regarding the sources, see M. Pütz. 1984. 'Max Webers und Friedrich Kürnbergers Auseinandersetzung mit Benjamin Franklin. Zum Verhältnis von Quellenverfälschung und Fehlinterpretation', *Amerikastudien/American Studies* 29, 297–310; G. Kamphausen, 2002. *Die Erfindung Amerikas in der Kulturkritik der Generation von 1890,* Weilerswist: Velbrück; H. Steinert. 2010. *Max Webers unwiderlegbare Fehlkonstruktionen. Die protestantische Ethik und der Geist des Kapitalismus,* Frankfurt, Main: Campus, 55–65; for a general critique, see P. Ghosh. 2008. *A Historian Reads Max Weber. Essays on the Protestant Ethic,* Wiesbaden: Harassowitz, 281–97.

37. The comparatively large denominations mentioned in the text represented 6.4 per cent of the population; see Hoppit, *Land of Liberty,* 220. On the Anglican work ethic, see C. J. Sommerville. 1981. 'The Anti-Puritan Work Ethic', *Journal of British Studies* 20, 70–81. For a general account, see R. J. Acheson. 1990. *Radical Puritans in England 1550–1660,* London: Longman.

38. 'The development of capitalism in Holland and England … was due, not to the fact that they were Protestant powers, but to large economic movements … Of course material and psychological changes went together, and of course the second reacted on the first. But it seems a little artificial to talk as though capitalist enterprise could not appear till religious changes had produced a capitalist spirit. It would be equally true, and equally one-sided, to say that the

religious changes were purely the result of economic movements.' R. H. Tawney. 1937 (1922). *Religion and the Rise of Capitalism,* Harmondsworth: Penguin, 312. W. D. Rubinstein explores further arguments against Weber that arise from English history in his 1998 'The Weber Thesis, Ethnic Minorities, and British Entrepreneurship', in D. J. Jeremy (ed.), *Religion, Business and Wealth in Modern Britain,* London: Routledge, 170–81.

39. Cf. Sombart, *Der moderne Kapitalismus,* vol. 2/1, 118–25.
40. Cf. B. S. Yamey. 1949. 'Scientific Bookkeeping and the Rise of Capitalism', *Economic History Review* 1, 110–11; M. Poovey. 1998. *A History of the Modern Fact. Problems of Knowledge in the Sciences of Wealth and Society,* Chicago: University of Chicago Press, 30–32. Muldrew points out that double entry bookkeeping was not very widespread in *Economy of Obligation,* 2; see also J. R. Edwards et al. 2002. 'British Central Government and "the mercantile system of double entry" Bookkeeping: a Study of Ideological Conflict', in *Accounting, Organizations and Society* 27, 637–58.
41. Anderson argues that these data, not the general calculability of economic activity, were decisive for the commercial sector; see 'Entrepreneurship', 158–59, 169.
42. Cf. P. Buck. 1977. 'Seventeenth-Century Political Arithmetic: Civil Strife and Vital Statistics', *Isis* 68, 83.
43. Cf. idem. 1982. 'People Who Counted: Political Arithmetic in the Eighteenth Century', *Isis* 73, 28. On the dating, see Glaisyer, *Culture of Commerce,* 4–5.
44. J. Hoppit. 2002. 'Checking the Leviathan, 1688–1832', in D. Winch and P. O'Brien (eds), *The Political Economy of British Historical Experience, 1688–1914,* Oxford: Oxford University Press for the British Academy, 274, 276–79, 291.
45. See Buck, 'Seventeenth-Century Political Arithmetic', 33; J. Hoppit. 1996. 'Political Arithmetic in Eighteenth-Century England', *Economic History Review* 49, 532–34.
46. Henri Misson de Valberg, *Memoirs and Observations in his Travels over England,* London 1719, 39–40, quoted in M. Ellis. 2008. 'An Introduction to the Coffee-House: a Discursive Model', *Language and Communication* 28, 158.
47. Cf. Ellis, *Coffee-House,* 172 (also with a discussion of the far higher figures circulating in the literature).
48. An overview of this literature can be found in ibid., 220–24.
49. J. Habermas. 1962. *Strukturwandel der Öffentlichkeit. Untersuchungen zu einer Kategorie der bürgerlichen Gesellschaft,* Frankfurt, Main: Suhrkamp (trans. 1989. *The Structural Transformation of the Public Sphere: An Inquiry into the Category of Bourgeois Society,* Cambridge: Polity) as well as P. Lake and S. Pincus (eds). 2007. *The Politics of the Public Sphere in Early Modern England,* Manchester: Manchester University Press.
50. Habermas, *Strukturwandel,* 89, 92 and, generalizing from his argument, J. van Horn Melton. 2001. *The Rise of the Public in Enlightenment Europe,* Cambridge: Cambridge University Press.
51. The argumentation that follows is based on Ellis's thorough study *Coffee-House,* esp. 185–206, as well as Pincus, *1688,* 74–81. See also the introduction to E. Mackie (ed.). 1998. *The Commerce of Everyday Life. Selections from The Tatler and The Spectator,* Boston, New York: Palgrave Macmillan, esp. 32.
52. The number comes from Ellis, *Coffee-House,* 173.
53. See ibid., 185–206; idem. 2001. 'The Coffee-Women, *The Spectator* and the Public Sphere in the Early-Eighteenth Century', in E. Eger et al. (eds), *Women, Writing and the Public Sphere,* Cambridge: Cambridge University Press, 27–52; Clery, E. J. 1991. 'Women, Publicity and the Coffee-House Myth', *Women. A Cultural Review* 2, 168–77.
54. Sales figures reflected the broad public response: *The Tatler* and *The Spectator* were published in print runs of up to three thousand per issue, and the collected issues of each year were bound in the provinces and sent to Continental Europe, where they disseminated the idea of the cof-

fee house and its discursive sociability – a commercial success unparalleled in the eighteenth century. Print run figures from Ellis, *Coffee-House*, 191–92.

55. Ibid., 190, 214; see also E. A. Lejeune. 1979. *The Gentlemen's Cubs of London*, London: Macdonald and Janes.

56. *Every Man his own Broker*, 81–82, quoted in Ellis, *Coffee-House*, 176–77.

57. Cf. Ibid., 214–15.

58. Cf. D. Zaret. 2000. Origins of Democratic Culture: Printing, Petitions and the Public Sphere in Early-Modern England, Princeton, NJ: Princeton University Press, 165.

59. Cf. C. J. Sommerville. 1996. *The News Revolution in England. Cultural Dynamics of Daily Information*, New York and Oxford: Oxford University Press, 84.

60. Cf. C. Heyl. 2004. *A Passion for Privacy. Untersuchungen zur Genese der bürgerlichen Privatsphäre in London*, 1660–1800, Munich: Oldenbourg.

61. Approximately three hundred thousand books and pamphlets appeared between 1660 and 1800, which added up to about 200 million copies; figures from R. Porter. 2000. *The Creation of the Modern World. The Untold Story of the British Enlightenment*, New York: W.W. Norton and Company, 73.

62. The percentage comes from L. Stone. 1969. 'Literacy and Education in England 1640–1900', *Past and Present* 42, 120. See also S. Pollard. 1973. 'Die Bildung und Ausbildung der industriellen Klassen Britanniens im 18. Jahrhundert', in R. Braun et al. (eds), *Gesellschaft in der industriellen Revolution*, Cologne: Kiepenheuer and Witsch, 147–61; T. Laqueur. 1976. 'The Cultural Origins of Popular Literacy in England 1550–1800', *Oxford Review of Education* 2, 255–75; K. Thomas. 1986. 'The Meaning of Literacy in Early Modern England', in G. Baumann (ed.), *The Written Word: Literacy in Transition*, Oxford: Clarendon Press, 97–131.

63. Cf. Porter, *Creation*, 77–78, as well as G. A. Cranfield. 1962. *The Development of the Provincial Newspapers 1700–1760*, Oxford: Clarendon Press. On distribution in the surrounding villages, see E. Pawson. 1977. *Transport and Economy: The Turnpike Roads of Eighteenth Century Britain*, London: Palgrave, 34 and passim.

64. Figures from B. Harris. 1996. *Politics and the Rise of the Press: Britain and France, 1620–1800*, London: Macmillan, 12.

65. Cf. R. Stöber. 2005. *Deutsche Pressegeschichte. Von den Anfängen bis zur Gegenwart*, Konstanz: UVK Verlagsgesellschaft, 79.

66. Cf. Sommerville, *News Revolution*, 15.

67. Cf. Glaisyer, *Culture of Commerce*, 144, 184; Ellis, *Coffee-House*, 192.

68. See, for example, Kramnick, J. B. 1998. *Making the English Canon. Print Capitalism and the Cultural Past, 1700–1770*, Cambridge: Cambridge University Press.

69. The argument is based on Sommerville, *News Revolution*, 3–4, 10, 162.

70. Cf. A. Harvey. 2004. *The Beginnings of a Commercial Sporting Culture in Britain, 1793–1850*, Aldershot: Ashgate, 16–17, 31–55; D. Brailsford. 1994. 'England 1775–1815: A Time for Play', in I. Blanchard (ed.), *Labour and Leisure in Historical Perspective, Thirteenth to Twentieth Centuries. Papers Presented at Session B-3a of the Eleventh International Economic History Congress, Milan, 12th–17th September 1994*, Stuttgart: Steiner, 101–09; I. Middleton and W. Vamplew. 2003. 'Horse-Racing and the Yorkshire Leisure Calendar in the Early Eighteenth Century', *Northern History* 40, 259–76.

71. Cf. McKendrick, 'The Commercialization of Fashion', 51. See also E. Wilson. 2005. 'Fashion and Modernity', in C. Breward and C. Evans (eds), *Fashion and Modernity*, Oxford: Berg.

72. See the overviews in Stöber, *Deutsche Pressegeschichte*, 73, 91. Stöber mentions only one daily newspaper, the *Einkommende Zeitung*, which appeared in Leipzig in the mid-seventeenth century.

73. For a wealth of examples, see U. Rosseaux. 2007. *Freiräume. Unterhaltung, Vergnügen und Erholung in Dresden (1694–1830)*, Cologne: Böhlau, 35–48.

74. See the survey article by P. Nolte. 2001. 'Modernization and Modernity in History', in *International Encyclopedia of the Social and Behavioral Sciences,* vol. 15, Amsterdam, 9958–59.
75. On these social functions of playing, see G. Gebauer and C. Wulf. 1998. *Spiel, Ritual, Geste. Mimetisches Handeln in der sozialen Welt,* Reinbek: Rowohlt, 188–89.
76. Cf. R. Caillois, 2001. *Men, Play and Games,* Urbana and Chicago: Chicago University Press.
77. Cf. S. H. Kurath (ed.). 1980. *Middle English Dictionary,* vol. O-P, Ann Arbor, MI: University of Michigan Press, 1032. See also H. Gillmeister. 1995. '*Not Cricket* und *Fair play*. Betrachtungen zum englischen Sportgedanken', in V. Gerhard and M. Lämmer (eds), *Fairness und Fair play: eine Ringvorlesung an der Deutschen Sporthochschule Köln,* 2nd ed., Sankt Augustin Academia Richarz, 129. In German, in contrast, in the course of the High German consonant shift there was a development from *plegian* to *pflegen* (care for, cultivate) and *Pflicht* (duty).
78. Cf. M. W. McConahey. 1974. *Sports and Recreations in Later Medieval France and England,* PhD Thesis University of Southern California, Los Angeles: University of Southern California Press; C. Reeves. 1995. *Pleasures and Pastimes in Medieval England,* Phoenix Mill, Gloucestershire: Anne Sutton Publishing Ltd.; G. M. Colón Semenza. 2003. *Sport, Politics and Literature in the English Renaissance,* Neward: University of Delaware Press; E. Griffin. 2005. *England's Revelry: A History of Popular Sports and Pastimes, 1660–1830,* Oxford: Oxford University Press; Wigglesworth, N. 1996. *The Evolution of English Sport,* London: Cass, esp. 13–24.
79. Cf. T. B. Leinwand. 1986. *The City Staged. Jacobean Comedy, 1603–1613,* Madison, WI: University of Madison Press; idem. 1999. *Theatre, Finance and Society in Early Modern England,* Cambridge: Cambridge University Press; W. Ingram. 1999. 'The Economics of Playing', in D. S. Kastan (ed.), *A Companion to Shakespeare,* Oxford: Blackwell, 313–27; M. White. 2004. 'London Professional Playhouses and Performances', in J. Milling and P. Thomson (eds), *The Cambridge History of British Theatre, vol. 1: Origins to 1660,* Cambridge: Cambridge University Press, 298–338; Reeves, *Pleasures and Pastimes,* 73–88.
80. Cf. K. Thomas. 1991 (1971). Religion and the Decline of Magic. Studies in Popular Beliefs in Sixteenth- and Seventeenth-Century England, London: Penguin, esp. 22–24, 157–65, 176–77, 569ff; R. Munting. 1996. *An Economic and Social History of Gambling in Britain and the USA,* Manchester: Manchester University Press, 6ff; D. Miers. 1989. 'A Social and Legal History of Gambling: From the Restoration to the Gaming Act 1845', in T. G. Watkin (ed.), *Legal Record and Historical Reality. Proceedings of the Eighth British Legal History Conference, Cardiff 1987,* London: The Hambledon Press, 107–120. See also the highly detailed historical review in C. Chinn. 1991. *Better Betting with a Decent Feller. Bookmaking, Betting and the British Working Class 1750–1990,* New York, London: Harvester Wheatsheaf, 6–30.
81. Cf. R. Woodhall. 1964. 'The British State Lotteries', *History Today* 14, 497–504.
82. According to Peter Burke, the number of publishers rose between 1730 and 1777 to 72, a figure exceeding that anywhere else at the time. 2001. *Papier und Marktgeschrei. Die Geburt der Wissensgesellschaft,* Berlin: Wagenbach, 193. See also R. Porter. 1996. 'Material Pleasures in the Consumer Society', in R. Porter and M. M. Roberts (eds), *Pleasures in the Eighteenth Century,* New York: New York University Press, 23, and the literature cited there. On women's cultural professions, see J. Brewer. 1997. *The Pleasures of the Imagination. English Culture in the Eighteenth Century,* New York: Farrar Straus Giroux, 78.
83. Copyright was introduced for authors and publishers in 1709, and for engravers in 1735 (on the initiative of William Hogarth); cf. J. A. Goltz. 2006. *Publizieren im 18. und frühen 19. Jahrhundert. Deutschland und England im Vergleich. Eine Untersuchung der spezifischen Entwicklung des Autorenrechts anhand der Rechtsquellen des deutschen Urheberrechts und des englischen Copyright Law,* Master Thesis, Humboldt-Universität zu Berlin, Institut für Geschichtswissenschaften; for the theatre, see Kewes, P. 2001. 'Plays as Property, 1660–1710', in A. Houston and S. Pincus (eds), *A Nation Transformed. England after the Restoration,* Cambridge: Cambridge University Press, 211–40.

84. The new vocabulary is mentioned in A. Houston and S. Pincus. 2001. 'Introduction. Modernity and Later Seventeenth-Century England', in A. Houston and S. Pincus (eds), *A Nation Transformed. England after the Restoration*, Cambridge: Cambridge University Press, 15.

85. Cf. J. H. Plumb. 1982. 'The Commercialization of Leisure', in N. McKendrick et al., *The Birth of a Consumer Society*, 275–76, as well as the works by Porter listed in the bibliography.

86. Cf. E. W. White. 1983. *A History of English Opera*, London: Faber and Faber; D. Alsop. 1996. '"Strains of New Beauty": Handel and the Pleasures of Italian Opera, 1711–28', in R. Porter and M. M. Roberts (eds), *Pleasure in the Eighteenth Century*, New York: New York University Press, 133–63.

87. Cf. J. Brewer. 1995. '"The Most Polite Age and the Most Vicious". Attitudes towards Culture as a Commodity, 1660–1800', in A. Bermingham and J. Brewer (eds), *The Consumption of Culture 1600–1800*, London: Routledge, 347.

88. For a detailed account of the rationalization of sport in the eighteenth century, see C. Eisenberg. 1999. *'English sports' und deutsche Bürger. Eine Gesellschaftsgeschichte 1800–1939*, Paderborn: Schöningh, 25–36.

89. C. L. de Secondat Baron de Montesquieu. 1977. *Persian Letters*, trans. C. J. Betts, Harmondsworth: Penguin, 65. See also T. M. Kavanagh. 1993. *Enlightenment and the Shadows of Chance: The Novel and the Culture of Gambling in Eighteenth-Century France*, Baltimore: Johns Hopkins University Press, 38.

90. Cf. G. Reith. 1999. *The Age of Chance. Gambling in Western Culture*, London: Routledge, 64–65. For examples and additional literature, see Eisenberg, *'English Sports'*, 29–36; D. Underdown. 2000. *Start of Play. Cricket and Culture in Eighteenth-Century England*, London: Penguin, 34ff.

91. See also Harvey, *Beginnings*, 155–56.

92. See the discussion in P. Mathias. 1969. *The First Industrial Nation. An Economic History of Britain 1700–1914*, London: Methuen, 131–32.

93. It is worth noting here that the Bubble Act was not a measure to prevent future speculative bubbles; rather, it was intended to provide the South Sea Company, which the government favoured, with a monopoly position over competing investors. In both public perception and historical memory, however, the temporal coincidence suggested a connection with the South Sea fraud. On the context in which the Bubble Act emerged, see Harris, *Industrializing English Law*, 60–81.

94. [D. Defoe] 1719. *The Anatomy of Exchange-Alley; or a System of Stock-Jobbing. Providing the Scandalous Trade, as it is Now Carry'd on, to be Knavish in its Private Practice, and Treason in its Publick: … By a Jobber*, 2nd ed., London: E. Smith., 43–44.

95. Cf. P. Williams. 1956. 'Lotteries and Government Finances in England', *History Today* 6, 559–60.

96. Cf. G. Clark. 1999. *Betting on Lives. The Culture of Life Insurance in England, 1695–1775*, Manchester: Manchester University Press.

97. See D. Hesmondhalgh. 2002. *The Cultural Industries*, London: Sage, 17–18.

98. Cf. S. McVeigh. 1993. *Concert Life in London from Mozart to Haydn*, Cambridge: Cambridge University Press, 3; Plumb, 'Commercialization of Leisure', 277, 282. Among the exceptions to this rule were, in particular, cooperative subscription societies of artists and athletes founded for the purpose of profit sharing. On the concert business, see McVeigh, *Concert Life*, 167. I am grateful to Ruti Ungar, who wrote her doctoral thesis on the culture of pugilism, for information on societies of boxers.

99. The example comes from J. Hall-Witt. 2003. 'Reforming the Aristocracy: Opera and Elite Culture, 1780–1860', in A. Burns and J. Innes (eds), *Rethinking the Age of Reform. Britain 1780–1850*, Cambridge: Cambridge University Press, 228; see, more generally, McVeigh, *Concert Life*, 6; D. Hunter. 2000. 'Patronizing Handel, Inventing Audiences. The Intersection of Class, Money, Music and History', *Early Music* 18, 36.

100. See also Brewer, 'Commercialization and Politics', 224.

101. Cf. the article 'Händel', in C. Dahlhaus and H. H. Eggebrecht (eds). 1979. *Brockhaus Riemann Musiklexikon,* Mainz: Brockhaus, 517; E. T. Harris. 2004. 'Handel the Investor', *Music and Letters* 85, 521–75.

102. Cf. Brewer, 'Commercialization and Politics', 6, 12; W. Weber. 1992. *The Rise of Musical Classics in Eighteenth-Century England. A Study in Canon, Ritual, and Ideology,* Oxford: Clarendon Press, 223–42 (on the concerts commemorating Handel as an expression of cultural commonalities between the clergy and the political class).

103. Towards the end of the eighteenth century, cultural events were, tellingly, increasingly financed by the sale of tickets; see McVeigh, *Concert Life,* 6, 12, 19, 171, as well as R. McGuinness and H. D. Johnstone. 1990. 'Concert Life in England I', in H. D. Johnstone and R. Fiske (eds), *The Blackwell History of Music in Britain the Eighteenth Century,* Oxford: Blackwell, 83. See also F. M. Scherer. 2001. 'The Evolution of Free-Lance Music Composition, 1650–1900', *Journal of Cultural Economics* 25, 310 (with reference to Handel's policy of also attracting the less well-off middle classes to his concerts).

104. Cf. Brewer, 'Commercialization and Politics', 224–25.

105. Cf. ibid., '"The Most Polite Age and the Most Vicious"', 349; J. Crump. 2005. 'The Perils of Play: Eighteenth-Century Ideas about Gambling', *Gaming Research Weblog* 27.1.2005 (http://www-histecon.kings.cam.ac.uk/docs/crump_perils.pdf, last accessed 21 September 2012).

106. Corresponding quotations are reproduced in M. Maurer (ed.). 1992. *O Britannien. Von Deiner Freiheit einen Hut voll. Deutsche Reiseberichte des 18. Jahrhunderts,* Munich: Beck and Kiepenheuer, 115–16, 193–94, 210–22 and passim; S. O. Müller, 2006. 'Friction, Fiction and Fashion: German Perceptions of Music Life in Britain in the "Long Nineteenth Century"', in A. Bauerkämper and C. Eisenberg (eds), *Britain as a Model of Modern Society? German Views,* Augsburg: Wißner, 224–41. See also Brewer, *The Pleasures of the Imagination,* 69; McVeigh, *Concert Life,* 60–64.

107. The opposition between play and work typical of Continental Europe, as expressed for example in the works of Jean-Jacques Rousseau and Friedrich Schiller, was wholly alien to them; see F. Oz-Salzberger. 1995. *Translating the Enlightenment. Scottish Civic Discourse in Eighteenth-Century Germany,* Oxford: Clarendon Press, 310–11, 319. The Ferguson quotations may be found there on 115, 154; see also 114–16. On the English Enlightenment more generally, see Porter, *Creation,* and idem. 1981. 'The English Enlightenment', in R. Porter and M. Teich (eds), *The Enlightenment in National Context,* Cambridge: Cambridge University Press, 1–18.

108. Cf. Hirschman, *Passions,* 60; idem. 1982. 'Rival Interpretations of Market Society: Civilizing, Destructive, or Feeble?', *Journal of Economic Literature* 20, 1464–66; Pocock, *Virtue;* E. Rothschild. 2002. *Economic Sentiments. Adam Smith, Condorcet, and the Enlightenment,* Cambridge, MA: Harvard University Press. It speaks for itself that Adam Smith uses the language of sport to explain the norm of 'fair play' for market actors: 'In the race for wealth, and honours, and preferments, he may run as hard as he can, and strain every nerve and every muscle, in order to outstrip all his competitors. But if he should jostle, or throw down any of them, the indulgence of the spectators is entirely at an end. It is a violation of fair play, which they cannot admit of.' Smith, *Theory of Moral Sentiments,* 101; see also F. Forman-Barzilai. 2010. *Adam Smith and the Circles of Sympathy. Cosmopolitanism and Moral Theory,* Cambridge: Cambridge University Press, 42.

109. Cf. K. Tribe. 1977. 'The "Histories" of Economic Discourse', *Economy and Society* 6, 314–44; I. Hont and M. Ignatieff. 1983. 'Needs and Justice in the Wealth of Nations: an Introductory Essay', in I. Hont and M. Ignatieff (eds), *Wealth and Virtue: The Shaping of Political Economy in the Scottish Enlightenment,* Cambridge: Cambridge University Press, 1–45; as well as N. Phillipson. 1983. 'Adam Smith as a Civic Moralist', in I. Hont and M. Ignatieff (eds), *Wealth and*

Virtue: The Shaping of Political Economy in the Scottish Enlightenment, Cambridge: Cambridge University Press, 179–203.

110. Cf. McKendrick, 'The Consumer Revolution of Eighteenth-Century England', 17–18.
111. This is demonstrated by T. C. W. Blanning's 2002 comparative study *The Culture of Power and the Power of Culture. Old Regime Europe 1660–1789,* Oxford: Oxford University Press, as well as by B. Cowan. 2004. 'An Open Elite: The Peculiarities of Connoisseurship in Early Modern England', *Modern Intellectual History* 1, esp. 156.
112. The argument is based on R. McGuinness's essay 2004. 'Gigs, Roadies and Promoters: Marketing Eighteenth-Century Concerts', in S. Wollenberg and S. McVeigh (eds), *Concert Life in Eighteenth-Century Britain,* Aldershot: Ashgate, 261–71.
113. Z. Bauman. 1994. 'Desert Spectacular', in K. Tester (ed.), *The Flâneur,* London: Routledge, 145–46. Tellingly, the figure of the flâneur is not mentioned in Brewer, *The Pleasures of the Imagination.*
114. Cf. H. Fürst von Pückler-Muskau. 1985. 'J.-A. Barbey d'Aurevilly and C. Baudelaire', in G. Stein (ed.), *Dandy – Snob – Flaneur. Dekadenz und Exzentrik. Kulturfiguren und Sozialcharaktere des 19. und 20. Jahrhunderts,* Frankfurt, Main: Fischer, 19–23; see also C. Breward. 2003. 'Masculine Pleasures: Metropolitan Identities and the Commercial Sites of Dandyism', 1790–1840, *London Journal* 28, 60–72.
115. Cf. Agnew, *Worlds Apart,* 170–71, as well as above, 83–84.

COMMERCIALIZATION AS
AN HISTORICAL PROCESS

Thus far in this study, individual sites of the commercialization process have been described: agriculture, industrial production, the financial sector and cultural life. On the heels of these portrayals, the question arises of the nature of the ligatures and connections that integrated these sites into a viable market society. Furthermore, it remains to be determined whether and in what way English market society can be characterized as capitalist. Finally, the direction of its development shall be analysed: did English market society transition seamlessly into modern industrialization, characterized by the centralization of workers in factories and the massive deployment of machines? Or would other categories better describe its characteristic pattern of development?

The following snapshot of the English economy at the turn of the nineteenth century attempts to answer these questions on a general level. Thereafter, a systematic section will address two further questions: whether and in what respect England represents a special case of market development in Europe; and what drivers, path dependencies, and developmental potentials of the process of commercialization in England should future comparative studies take into account?

English Market Society in 1800: Regulatory Mechanisms and Direction of Development

One of the outstanding characteristics of English market society around 1800, and one that requires no further discussion, was its modernity. A (male) time traveller from a Western country in the advanced twentieth or early twenty-first century

---

Notes from this chapter begin on page 126.

would be able to find his bearings without any difficulty – indeed, presumably better than a contemporary visitor from an economically less developed region of Continental Europe would have. The rhythm of life, dictated by commerce and the media; the tendency towards the levelling of differences between high and popular culture; and the general tenor of life in consumer society would all seem quite familiar to the time traveller. The social structure – based in large part on the factors of ownership and money, and therefore relatively fluid – would enable him to form connections with people and integrate into English social life. The time traveller would not necessarily register the absence of factories and smoking chimneys, which were not yet a feature of the cityscape, as he is no longer used to seeing them at home. All he would miss would be technical developments such as the railroad, the automobile and the electronic media. As a political observer, he might find the alliance between the Crown, Parliament and the other players in the pursuit of 'gentlemanly capitalism' to be problematic. Furthermore, he would be struck by the profound inequalities of wealth and – unless he were a staunch neoliberal – see the desirability of a welfare-state-style redistribution. On the other hand, the time traveller would be able to explain these deficits in terms of the fact that the society he was visiting was already a capitalist one, and that capitalism, democracy and social justice do not always go hand in hand, not even in the early twenty-first century.

English market society did indeed display key elements of capitalism around 1800, although most contemporaries had no real concept of the principles according to which such a society functioned, nor would they have been familiar with the word 'capitalism' itself.[1] After all, the framework conditions for doing business – from the guarantee of private ownership rights to the existence of a single currency, from free markets in land and money to the generalization of wage labour, from the protection of trade routes by the Royal Navy to presence of the Bank of England and the London Stock Exchange – not merely made profit maximization and reinvestments (i.e., capitalist relations of exchange) possible but in fact made them the norm. Even on the financial markets, family ties and informal relationships had diminished in importance, as bank-mediated discount loans for high and short-term obligations came on the market following the foundation of the Bank of England in 1694.[2]

What distinguished the capitalist market society of England from modern industrial capitalism was its clear emphasis on agriculture, on the one hand, and on trade and finance, on the other. While manufacturing was integrated into the capitalist economy, as has been demonstrated, it did not develop autonomously but rather in close symbiosis with these dominant economic sectors. Due to its incomplete differentiation as well as its decentralized organizational structure based on a complex division of labour, it escaped the notice of contemporary observers, who would have had little to say about it anyway. As the nineteenth century wore on, political economists and theoreticians of capitalism would con-

Figure 4.1. Street traffic in front of the Royal Exchange, 1751.

centrate their attention on modern factory work, with its spectacular technology as well as its alienating and exploitative aspects. This means that when economists started to think systematically about capitalism and its concomitant effects, they identified the factory rather than the market as the main feature of modern capitalism and the factory owner rather than the businessman as the capitalist par excellence.

That in the long term England would develop in the direction of an industrial society, as these later authorities took as a given, was by no means a foregone conclusion in the decades straddling the turn of the nineteenth century, however. This is testified to not least by *The Wealth of Nations* (1776), Adam Smith's astute description of contemporary conditions, which focused on the market and commercial society rather than on industrial production.[3] In my subsequent analysis of the capitalist market economy in England around 1800, I shall also argue that the development towards an industrial society was quite unlikely and in any event did not result from the market economy itself. For if one analyses the business rationale of merchants, traders and other economic actors in the Early Modern period according to certain criteria, one sees that it was rational for them not to overstep the boundaries of commercial capitalism.

Profit and Control. The profit orientation of the business activity of merchants, traders and many others who were professionally involved in the system of commercial capitalism found expression in the way they factored time into their business decisions. For them, speculation about future market developments was a central element of doing business.[4] For traders and financiers, capital and credit were instruments, either for withholding their supply in the face of insufficient demand until prices rose again or for increasing it temporarily as demand increased. Their business practices therefore included maintaining storage capacity or, in the case of financial transactions, liquidity. Merchants also had to possess a certain base amount of monetary capital to undertake commercial transactions and credit operations and to be able to serve specialized, geographically distant markets, as investments in the transport of goods as well as in additional manpower were regularly required. To organize such transactions at the scale demanded was at once the entrepreneurial challenge and the source of the profits. In contrast, the supervision of the production process and of workers in the putting-out system appeared as a problem of secondary importance – quite apart from the fact that in a decentralized production system, it was generally difficult to establish and maintain control. Instead, merchants organized their firms around contractual networks of individual producers and in so doing placed great value on the design of contracts.[5]

Speculation and Calculability. For merchants, the concrete conditions of the production of industrial and agricultural goods were also of limited interest because the profits that they could anticipate were relatively independent of such factors. Nor does the particular branch in which an entrepreneur was active appear to have been particularly significant. Rather, profits accrued out of the short-term identification and exploitation of price fluctuations, similar to arbitrage profits on the stock market. The chances of earning such profits were extraordinarily good in England, not least due to regional specialization and the permeable social structure, both of which favoured the segmentation of markets.[6] In this environment, what was important for the merchant was that he was in possession of the information he needed to recognize his market opportunities and that he always had access to the credit and transport options necessary to realize them. In view of the permanent changes in the markets and the pressure to conform to ever-new situations, it appeared relatively futile to attempt to optimize profits through bookkeeping, detailed analyses of price records and exchange rates, or a reordering of business practices. This explains the finding from the field of historical management research that in Early Modern England, such rationalization methods were generally not applied, as well as the opinion that no impulses for industrialization came from this direction.[7]

Investment and Risk. To the extent that a merchant invested a share of his capital in fixed assets to centralize certain work processes, he remained but one of many resource owners in the system of decentralized production, and little changed in terms of the overall risk of his market-orientated transactions. Should he shift completely to production, his risk might even increase, because he now became all the more dependent on the decisions of outside middlemen and other market experts.[8] As this study has emphasized, English merchants in this situation invested predominantly in the infrastructure of market society: in enterprises like banks, stock exchanges and insurance companies; in streets, canals and other transport systems; in information services and newspapers. It was also rational for them to cultivate a large number of cultural and social relations to engender trust and goodwill. In the area of consumer goods and in the cultural industry, such relations could also contribute to the early recognition of trends and to the launching of new fashions.[9]

Infrastructure as a Collective Good. Viewed from an historical perspective, the specific effect of all these investments lay in the fact that their fruits also benefitted people other than the investors. In this manner, a yield for society resulted even when the individual investor failed with his project and disappeared from the market – a further element of 'doux commerce' in the capitalist economy of England. Alongside investors and the general public, the users and beneficiaries of the infrastructure as a collective good also included a large number of market coordinators, so-called middlemen. They were largely self-employed and influenced market activity indirectly. In addition, there were members of professions that influenced the market directly, such as currency and bond traders, money-lenders, bankers, stock brokers, warehouse workers, salesmen; legions of waggoners, peddlers and travelling salesmen (the 'itinerant class') and – last but not least – hundreds of thousands of shopkeepers. Furthermore, publishers and journalists as well as members of the professions, such as lawyers and notaries, tax collectors and even those members of the armed forces assigned to open up and protect international trade routes, could be counted among such intermediaries of market exchange. Many of these persons lived in the growing cities, which, due to their complex social relationships, created a greater need for coordination.[10] And yet one characteristic of English market society consisted in the fact that the thoroughly commercialized and regionally specialized agricultural sector, whose (sales) markets were equally located at home and abroad, was also dependent on the services of the abovementioned intermediary professions.

It was these 'commercial classes' that gave the English economy in the Early Modern period its face. Due to their omnipresence, contemporary observers were of the opinion that they were far too numerous and that England had two to three times as many merchants 'as all the rest of Europe put together'. Observers recognized a particular problem in the fact that so many 'downright Merchants' had to finance their businesses 'upon their own Capital', i.e., without access to credit.[11]

The lament over the excess numbers of persons brokering market exchange was not unfounded, seeing as this population had grown steadily since the late Middle Ages and then risen sharply, especially in the course of the eighteenth century. According to an analysis of contemporary statistics by the American historian Ray B. Westerfield, who in 1915 published an extraordinarily informative social and economic history of middlemen, between 1688 and 1750, a period when the general population grew by about 10 per cent, the commercial classes increased by between 32 and 63 per cent, according to profession (table 4.1).

Table 4.1. Estimated Growth of the Commercial Classes Compared with General
Population Growth, 1688–1750 (in per cent)

	Families	Persons
Large-scale ('eminent') merchants	45.0	63.0
Small-scale ('lesser') merchants	39.0	39.0
Traders, shop owners	18.0	32.0
Population growth	9.9	9.8

Source: R. B. Westerfield. 1968. *Middlemen in English Business Particularly Between 1660–1760,* New Haven, CT: Yale University Press. 1915, Reprint New York: David and Charles Reprints., 414. Westerfield's calculations are mainly based on figures from the statisticians Gregory King (1688) and Andrew Young (1769).

In the further course of the eighteenth century, this growth accelerated once again. The causes of this were threefold: Firstly, the demand for market personnel increased because the growth in population contributed to the consolidation of market relations and because, stimulated by the consumer revolution, new branches of the economy developed and new types of goods were traded. On top of that, the expansion of the empire opened up new markets, including on the British Isles.[12]

A second reason for the growth of the commercial classes was the supply-driven increase in the so-called 'excess population', which was created by population growth and accumulated especially in the cities: Migrants in search of work gravitated as a matter of course towards trade or the transport industry, and those without capital could find employment in these branches as wage labourers.[13]

A third reason was structural: the commercial classes of the eighteenth century would generally have been subject to the same limits to rationalization that more recent sociology has diagnosed for modern service-sector work. Such activities are in general difficult to standardize and can be neither transported nor stored. Often – particularly in the case of cultural and personal services – production and consumption occur at the same time (the 'uno actu principle'). Above all, however, due to the uncertainty characteristic of the market economy, one cannot measure a priori how many services a society really needs, with the result that an overcapacity is often produced.[14] In some cases, the 'invisible hand' of the market can induce marginal sellers to withdraw. And yet not even Adam Smith believed that this took place automatically. He described services as simply 'unproductive': They 'generally perish in the very instant of their performance, and seldom leave any trace of value behind them, for which an equal quantity of service could afterwards be procured'.[15]

Around the turn of the nineteenth century, these growth conditions found statistical expression in the occupational structure. The estimates provided in table 4.2,[16] which in the case of England and Wales are based on the census of

Table 4.2. Occupational Structure of Several Northwest European Countries, around 1800 (in per cent)

	Agriculture	Manufacturing	Services
England and Wales 1801	36	30	34
Republic of the Netherlands 1750–1800	41	32	27
'Germany' 1800	62	21	17

Source: J. de Vries and A. van der Woude. 1997. *The First Modern Economy. Success, Failure and Perseverance of the Dutch Economy, 1500–1815*, Cambridge: Cambridge University Press, 528–29.

1801, bring two noteworthy circumstances to light: on the one hand, the considerable decline in the agrarian sector, which encompassed only 36 per cent of the workforce; on the other – and this is the significant point here – that among the sectors of the economy that would dominate in the future, services, at 34 per cent, were more strongly represented than manufacturing, at 30 per cent.

As the international comparison shows, a service sector of this scope was not in evidence in any other European country at this time. Even the advanced Netherlands lagged considerably behind England, with a figure of 27 per cent. Furthermore, the estimates for the German states, which in the table stand as a proxy for the rest of Western and Central Europe,[17] brought up the rear at 17 per cent. How exceedingly modern the occupational structure of England and Wales was at the turn of the nineteenth century reveals itself most clearly when one considers that at 34 per cent of the workforce, its service sector was approximately equal in size to that of the United States around 1900 (32 per cent), of the German Empire in 1936 (36 per cent) and of France in 1937 (37 per cent).[18]

At the turn of the nineteenth century, the service sector in England and Wales overtook the manufacturing sector – and not only in terms of the size of the workforce. It also made the largest contribution of the three sectors to the gross domestic product. As table 4.3 shows, the share of the manufacturing sector exceeds that of the service sector only for the period 1760–80 (and only according to the calculations of Nicholas F. R. Crafts, which reflect commercial services quite inadequately). Only in the first decades of the nineteenth century – that is, towards the end of the time frame of this study – did the growth rates of the manufacturing sector experience a notable rise. And yet according to calculations of Charles H. Feinstein, which are presented in the table, over the long term they also ranked lower than those of the service sector.[19]

Table 4.3 furthermore shows that the greatest growth spurts in the service sector occurred in the decades after 1760. According to the research findings of Robin Pearson und David Richardson, this date marks the beginning of a period in which – despite the unfavourable legal framework conditions on the local and regional levels – British entrepreneurs began to form joint ventures. The Bubble Act of 1720 had denied legislative protection to joint stock companies operating

Table 4.3. Weighted Sectoral Output Growth Rates of the GDP in Great Britain, 1700–1860 (in per cent per year)

	Agriculture	Manufacturing	Services	Gross domestic product
Calculations of N. F. R. Crafts				
1700–1760	0.22	0.14	0.33	0.69
1760–1780	0.04	0.38	0.28	0.70
1780–1801	0.24	0.53	0.55	1.32
1801–1831	0.31	0.95	0.70	1.97
Calculations of C. K. Harley				
1700–1770	0.19	0.16	0.21	0.56
1770–1815	0.26	0.40	0.65	1.31
1815–1841	0.36	0.99	0.88	2.23
Calculations of C. H. Feinstein				
1831–60	0.36	0.97	1.17	2.50

Source: C. H. Lee. 1986. *The British Economy since 1700: a Macroeconomic Perspective,* Cambridge: Cambridge University Press, 10.

without a royal or parliamentary charter, and such charters were generally not easy to come by. However, entrepreneurs who wanted to cover higher capital demands, take advantage of economies of scale and make better use of their know-how were not dissuaded by this, but increasingly formed unchartered partnerships, trusts or limited liability companies, with which they entered the market. They created detailed statutes for themselves and allowed shareholders to participate in corporate governance as a guarantee of control ('shareholder democracy'). This development likewise primarily took place not in manufacturing but rather in the service sector. It led to the foundation of large insurance companies, new well-funded canal-building societies, and soon also gas-lighting and water companies, and went hand in hand with cooperation among companies, the creation of cartels and not infrequently the acquisition of a quasi-official status.[20] The close of the eighteenth century therefore marked a point in the development of English market society at which organizations supplemented and supplanted individuals as market actors.[21]

The finding that the service sector carried great weight in the British economy – a characteristic that endured far into the nineteenth century[22] – is confirmed by recent research in economic and social history, with its tendency to turn away from the concept of the Industrial Revolution. The present study has radicalized this research trend not only by strengthening the long-standing doubts as to the revolutionary quality of the development in the core time period of 1760–1830, but also by calling into question the very industrial character of the British economy at this time. The isolated analysis of individual, successfully industrialized regions and branches – such as the textile industry in Lancashire, where certain towns could boast multiple steam-powered factories – could relativize this interpretation a bit. However, one must keep in mind that at the beginning of the nineteenth century, even in Manchester, the 'Cottonopolis' of the English textile industry, considerably more capital was being invested in warehouses and public houses – that is, in the service sector – than in factory production.[23] Both types of buildings served as clearing houses (quality control) and as business premises for producers living in scattered locations in the countryside, who had temporarily taken up residence in cities to gain access to national and international markets. The statement that the commercialization process in England in the early nineteenth century culminated not in an industrial but rather in a service society therefore appears entirely justified.

Thus, if one were to propose a meaningful follow-up to the present study, it would not be yet another history of the industrialization of England and/or Great Britain, supplemented by a market-related analysis. A more appropriate next step would be to revisit the long-neglected topic of the provision of services and in a manner that from the outset not only researches the subject in its economic social and cultural historical context but also takes into account the longer-term trend towards the integration of services into businesses and other organizations. Precisely for the industrial pioneer Britain, the term productivity, which is utilized in (neo)classical economics and is narrowly oriented towards the production of goods, would appear to be entirely insufficient for the investigation of such an ambivalent and puzzling topic.[24]

Throughout, attention should also be paid to the indirect contribution of services to economic productivity and societal integration. As this study has shown, in the Early Modern period this consisted especially in organizing and safeguarding the flow of information and communication as well as other brokerage services. In the longer term, the contribution of service providers to the supervision and overseeing of these functions, to the conservation of natural resources and to the synthesizing of societal self-understanding would have to be included.[25] Above all, any research seeking to build upon the present study of market society would have to answer two questions.

With a view towards the further economic and societal development of England and/or Great Britain, the functional relationship between market-related services and industrial production, which might have assumed a different shape at different periods, would have to be determined. When were the two areas complementary, and when were they not? When did they stimulate one another, and where did they compete? Can one go so far as to argue that for England and/or Great Britain, the characteristically slow progression of industrialization in the eighteenth and early nineteenth century can be traced back to the high percentage of service professionals among the workforce? This argument has already been put forward in the literature; however, thus far only in studies of Great Britain's backward slide in the Second Industrial Revolution since the turn of the twentieth century (chemical and electrical industry, the use of petrol as a new form of energy). Stephen Broadberry, who has researched the problem in a comparative study of Britain, Germany and the United States, argues that at this time, the level of organization and technology among British services was too low.[26] One needs to determine if this interpretation also holds true for the early period under investigation – and thereby for the phase of industrialization as a whole. After all, the development of services could provide a plausible explanation for the longer-term decline of the British economy, i.e., the 'falling behind' of the industrial pioneer relative to economies that industrialized after it.

From an international perspective, it would ultimately be desirable to know if the order in which the service and manufacturing sectors developed in England can be generalized or if elsewhere in Europe and in the world as a whole, empirical evidence can be found for the broadly accepted 'three-sector hypothesis' of the French economist Jean Fourastié (1907–1990), according to which the occupational structure of modern economies fundamentally follows a development from the agrarian to the industrial and, only at an advanced stage, to the service sector. Should this be the case, then market economies outside of England would presumably be structured very differently.[27]

Driving Forces, Path Dependencies and Development Potential: Perspectives for a Long-term European Comparison

The preceding snapshot of the English market economy around 1800, with the characteristic dominance of the service sector, shows that the process of commercialization did in many ways contribute to a modernization of cultural, social and societal conditions in England: against the background of a rapidly growing population, it made it possible to overcome traditional food crises and, through its contribution to sustainable economic growth, helped the country to achieve a level of prosperity far above the standard in the rest of Europe.[28] And yet with respect to production methods, no revolutionary force was unleashed by the process. Therefore, in the results of this study, the commercialization of England can be characterized only as a necessary but not as a sufficient precondition for industrialization.[29]

This ultimately negative finding might be perplexing; in the context of this study, however, it seems plausible, since any less cautious depiction of the situation would raise the question of why the breakthrough of industrialization in England did not take place at an earlier point in the 750-year-long commercialization process outlined here. The obvious objection that the shift from quantity to quality did not take place until the middle of the nineteenth century would, according to the structure of the argument, be a circular one. This objection would furthermore inevitably leave the question unresolved of why, around the middle of the nineteenth century, England experienced the breakthrough to industrial society years or even decades before other European and non-European countries, which had not gone through so early and comprehensive a preliminary phase of commercialization.

For the history of English industrialization, this means that to explain its pioneering character, other contributing factors must be weighted more heavily than the preliminary process of commercialization. The factors that emerged in the preceding study include above all the development of new technologies, which in part built on the transfer of European knowledge and technology and, in coal-rich Great Britain, were utilized especially to improve the production of energy (steam engines).[30] A second factor was the comparatively high level of wages in manufacturing, particularly in the textile industry, in Great Britain – a result in part of union organization and strikes – which represented a considerable cost factor, and in the long term under world market conditions encouraged the replacement of human labour with machines.[31] Finally, the stimulation of demand for certain commodities (e.g., cotton fabrics), which went hand in hand with imperial expansion, will also have made its contribution, as exports accounted for nearly half of the growth in industrial production that England experienced in the course of the eighteenth century. This point calls attention to the role of the Crown and Parliament in promoting industrialization, and recalls the Financial Revolution as well as additional encouraging measures on the part of the government.[32] Thus, the self-same politics that served as a driving force behind commercialization were also an impetus to industrialization.

With regard to the process of commercialization itself, one can summarize the finding of this study by stating that even 750 years after it had begun – by which time England and/or Great Britain had long since developed a fully fledged market society – a qualitative intensification of commercialization failed to materialize. Developments appeared to be heading in the direction of more of the same and possibly even towards a period of busy idling. The following summary of the progression and most important characteristics of the commercialization process in England can therefore not be limited to highlighting its merits and achievements. It must at the same time identify and – to the extent possible – attempt to explain its deficits as well as the limits of its malleability within the context of the unfolding of the process itself. Only on this basis can hypotheses for future comparative studies be formed.

The process of commercialization in England did not spring from any specifically English peculiarities. Rather, its decisive initial push came from a very external event: the victory of William the Norman over the English king Harald II in the Battle of Hastings in 1066. One should be wary of overestimating the long-term effects of singular historical events. In this case, however, the campaign of conquest that followed this victory led in a short span of time to the violent destruction of the political system of the Anglo-Saxons, so that a cooperation between the old and new elites was as unthinkable as a return to the former status quo. A new system of authority was thus able to develop unhindered; one that was centralist in its orientation and united traditional elements of European feudalism – such as feudal tenure and the concept of personal loyalty – with novel methods of safeguarding authority, which were precisely tailored to the king. From the beginning, these were based on contractual and monetary relationships. Thus, in its capacity as the bare owner of the English territory, the Crown had to execute both political and economic functions, and in some situations was confronted with demands that required contradictory responses.

The centrifugal effects of monetary relationships unleashed a commercial dynamic and eroded the political power of the Crown. This mechanism first took hold of the land and capital markets, and subsequently also the rural labour markets. The joint experience of landowners and tenants that the productivity of villeins was less than that of freemen hastened the rationalization of agricultural production. Furthermore, the end of serfdom and concomitant inflow of manumitted rural labourers into urban labour markets put cities under great pressure. As in the state building process, cities had not succeeded in acquiring judicial autonomy, their authorities saw no means of defending themselves against this development. Hence, the permeability of the borders between cities and their environs accelerated the decline of the guilds and the generalization of the characteristic asymmetry in the labour market between supply and demand. To counteract this asymmetry, trade unions had begun to take shape by the eighteenth century, although their organizational scope still remained local.

In other concrete situations it was the Crown itself – motivated by pure self-interest in safeguarding its power and securing the financial means that this required – that gave impetus to market development, both directly and indirectly. The motive of creating revenue stood behind measures such as the systematic sale of market rights since the second half of the thirteenth century, the relatively uncomplicated manner in which the royal courts dealt with matters of domestic and international trade (merchant law, or *lex mercatoria*), as well as the Crown's patronage of the Royal Exchange, which was built in 1565 as a multifunctional business centre in the City of London. Furthermore, through numerous strategic laws, the Crown increased the pressure on the poor and needy to make themselves available to the market. Particularly noteworthy in this regard are laws dating from the sixteenth century, including the Statute of Artificers (1563), which demanded access to craft apprenticeships for the children of the poor, but above all the Poor Laws, which obligated municipal administrations to support vagrants and other paupers and at the same time served as a kind of rudimentary unemployment insurance during seasonal and cyclical downturns in the economy. Moreover, the relief benefits were linked to outrageous impositions, so that the needy would feel obliged to accept any offer of employment, however unpleasant.[33] After the revolutions of the seventeenth century sharply limited the ability of the Crown to shape politics, it, together with Parliament, ultimately initiated a reorganization of state finances (the Financial Revolution), which created a new instrument for steering the English economy: the national debt. Therewith, the role of promoter of the market economy was transferred from the Crown to the modern British state.

As both the Crown and the State were active participants in the market, one should not characterize the interventions they spearheaded as exogenous impulses with regard to the process of commercialization. Nor did any truly external or extra-economic entity either disrupt or add momentum to this development after 1066. As was argued above, an important reason for this was England's island location, which not only thwarted would-be conquerors but also shielded the continuous development of its market from the adverse effects of war and the introduction of epidemics. One of the findings of this study is thus that the commercialization of England, which began with a single impulse emanating from abroad, was then able to unfold over centuries as a largely indigenous, self-propelling process. That the Netherlands served as a model for the Financial Revolution of the late seventeenth century, and that London was consequently associated with the financial market in Amsterdam, does not detract from this general impression. The finding of this study is rather that, as is frequently observed in connection with the phenomenon of cultural transfer, in this situation the concrete interests of recipients with respect to the shape of things to come trumped the foreign model, so that the latter's significance as an instigator was relativized.[34]

All in all, the commercialization process in England developed steadily and with no recognizable setbacks. However, at an advanced stage of the process, there was a certain acceleration effect that derived from the exchange of individual markets with their social environment. This study examined the reciprocal and synergic effects of this in detail with regard to manufacturing and determined that the expansion of modern industry, especially since the end of the seventeenth and beginning of the eighteenth century, led to an upturn, albeit a slow one. This was bolstered by a considerable growth in population, which also contributed to the consolidation of market exchange, a drop in transaction costs, the encouragement of a division of labour and thereby a more efficient economy. That contemporary observers as well as historians of this period began to characterize English society as a consumer society can be taken as proof that the process of commercialization was able, through a quantitative increase, to lend economic relations of exchange a quality that at the time was perceived as novel. However, the satisfaction of everyday needs via the market was by no means a new phenomenon, but rather had been expanding continuously since the Middle Ages.

On a general level, the innate ability of the commercialization process to anchor its principles in ever-changing social and cultural conditions grew out of the experience of contemporaries that there were also existential disadvantages to not being connected to the network of the market. Furthermore, one can argue, with reference to modern network theory, that the network became more sustainable, more efficient and therefore also more attractive the more indirect contacts it brokered. That's why, paradoxically, sociological studies have been able to demonstrate that informal, so-called 'weak' ties facilitated through the market (and the media) contribute more to communication than do close, interpersonal relationships.[35] Finally, the commercialization process took centuries to unfold, so that a habituation effect must also have set in.

Market relations were furthermore able to successfully embed themselves in existing social and cultural contexts – a quality that can be traced back to active brokering efforts on the part of market participants. These efforts arose through the circumstance that individual actors sought, through collective behaviour and organization, to make it possible to coordinate with one another and forge an environment that was tailored precisely to their specific economic interests. The examples that were presented in this study include the following: the efforts of stock market and insurance experts at professionalization, which led to the separation of the London Stock Exchange and modern insurance companies from the Royal Exchange; the turnpike societies and the profit interests of private developers that were behind the trend in urban improvement; the strikes and attempts at organization on the part of unions; and finally, the innumerable friendly societies for mutual aid in the event of illness or other life crises, which in a market society can quickly spiral into existential crises.

A particular contribution to the self-perpetuation of the commercialization process as well as to its embedding in existing social and cultural environments was made by the press and the cultural industries. In England, both branches were from the outset profit orientated, and business was done in the interest of the owners as well as the – largely self-employed – journalists and cultural professionals working in these fields. In pursuing these interests, it was helpful for the two branches to exchange information and cooperate closely. The press needed the cultural industries due to its incessant demand for current information, and conversely the cultural industries profited from the public relations work of the press, which directed audiences to them and helped to create the special aura that would come to surround many regularly staged events. By together assisting various sectors of the market – betting and sports, fashion and consumption as a whole – in their efforts to institutionalize, the press and the cultural industries additionally generated another mutually beneficial effect: they supported cultural and psychological efforts to adapt to market activities, also among those contemporaries who were not themselves professionally involved in them.

Was the commercialization of England since the end of the Middle Ages a path-dependent process? This question, which refers to a discussion that first took place in the field of economics, encompasses three subquestions: to what extent can it be said that the – potentially random – constellation of circumstances at the outset continued to shape the long-term development of the process? Did this constellation, in the further course of its evolution, become subject to a self-reinforcing 'lock-in' effect, which might have secured its irreversibility? And finally: was the process able to fulfil its functions in the long term, or did its marginal utility begin to diminish over time? Or did emerging dysfunctions, internal contradictions or innovations in the environment gradually lead to less-than-ideal results?[36]

The answer to the first question regarding the influence of the initial constellation of factors is already known: the commercialization process was instigated in 1066 by the victory of William the Conqueror over the Anglo-Saxons and developed henceforth more or less as a side effect of the new system of rule that he established. To that extent, chance – defined by Niklas Luhmann as 'the absence of advance coordination between events and systems' – played an important role, quite apart from the fact that the Norman Invasion could have ended in failure.[37]

A 'lock-in' situation was created through the campaign that followed the conquest, which resulted in the nearly complete liquidation of the old Anglo-Saxon elite. A commander who has thus created a tabula rasa must not only establish a new, differently constituted structure of rule, but must also be able to manage it when unintended consequences and contradictions arise. This self-imposed predicament is not the least of the factors that can help to explain why even in the longer term, the Crown remained the driving force behind the commercialization process, even though it relatively early on became clear that the process was undermining its authority.

In this study, the 'lock-in' situation of the Crown has been sketched out for the erosion of feudal domination. It would be a worthy topic for another study to make clear in what manner the same mechanism produced positive consequences for the history of civil liberties. After all, the Magna Carta, which was imposed upon King John in 1215 by a group of his most privileged barons from Normandy, already settled a whole slew of economically relevant questions, including the treatment of debtors, questions relating to insolvency proceedings and relations with foreign merchants. In the history of parliamentarization, as well, one can repeatedly identify situations – beginning with Simon de Monfort and the opposition he led to the foreign policy plans of Henry II in 1254 – in which the barons (and later also members of the middle classes) took advantage of fiscal emergencies on the part of the Crown in order to 'purchase' new rights by consenting to the levying of taxes. Viewed in this manner, the 'Financial Revolution', following on the heels of the Glorious Revolution, was merely the culmination of a practice that had been going on for centuries.[38]

However, the automatic weakening of the Crown as a consequence of expanding market relations is not the topic of this study. Rather, its concern is with the path dependency of the process of commercialization and in particular with the question of whether and in what regard this process produced side effects and dys-functions that negatively impacted on its own functioning. The answer to this is negative, since over the centuries the market grew increasingly better at fulfilling its task of guaranteeing the allocation of goods and services and of coordinating the transactions this required. Its only recognizable side effect was the integration of English society by means of the fleeting and largely anonymous social relations that it forged. This, in turn – to phrase it in the language of path-dependency – was not a dysfunction, but rather an example of positive feedback.

It does not contradict this finding to acknowledge that crises repeatedly occurred or that for the majority of people in the Early Modern era, as wage earners, small employers and consumers, the market economy created fewer opportunities than it did for employers and merchants, thereby limiting their quality of life. Even within the framework of the thoroughly one-sided rules for the making of labour contracts, laid down by legislators and courts, the market principle functioned in an unfettered manner; indeed, during the period under investigation, it inspired neither a popular protest movement nor any noteworthy intellectual criticism.[39] Significantly, the English Enlightenment took market society as a given and did not allow itself to be put off by the latter's morally more questionable effects, such as corruption or the passion for gambling. Indeed, instead of subjecting it to a fundamental critique, the relevant authors celebrated 'doux commerce' as an evolutionary step forward. To this extent, one can say that the path dependency of the commercialization process was supported by the perception that it was omnipresent and unavoidable.

To underscore the argument, one could cite the tacit agreement of the English to exempt certain areas of everyday life and culture from the market mechanism. Towards the end of the eighteenth century, this tendency emerged in connection with the ideal of romantic love and the ideologically inflated understanding of the family as the counterworld to market society.[40] In some branches of culture, such as sport and the performing arts, this was joined in the nineteenth century by the 'amateur ideal', with committees and governing bodies dispensing with cash prizes in favour of symbolic awards.[41] It is also noteworthy that even in long term, the ideal of the gentleman – so important for the political culture of England – retained a certain anti-commercial flavour, despite the active participa-tion of gentlemen in market activity.[42] Behaviour in conformity with the market was all of that, insofar as – in the language of the much-cited study of Albert O. Hirschman – it showed a preference for the option of 'exit' rather than of 'voice'. 'Exit' – i.e., voting with one's feet – is the typical reaction of dissatisfied customers, consumers and other market participants. 'Voice', in contrast, is 'the act of complaining or protesting in order to obtain a change … which will lead to a recuperation of the quality of the product or service'.[43] This second option presupposes a concrete addressee, who, however, is barely discernible amidst the largely anonymous operations of the market system.

These reflections strengthen the overall impression that the commercialization process in England functioned smoothly and experienced no notable disruption from its environment. It cannot, however, be argued that the relations of exchange that it engendered did more than merely assure its own self-perpetuation. This study, at any rate, could not diagnose any marked development dynamic. In particular, commercialization as such made no recognizable contribution to the English economy's transition to industrial capitalism. How are we to explain these limits to its creative power? What explanations can be derived from the specific course taken by the commercialization process?

An initial explanation arises from its temporal length alone. In England the process began not with Napoleon – with whom, following a convention of Continental European research, a parallel study of Central Europe could begin – but rather with William the Conqueror. Therefore, by around 1800 the commercialization process had had some 750 years in which to create a fully fledged market society. The accompanying processes, as well – population growth, the development of transport, urbanization, the rise of wage labour and the formation of a consumer society – were protracted, and the distorting effects on the economy, society and culture were ironed out. Institutions of modern capitalism such as the stock exchange and the Bank of England only emerged at a more advanced stage in the process.

This pattern of development had ambivalent consequences. On the one hand, as we have seen in various contexts, the leisurely pace made it possible for the economic, social and cultural changes that it wrought to be experienced as gentle: indeed, as 'doux commerce'. On the other hand, the lengthy nature of the commercialization process meant that strategic impulses that it sent out into its environment took place early on, when the market network was first emerging and still patchy, so that initially only subsections of the economy and society were affected. The lack of dynamism and marked self-referentiality of English market society were therefore both concomitant and posterior effects of its early start.

A second explanation at once links and defamiliarizes the interpretations of the relationship between tradition and modernity in the commercialization process offered by Jürgen Habermas and Eric Hobsbawm, which were sketched out in the introduction. To recapitulate: while Habermas, taking up an argument of Karl Marx's, recognized the 'exhaustion' of traditions in the course of the process as an existential problem of market society, Hobsbawm pointed to the opportunities for 'inventing' new traditions that just such a society opened up.[44] If we apply these interpretations to the English case described in this study, and particularly to the specifically English type of feudalism, the following diagnosis emerges: in England, the commercialization process already eroded its feudal foundations in the Middle Ages, so that in the long run it could not find enough sources of friction from which to obtain new energies. The argument may also be applied to the feudal system of rule set up after the Conquest, which rapidly degenerated into so-called bastard feudalism,[45] as well as to both the comparatively permeable social structure, which stood in opposition to a rigid estate order and through the anchoring in trust law of rights of disposal; the principle of primogeniture, which discouraged the subdivision of property through inheritance into increasingly smaller parcels; and a high level of geographic mobility, which made it more difficult to exploit family connections, the developing market relations drove this development forward. The 'invention' of new traditions did not impede this process, as, under the circumstances described, the framing conditions were generally in line with the market, i.e., produced no friction.[46] In the course of the self-reproduction of the commercialization process, this conformity resulted in a certain tendency towards inefficiency: the engine ran smoothly, in fact too smoothly, on occasion idling, because there was not enough drag in its environment to enable it to convey the power to the transmission.

To illustrate this argument, it is helpful to generate a concrete idea of what such sources of drag would have looked like. Here, the European continent offers us a number of specific examples. The region's distinctive pattern of small states led to the accumulation of a multitude of customs barriers, currencies and legal ordinances that hindered the development of market exchange in a variety of ways.[47] Furthermore, many of these small-scale potentates engaged in power games with their subjects, with the result that cartel privileges were granted to specific guilds of merchants and producers, enabling them to intervene in and regulate local markets in their own interest. The plethora of legal restrictions on trade, which were issued on behalf of these privileged parties, banned certain sections of the population, such as feudal dependents, foreigners, Jews and women, from participating in markets either as vendors or consumers, thereby making it impossible for them to take part in even the most basic forms of everyday market exchange. The rulers also imposed feudal levies, issued sumptuary laws and placed restrictions on residence and citizenship, which were often anchored in local laws. Such measures were implemented by local authorities such as feudal lords, officials, military officers, heads of guilds, schoolmasters and husbands.[48]

Thus far, this study has always referred to such framing conditions when explaining the early modern weakening of feudal structures as an important factor in the formation and unproblematic establishment of English market society. This pioneering market society was able to develop freely, so the argument runs, because its unfolding was not hindered by feudal structures. If one turns from the institutional level to the level of social action and mentalities, however, it emerges that the absence of feudal structures could also, under certain circumstances, have problematic effects. This emerges when we link the analysis with a question that scholars have repeatedly posed: 'What is it that made catching up [with England] for most countries in Western Europe, like Germany and France, so relatively easy?'[49]

In the countries of Continental Europe, monarchs, princes and dukes tended to delegate responsibility for controlling social discipline, increasing efficiency and influencing social selection to local authorities, thereby obliging the latter to impose concrete standards of behaviour and performance, continually readjust them – usually upwards – and punish violations thereof.[50] The manner of conduct and thinking thereby formed corresponded to the high esteem in which Enlightenment thinkers held 'perfectibilité', and thus habitual comparison became a central element of Continental European political culture. Therefore, when princely rule and graduated power relations were gradually done away with in the context of the rise of national states – in Central Europe beginning in the early nineteenth century and later also in Eastern Europe – this did not only result in the unleashing of pent-up competitive energies. At the same time, the habit of comparison also transferred a pattern of behaviour to a new framework, one suited to lending a dynamic component to market exchange.

The reason why this pattern of behaviour, the *Leistungsprinzip,* has not yet been mentioned in this study is that it traditionally enjoyed little esteem in the British Isles and, perhaps for a lack of intermediate authority relations, never developed to the same degree as elsewhere in Europe. For in England, each individual was directly subject to the monarch, so that subordinate disciplining authorities, to the extent that they existed, had no extensive opportunities for intervention. This is an important explanatory factor for the opinion of contemporary foreign observers (and some present-day historians) that Englishmen and women had a laxer and lazier attitude towards work than did other European peoples.[51] The finding that the thinkers of the English (and Scottish) Enlightenment had little time for their Continental colleagues' enthusiastic embrace of 'perfectibilité' and other glorifications of individual 'striving', and that some of their views, such as the indulgent tolerance for gambling, even amounted to a mockery of personal effort points in the same direction.[52]

How very alien the category of the *Leistungsprinzip* must have been for English Enlightenment thinkers is evident not least in the fact that the English language has no translation for the German verb *leisten* that would express the feudal context in which it arose: '*jemandem einen Dienst leisten*' ('to render someone a service'), or '*sich etwas leisten*' ('to behave in a presumptuous manner'). The usual translations for *Leistung,* 'achievement' and 'performance', refer to the results of an action as well as the individual effort involved in and mastery of a task. However, they fail to grasp the aspect of fulfilling a duty, including to oneself. Nor do these translations effectively convey the meaning implied in the term *Leistungsvergleich* (comparison of proficiency), i.e., outdoing others in competitions in environments organized by authorities such as rulers, employers or governing bodies of sport.[53] In the context of the argument sketched here, one can regard this enduring lacuna in the vocabulary as evidence that the English language has not produced such a 'superstructure' retroactively – perhaps also because there has been no need to do so: in a developed market society, the actors are generally interested in results and remain 'blind' to the circumstances under which they were achieved.[54]

It is scarcely surprising that in nineteenth- and early-twentieth-century England, the *Leistungsprinzip* was not an essential benchmark in certain fields of activity in which on the Continent this would have been self-evident.[55] At any rate, several German-British comparisons on relevant topics undertaken by historians in recent years would seem to suggest this. Thus a study of labour relations in the textile sector at the time of the Industrial Revolution concludes that English textile manufacturers purchased the product from their workers, while their German competitors paid, as a matter of course, for the workers' labour power (*Arbeitskraft* in the Marxist sense); that is, for their personal performance.[56] Another comparative study of the principles and practices of middle-class education cites ample evidence on the German side that striving and the capacity for achievement were highly prized in middle-class families, whereas the English section of the study ignores this topic because the sources offer no material.[57] Historians of sport have also noticed that the *Leistungsprinzip* cannot truly be reconciled with the English notion of sportsmanship. While the English 'invented' the rules and organizational framework for popular sporting competitions in the eighteenth and nineteenth centuries, the striving for records and the concept of *Leistungssport* (literally, 'achievement sport') that was based upon it was initially foreign to them. When the English understanding of sport did expand to encompass these components at the turn of the twentieth century, this took place without their direct cooperation – and to the dismay of many sportsmen – in response to the cultural transfer of the English sporting model to Continental Europe and the United States.[58]

The now common English translation of *Leistungssport*, 'competitive sport', tellingly arose by translating the associated behavioural demand into terminology in keeping with the market. This is an interesting finding if, as I have done in this book, one regards England as a case study of an early and fully developed market society. The translation nicely illustrates the boundaries of such a market society: its great advantage, as has been explained, resides in its continual provision of new impulses for the economy, culture and politics, so that what is new and alien can be adopted quickly and flexibly and transformed into opportunities. The specific weakness of such an early and fully developed market society, in contrast, must be seen in the fact that, as it became universally established, it increasingly lost the ability to truly respond to the new. After all, it tends to subordinate stimuli of all kinds to its specific functional principle: competition. Following David Marquand, a keen analyst of contemporary British society, we can describe this mechanism as a trap that is continually snapping shut because it is impossible '[to apply] some other test to the whole pattern than that of the market rationality of the individual decisions which had created it'.[59]

For Marquand, this snapping mechanism is an important explanation for the tendencies towards stagnation and oft-cited decline of Britain, which he sees in a number of areas. We need not accept the absolute nature of his diagnosis of the present (political interventions remain an option, after all) to derive inspiration for future historical research on English society. Particularly in regard to studies comparing England to other early-developing market societies, testing this explanatory model might prove illuminating. Thus far, England has as a matter of course represented the superior model for success in such studies – for instance, in research on the causes of the stagnation in Dutch economic development in the seventeenth and eighteenth centuries or in the recent debate on the 'Great Divergence' between England and the economically advanced regions of the Chinese Qing Dynasty (standing in as proxies for Asia and Europe). Instead of constantly asking 'Why did England industrialize first?' – that is, seeking factors to explain the differences – scholars would systematically look for similarities between countries and regions with slow economic development based on the reflections outlined here.

This field of research could certainly also include the Western economies of the present day. Scholars engaged in such research would likely need to pay special attention to one possible cause of the differing dynamics: the market mechanism as such, which, as the English example shows, provided countless developmental impulses to the environment, which could however also encourage stagnation.

Notes

1. Cf. H. Grossman. 1948. 'W. Playfair, the Earliest Theorist of Capitalist Development', *Economic History Review* 18, 65–83. The word 'capital' was not yet even in common use in the seventeenth century. People spoke instead of a 'stock' or 'fund'; see Glaisyer, *Culture of Commerce*, 122–23, and H. Levy. 1932. 'Wirtschaftssprachliche Materialien aus der englischen Geschichte des 17. und 18. Jahrhunderts', *Neuphilologische Monatsschrift* 3, 112–13.
2. Private banks only became widespread in the second half of the eighteenth century, when their number rose from about a dozen to around 650. Figures from Y. Cassis. 2007. *Metropolen des Kapitals. Die Geschichte der internationalen Finanzzentren 1780–2005,* Hamburg: Murmann Verlag, 42. One reason for the delay was that until 1825 the monopoly of the Bank of England as a bank of issue was protected by law; cf. R. Tilly. 2003. *Geld und Kredit in der Wirtschaftsgeschichte,* Stuttgart: Steiner, 57.
3. See C. P. Kindleberger. 1976. 'The Historical Background: Adam Smith and the Industrial Revolution', in T. Wilson and A. S. Skinner (eds), *The Market and the State. Essays in Honour of Adam Smith,* Oxford: Clarendon Press, 1–25.
4. 'The dealing in time markets may be regarded as the "capitalist function"', writes Westerfield, *Middlemen,* 349; see also 369–70.
5. Cf. S. Pollard. 1965. *The Genesis of Modern Management. A Study of the Industrial Revolution in Great Britain,* London: Edward Arnold, 38–47; F. C. Lane. 1969. 'Meanings of Capitalism', *Journal of Economic History* 29, 6, 9; Anderson, 'Entrepreneurship', 176. On the secondary significance of control in the cotton industry, the leading sector of English industrialization,

M. B. Rose. 1996. 'Introduction: The Rise of the Cotton Industry in Lancashire to 1830', in M. B. Rose (ed.), *The Lancashire Cotton Industry,* Preston: Lancashire County Books, 11–12.

6. Anderson makes this argument in 'Entrepreneurship', 160–61.

7. Pollard explicitly makes this point in *Genesis*, 271–72.

8. This consideration delayed the transition to the factory system in the Lancashire cotton industry, for example. See S. Chapman. 1996. 'The Commercial Sector', in M. B. Rose (ed.), *The Lancashire Cotton Industry,* Preston: Lancashire County Books, 59–60.

9. The argumentation follows Price, 'What Did Merchants Do', 283–84. See also Anderson, 'Entrepreneurship', 169; A. M. Carlos and L. Neal. 2006. 'The Micro-Foundations of the Early London Capital Market: Bank of England Shareholders during and after the South Sea Bubble, 1720–25', *Economic History Review* 59, 531–32.

10. A. Hann undertakes a statistical analysis by city type in 2005. 'Industrialisation and the Service Economy', in J. Stobart and N. Raven (eds), *Towns, Regions, and Industries: Urban and Industrial Change in the Midlands, c. 1700–1840,* Manchester: Manchester University Press, 42–61.

11. J. S. Brewer, *British Merchant; or, Commerce preserved,* London 1721, quoted in Westerfield, 412–13.

12. See ibid., 124, 331–32, as well as Weatherill's case-study 'The Business of Middlemen'.

13. Cf. Westerfield, 414–15, 416–28.

14. For an impression of the complexity of the subject, see the handbook article by U. Berger and Engfer, 'Strukturwandel der gesellschaftlichen Arbeit'; see also U. Berger and C. Offe. 1984. 'Das Rationalisierungsdilemma der Angestelltenarbeit. Arbeitssoziologische Überlegungen zur Erklärung des Status von kaufmännischen Angestellten aus der Eigenschaft ihrer Arbeit als Dienstleistungsarbeit', in C. Offe, *"Arbeitsgesellschaft": Strukturprobleme und Zukunftsperspektiven,* Frankfurt, Main: Campus, 271–90. On personal services, see P. Gross and B. Badura. 1977. 'Sozialpolitik und soziale Dienste: Entwurf einer Theorie personenbezogener Dienstleistungen', in C. v. Ferber and F.-X. Kaufmann (eds), *Soziologie und Sozialpolitik,* Opladen: Westdeutscher Verlag, 362–63.

15. Smith, *Inquiry,* vol. 1, 330. In the sentence quoted, Smith is referring to the services provided by servants.

16. The figures should be used with caution because they are based on data gathered according to differing criteria. We have no better data, however. For England and Wales, J. de Vries und A. van der Woude. 1997. *The First Modern Economy. Success, Failure and Perseverance of the Dutch Economy, 1500–1815,* Cambridge: Cambridge University Press, 528–29, have adopted the estimates of P. Deane and W. A. Cole. 1967. *British Economic Growth 1688–1959: Trends and Structure,* 2nd ed., Cambridge: Cambridge University Press, 142. These are same basic data that younger British historians also use, for instance to calculate economic growth.

17. In the period under examination relevant statistics were not yet kept in many European countries, in part because the process of state formation was incomplete.

18. Figures from C. Buchheim. 1994. *Industrielle Revolution. Langfristige Wirtschaftsentwicklung in Großbritannien, Europa und Übersee,* Munich: Deutscher Taschenbuch Verlag, 33.

19. C. H. Lee, who compiled the figures in table 4.3 and published them in 1986. *The British Economy since 1700: a Macroeconomic Perspective,* Cambridge: Cambridge University Press, 10, weights the growth rates of each sector by multiplying them by the size of the respective sector. He takes his data from N. F. R. Crafts. 1983. 'British Economic Growth 1700–1831: A Review of the Evidence', *Economic History Review* 36, 177–99, 187, 189, 191; C. K. Harley. 1982. 'British Industrialisation before 1841: Evidence of Slower Growth during the Industrial Revolution', *Journal of Economic History* 42, 284–86; C. H. Feinstein. 1978. 'Capital Formation in Great Britain', in P. Mathias and M. M. Postan (eds), *Cambridge Economic History of Europe,* vols 7(1), Cambridge: Cambridge University Press, 84. For the weakness of Craft's data

in respect of services, see M. Berg and P. Hudson in 'Rehabilitating the Industrial Revolution', *Economic History Review* 45, 29.

20. See R. Pearson and D. Richardson. 2001. 'Business Networking in the Industrial Revolution', *Economic History Review* 44, 657–79; R. Pearson. 2002. 'Shareholder Democracies? English Stock Companies and the Politics of Corporate Governance during the Industrial Revolution', *English Historical Review* 117, 840–66; R. Harris, *Industrializing English Law,* 168–200. On the Bubble Act, whose effects were often exaggerated in the older literature, see ibid., 60–81. The continuation of these developments in the Victorian era is the topic of P. Johnson's book *Making the Market.*

21. To use terminology that has fallen out of fashion in England the late eighteenth century marked the transition to organized capitalism – a characteristic overlooked by the traditional perspective that remains fixated on manufacturing; see, for example, H. Medick. 1974. 'Anfänge und Voraussetzungen des Organisierten Kapitalismus in Großbritannien', in H. A. Winkler (ed.), *Organisierter Kapitalismus. Voraussetzungen und Anfänge,* Göttingen: Vandenhoeck and Ruprecht, 58–83.

22. See C. H. Lee. 1984. 'The Service Sector, Regional Specialisation and Economic Growth in the Victorian Economy', *Journal of Historical Geography* 10, 139–55; idem. 1994. 'The Service Industries', in R. Floud and D. N. McCloskey (eds), *The Economic History of Britain since 1700, vol. 2: 1860–1939,* 2nd ed., Cambridge: Cambridge University Press, 117–44; N. Gemmell, 1990. 'The Contribution of Services to British Economic Growth, 1856–1913', *Explorations in Economic History* 27, 299–32; Thomas, 'The Service Sector'.

23. According to Chapman, in the years after 1815 investments in warehouses were six times that of investments in factories. 'The Commercial Sector', 75. See also R. Lloyd-Jones and M. J. Lewis. 1988. *Manchester and the Age of the Factory: the Business Structure of Cottonopolis in the Industrial Revolution,* London: Croom Helm, 30–32, 36, 46, as well as the data provided by King and Timmins, *Making Sense of the Industrial Revolution,* 49–59, and also Rose's sobering assessment of the degree of industrialization in Lancashire before 1830–50: 'Lancashire certainly became the single most important centre of the British cotton industry by 1830. However, throughout the nineteenth century, the majority of Lancashire's population was employed in other sectors, with vast tracts of the county virtually untouched by cotton. During the industrial revolution the quest for water power sent industrialists to the very margins of the country. However the lasting and cumulative impact of the cotton industry was increasingly restricted, as the nineteenth century progressed, to its south-easternmost corner. Even amongst the cotton towns there were, by 1830, considerable variations in their employment profile. Before the middle of the nineteenth century, factories did not dominate Lancashire industry'. 'Introduction', 27.

24. This may help to explain the failure of leading economic historians in the later twentieth century to pay serious attention to the phenomenon of services in the industrialization process. The data provided here have been known for decades, but they have been banished to the footnotes of surveys of economic history or ignored altogether. As one example among many, see P. Mathias. 1988. 'The Industrial Revolution – Concept and Reality', in A. M. Birke and L. Kettenacker (eds), *Wettlauf in die Moderne. England und Deutschland seit der industriellen Revolution/The Race for Modernisation. Britain and Germany since the Industrial Revolution,* Munich: Saur, 25–26. This *déformation professionnelle* of economic historians seems all the more bewildering nowadays given the fact that the crème de la crème of the discipline were already discussing the subject in the early 1970s; see R. M. Hartwell. 1972. 'The Tertiary Sector in the English Economy during the Industrial Revolution', in P. Léon et al. (eds), *L'industrialisation en Europe au XIXe siècle. Carthographie et Typologie,* Colloques internationaux du Centre National de la Recherche Scientifique, Nr. 540, Paris: C.N.R.S., 218–19, 226. The finding that the subsequent generation of scholars continued to show little interest in the topic

confirms Cannadine's suspicion that the study of industrialization, a historical subdiscipline whose relevance was waning, tried to retain its focus; see D. Cannadine. 2008. 'Economy: The Growth and Fluctuations of the Industrial Revolution', in D. Cannadine, *Making History Now and Then, Discoveries, Controversies and Explorations,* Houndmills: Macmillan, 110–11. Meanwhile, Joel Mokyr has rediscovered services; cf. 2002. *The Gifts of Athena. Historical Origins of the Knowledge Economy,* Princeton, NJ: Princeton University Press, and 2009. *The Enlightened Economy. Britain and the Industrial Revolution,* London: Penguin, 198–220.

25. These and other functions have been summarized under the heading of *Gewährleistungsarbeit,* work that guarantees the functioning of the whole; see J. Berger and C. Offe. 1984. 'Die Entwicklungsdynamik des Dienstleistungssektors', in C. Offe (ed.), *"Arbeitsgesellschaft". Strukturprobleme und Zukunftsperspektiven,* Frankfurt, Main: Campus, 229–70.

26. See S. Broadberry. 2006. *Market Services and the Productivity Race, 1850–2000. British Performance in International Perspective,* Cambridge: Cambridge University Press; idem. 1998. 'How Did the United States and Germany Overtake Britain? A Sectoral Analysis on Comparative Productivity Levels, 1870–1990', *Journal of Economic History* 58, 375–407. See also M. Thomas. 2003. 'The Service Sector', in *The Cambridge Economic History of Modern Britain, vol. 2: Economic Maturity 1860–1939,* ed. R. Floud and P. Johnson, Cambridge: Cambridge University Press, 132.

27. J. Fourastié. 1989 (1949). *Le grand espoir du XXe siècle,* Paris: Gallimard. H. Kaelble already discussed the problem in a 1989 essay, unfortunately only for the period after 1850–60; see his 1989. 'Was Prometheus Most Unbound in Europe? The Labour Force in Europe During the Late XIXth and XXth Centuries', *Journal of European Economic History* 18, 65–104.

28. Gregory Clark impressively reformulated this finding in 2007. *A Farewell to Alms. A Brief Economic History of the World,* Princeton, NJ: Princeton University Press, 240–41.

29. Interestingly, Peer Vries reaches a similar conclusion in his comparison between Britain and China; see *Via Peking Back to Manchester,* 59.

30. See above 49–50 as well as J. Mokyr. 2002. *The Gifts of Athena. Historical Origins of the Knowledge Economy,* Princeton, NJ: Princeton University Press; idem, 'The Intellectual Origins'; A. E. Musson. 1975. 'Continental Influences on the Industrial Revolution in Britain', in B. E. Radcliffe (ed.), *Great Britain and her World 1750–1914. Essays in Honour of W. O. Henderson,* Manchester: Manchester University Press, 71–85; C. McLeod. 2004. 'The European Origins of British Technological Predominance', in Prados de la Escosura, *Exceptionalism and Industrialisation,* 111–27; Allen, *The British Industrial Revolution,* 272–75.

31. See above 54–55; see also R. A. Allen. 2007. *The Industrial Revolution in Miniature: The Spinning Jenny in Britain, France, and India.* Discussion Paper Nr. 375, Oxford: University of Oxford, Department of Economics.

32. See above 59–62 as well as P. O'Brien. 1997. 'The Britishness of the First Industrial Revolution and the British Contribution to the Industrialization of "Follower Countries" on the Mainland, 1756–1914', *Diplomacy and Statecraft* 8, 55; on the cotton industry in particular, see idem et al. 1991. 'Political Components of the Industrial Revolution: Parliament and the English Cotton Textile Industry, 1660–1774', *Economic History Review* 44, 395–423.

33. D. W. Galenson's interpretation in 1994. 'The Rise of Free Labor: Economic Change and the Enforcement of Service Contracts in England, 1351–1875', in J. A. James and M. Thomas (eds), *Capitalism in Context. Essays in Economic Development and Cultural Change in Honor of R.M. Hartwell,* Chicago: The University of Chicago Press, 114–37, that the exercise of direct and indirect force legitimized by these laws delayed the emergence of free wage labour in England seems implausible from the perspective of market history. What Galenson describes is the institutionalization and intensification of the asymmetrical power relations between the suppliers and demanders inherent in labour markets. In this context, it has to be mentioned that certain provisions of the Master and Servant Laws, which were integrated into criminal

and contract law (and which are not analyzed in detail in the present study), made it difficult for workers to dissolve labour contracts. See Steinfeld, *Invention of Free Labor*. The examples of this increased, tellingly, from the second quarter of the nineteenth century, when industrialization gave a new impetus to the emergence of wage labour and employers developed relevant strategies with the support of legislation. See D. Hay. 2004. 'England, 1562–1875: The Law and its Uses', in D. Hay and Paul Craven (eds), *Masters, Servants, and Magistrates in Britain and the Empire, 1562–1955*, Chapel Hill, NC: University of North Carolina Press, 82–110.

34. See above 61–62. For a detailed account of this pull mechanism which is characteristic of cultural transfers, see C. Eisenberg. 2003. 'Kulturtransfer als historischer Prozess. Ein Beitrag zur Komparatistik', in H. Kaelble and J. Schriewer (eds), *Vergleich und Transfer. Komparatistik in den Sozial-, Geschichts- und Kulturwissenschaften*, Frankfurt, Main: Campus, 399–417.

35. See M. S. Granovetter. 1973. 'The Strength of Weak Ties', *American Journal of Sociology* 78, 1360–1380. See also H. Lübbe. 1996. 'Netzverdichtung. Zur Philosophie industriegesellschaftlicher Entwicklungen', *Zeitschrift für philosophische Forschung* 50, 133–50; B. Holzer. 2006. *Netzwerke*, Bielefeld: Transcript, 103.

36. These are the most important criteria for path-dependent processes; see P. A. David. 1985. 'Clio and the Economics of QWERTY', *American Economic Review* 75, 332–37; W. B. Arthur et al. 1987. 'Path-Dependent Processes and the Emergence of Macro-Structure', *European Journal of Operations Research* 30, 294–303; J. A. Goldstone. 1998. 'Initial Conditions, General Laws, Path Dependence and Explanation in Historical Sociology', *American Journal of Sociology* 104, 829–45; J. Mahoney. 2000. 'Path Dependence in Historical Sociology', *Theory and Society* 29, 507–48. See also the recent survey by J. Beyer. 2006. *Pfadabhängigkeit. Über institutionelle Kontinuität, anfällige Stabilität und fundamentalen Wandel*, Frankfurt, Main: Campus.

37. N. Luhmann. 1978. 'Geschichte als Prozess und die Theorie sozio-kultureller Evolution', in Faber and Meier, *Historische Prozesse*, 422. It is worth mentioning here that William vanquished the Anglo-Saxon Harold not least because the latter's troops had been weakened by victories in battles against the Norwegian King Harald. The two assaults were apparently not coordinated. See S. Körner. 1964. *The Battle of Hastings, England, and Europe 1035–1066*, Lund: Skanska Centraltryckeriet, 282–84.

38. Douglass C. North makes a similar argument in 1990. *Institutions, Institutional Change and Economic Performance*, Cambridge: Cambridge University Press, 113, 138–39. See also Simmel's self-advertisement for his 1989 (1900). *Philosophie des Geldes* (Georg-Simmel-Gesamtausgabe, vol. 6, ed. D. P. Frisby and K. C. Köhnke), Frankfurt, Main: Suhrkamp, 720: '[T]he liberty of the English people vis-à-vis its monarchs rests in part on the fact that it struggled with them over and secured certain rights once and for all by payments of capital. Not despite, but precisely because such negotiations concerning the people's liberties have a rather brutal and mechanical character, they represent a pure coming to terms so diametrically opposed to the king's sentiment that 'no piece of paper shall come between him and his people' – but for that very reason also a radical removal of all of the imponderables of sentimental relations, which in a less monetary acquisition of liberties often provide a means of taking them back or rendering them illusory.'

39. The absence of criticism is difficult to prove. An important piece of ex negativo evidence can be found in the fact that even studies by those authors who describe the transformation of the labour contract in the Master and Servant Acts document no misgivings about labour contracts as such; see Steinfeld, *Invention of Free Labor*, and Steinmetz, *Begegnungen vor Gericht*. Steinmetz also emphasizes the long-term tendency of English labour law to dispense with any regulation of labour contracts. This tendency underlines not just the desire of market actors to be able to negotiate their own contracts, but also the essential acceptance of the market principle.

40. See L. Davidoff and C. Hall. 1987. *Family Fortunes. Men and Women of the English Middle Class, 1780–1850,* Chicago: The University of Chicago Press.

41. See R. Holt. 1989. *Sport and the British. A Modern History,* Oxford: Oxford University Press, 74-134; D. Brailsford. 1991. *Sport, Time, and Society. The British at Play,* London: Routledge, 65; C. Eisenberg. 2011. 'Playing the Market Game: Cash Prizes, Symbolic Awards and the Professional Ideal in British Amateur Sport', *Sport in History* 31, 197–217.

42. See Cain and Hopkins, *British Imperialism,* vol. 1; W. D. Rubinstein. 1991. '"Gentlemanly capitalism" and British Industry, 1820–1914', *Past and Present* 132, 150–70. See also H. Perkin. 1989. *The Rise of Professional Society. England since 1880,* London: Routledge, 84 and passim.

43. A. O. Hirschman. 1970. *Exit, Voice, and Loyalty. Responses to Decline in Firms, Organizations, and States,* Cambridge, MA: Harvard University Press, 43, see also 22–25.

44. See above 8.

45. See above 25.

46. Hirschman has made a similar argument with regard to American developments, which are untouched by feudal traditions and thus in some respects 'sterile'. According to him, America lacks the traditions of 'feudal society with its complex institutional structure and built-in conflicts, as the indispensable seedbed of both Western democracy and capitalist development'. 'Rival Interpretations of Market Society', 1480. For empirical confirmation of this observation see J. L. van Zanden. 2009. *The Long Road to the Industrial Revolution. The European Economy in a Global Perspective, 1000–1800,* Leiden: Brill, 57–58, and Osterhammel, *Verwandlung der Welt,* 955.

47. Oliver Volckart has researched these factors systematically; see his 2001 article 'Zur Transformation der mitteleuropäischen Wirtschaftsordnung, 1000–1800', *Vierteljahrschrift für Sozial- und Wirtschaftsgeschich*te 68, 277–310, and his 2002 monograph *Wettbewerb und Wettbewerbsbeschränkung im vormodernen Deutschland 1000-1800,* Tübingen: Mohr.

48. The best overview for English readers is S. Ogilvie. 2011. *Institutions and European Trade. Merchant Guilds, 1000–1800,* Cambridge: Cambridge University Press. See also the same author's works *State Corporatism and Proto-Industry;* 2002. *A Bitter Living. Women, Markets, and Social Capital in Early-Modern Germany,* Oxford: Oxford University Press; 2010. 'Consumption, Social Capital, and the "Industrious Revolution" in Early Modern Germany', *Journal of Economic History* 70(2), 287–325.

49. P. Vries. 2010. 'Review article of Jürgen Osterhammel, Die Verwandlung der Welt', *Comparativ* 20, 37.

50. See A. J. La Vopa. 1988. *Grace, Talent, and Merit: Poor Students, Clerical Careers, and Professional Ideology in Eighteenth-Century Germany,* Cambridge: Cambridge University Press; J. M. Smith. 1996. *The Culture of Merit: Nobility, Royal Service, and the Making of the Absolute Monarchy in France, 1600–1789,* Ann Arbor, MI: University of Michigan Press; H.-E. Mueller. 1984. *Bureaucracy, Education and Monopoly. Civil Service Reforms in Prussia and England,* Berkeley: University of California Press, 224–34.

51. Paul Langford has assembled a large number of such quotations in 2000. *Englishness Identified. Manners and Characters 1650–1850,* Oxford: Oxford University Press, 29–36. See also Ogilvie's sceptical reflections regarding the transferability of Jan de Vries's notion of the 'Industrious Revolution' to Continental Europe, in her article 'Consumption', 321. According to de Vries, the new consumer habits that arose in eighteenth-century England were combined with a new industrious behaviour, which fostered the Industrial Revolution. On the limited means of intervention of subordinate disciplining authorities in England, see also above 64–65 (on the autonomy of medieval and early-modern popular culture in England).

52. See Oz-Salzberger, *Translating the Enlightenment,* 123–24, 159–60, 161, 165–66, 250, 256. See also above 69 on the linguistic history of the mediaeval word 'plegian', which developed into 'play' in English and *Pflicht* (duty) in German.

53. See G. Gebauer. 1972. '"Leistung" als Aktion und Präsentation', *Sportwissenschaft* 2, 183; K. M. Bolte. 1979. *Leistung und Leistungsprinzip. Zur Konzeption, Wirklichkeit und Möglichkeit eines gesellschaftlichen Gestaltungsprinzips. Ein Beitrag zur Sozialkunde der Bundesrepublik Deutschland*, Opladen: Leske and Budrich, 20–21, 24–27; F. Schlie. 1988. 'Die Vielfalt der Leistungsbegriffe', in K.-O. Hondrich et al., *Krise der Leistungsgesellschaft? Empirische Analysen zum Engagement in Arbeit, Familie und Politik*, Opladen: Westdeutscher Verlag, 50–67.

54. That the two principles have come into conflict in Germany's present-day political culture is evident from the publications that emerged from the recently completed sociological research project under the direction of Sighard Neckel, '"Leistung" in der Marktgesellschaft?' (http://www.ifs.uni-frankfurt.de/forschung/leistung/index.htm, last accessed 24 January 2013). See also S. Neckel, 2002. 'Ehrgeiz, Reputation und Bewährung. Zur Theoriegeschichte einer Soziologie des Erfolges', in G. Burkart and J. Wolf (eds), *Lebenszeiten. Erkundungen zur Soziologie der Generationen*, Opladen: Leske and Budrich, 103–17; idem and K. Dröge. 2002. 'Die Verdienste und ihr Preis: Leistung in der Marktgesellschaft', in A. Honneth (ed.), *Befreiung aus der Mündigkeit. Paradoxien des gegenwärtigen Kapitalismus*, Frankfurt, Main: Campus, esp. 100–01.

55. Ralf Dahrendorf also formulates this impression, noting that England is a country where the individual is identified in terms of belonging rather than achievement. See his 1979. *Lebenschancen. Anläufe zur sozialen und politischen Theorie*, Frankfurt, Main: Suhrkamp, 65.

56. Cf. R. G. Biernacki. 1995. *The Fabrication of Labor: Germany and Britain, 1640–1914*, Berkeley: University of California Press. esp. 56–73.

57. Cf. G. F. Budde. 1994. *Auf dem Weg ins Bürgerleben. Kindheit und Erziehung in deutschen und englischen Bürgerfamilien 1840–1914*, Göttingen: Vandenhoeck and Ruprecht. This negative finding is confirmed by another study on the history of paedagogy in England; see C. Quesel. 2005. *Pädagogik und politische Kultur in England 1870–1945*, Berne: Peter Lang. I would like to thank Gunilla Budde and Carsten Quesel for their willingness to discuss their research with me.

58. Cf. C. Eisenberg. 2008. '"Representing the Very Best': Anglo-German Competition and Transfers in Sport', in D. Geppert und R. Gerwarth (eds), *Wilhelmine Germany and Edwardian Britain Essays on Cultural Contacts and Transfers*, Oxford: Oxford University Press, 400–10; eadem. 'Playing the Market Game', 209.

59. D. Marquand. 1988. *The Unprincipled Society. New Demands and Old Politics*, London: Fontana Press, 123. See also the attempts at a sociological explanation in E. Buß. 1973. *Der Wettbewerb. Eine rechtssoziologische Untersuchung*, Tübingen: Mohr, 160–61.

WORKS CITED

Abelshauser, W. 2006. 'Von der Industriellen Revolution zur Neuen Wirtschaft. Der Paradig-
menwechsel im wirtschaftlichen Weltbild der Gegenwart', in J. Osterhammel et al. (eds),
Wege der Gesellschaftsgeschichte, Göttingen: Vandenhoeck and Ruprecht, 201–18.
Acheson, R. J. 1990. *Radical Puritans in England 1550–1660,* London: Longman.
Agnew, J.-C. 1988. *Worlds Apart: The Market and the Theater in Anglo-American Thought,
1550–1750,* Cambridge: Cambridge University Press.
Albert, W. 1972. *The Turnpike Road System in England 1663–1840,* Cambridge: Cambridge
University Press.
Allen, M. 2004. 'The English Currency and the Commercialisation before the Black Death',
in D. Wood (ed.), *Medieval Money Matters,* Oxford: Oxbow Books, 31–45.
Allen, R. C. 2001. 'The Great Divergence in European Wages and Prices from the Middle
Ages to the First World War', *Explorations in Economic History* 38, 411–47.
———. 2007. The Industrial Revolution in Miniature: The Spinning Jenny in Britain,
France, and India. Discussion Paper Nr. 375, Oxford: University of Oxford, Department
of Economics.
———. 2009. *The British Industrial Revolution in Global Perspective*, Cambridge: Cambridge
University Press.
Alsop, D. 1996. '"Strains of New Beauty": Handel and the Pleasures of Italian Opera,
1711–28', in R. Porter and M. M. Roberts (eds), *Pleasure in the Eighteenth Century,* New
York: New York University Press, 133–63.
Aminzade, R. 1992. 'Historical Sociology and Time', *Sociological Method and Research* 20,
456–80.
Anderson, B. L. 1970. 'Money and the Structure of Credit in the Eighteenth Century', *Business History* 12(2), 85–101.
———. 1975. 'Law, Finance and Economic Growth in England: Some Long-Term Influences', in B. M. Ratcliffe (ed.), *Great Britain and Her World 1750–1914. Essays in Honour
of W. O. Henderson,* Manchester: Manchester University Press, 99–124.
———. 1986. 'Entrepreneurship, Market Process and the Industrial Revolution in England',
in B. L Anderson and A. J. H. Latham (eds), *The Market in History. Papers Presented at
a Symposium Held 9–13 September 1984 at St George's House, Windsor Castle, under the
Auspices of the Liberty Fund,* London: Croom Helm, 155–200.
———, and A. J. H. Latham (eds). 1986. *The Market in History. Papers Presented at a
Symposium Held 9–13 September 1984 at St George's House, Windsor Castle, under the
Auspices of the Liberty Fund,* London: Croom Helm.
Appleby, J. O. 1978. *Economic Thought and Ideology in Seventeenth Century England,*
Princeton, N.J.: Princeton University Press.
Arthur, W. B. et al. 1987. 'Path Dependent Processes and the Emergence of Macro-
Structure', *European Journal of Operations Research* 30, 294–303.

Ashworth, W. J. 2003. *Customs and Excise. Trade, Production, and Consumption in England, 1640–1845,* Oxford: Oxford University Press.

Aston, T. H., and C. H. E. Philpin (eds). 1985. *The Brenner Debate: Agrarian Class Structure and Economic Development in Pre-Industrial Europe,* Cambridge: Cambridge University Press.

d'Avray, D. 2008. 'Roman Law and Common Law: Medieval England and Germany in Weber's Wirtschaft und Gesellschaft', in M.-L. Heckmann and J. Röhrkasten (eds), *Von Nowgorod bis London. Studien zu Handel, Wirtschaft und Gesellschaft im mittelalterlichen Europa. Festschrift für Stuart Jenks zum 60.* Geburtstag, Göttingen: Vandenhoeck and Ruprecht, 343–57.

Bailey, M. 1998. 'Historiographical Essay: the Commercialisation of the English Economy, 1086–1500', *Journal of Medieval History* 24, 297–311.

Baker, J. H. 1979. 'The Law Merchant and the Common Law before 1700', *Cambridge Law Journal* 38, 295–322.

———. 2002. *An Introduction to English Legal History,* 2nd ed., London: Butterworths.

Baker, J. J. 2005. *Securing the Commonwealth. Debt, Speculation, and Writing in the Making of Early America,* Baltimore: The Johns Hopkins University Press.

Bauman, Z. 1994. 'Desert Spectacular', in K. Tester (ed.), *The Flâneur,* London: Routledge, 138–57.

Beckert, J. 2002. 'Vertrauen und die performative Konstruktion von Märkten', *Zeitschrift für Soziologie* 31, 27–43.

Beckett, J. V. 1994. 'The Peasant in England. A Case of Terminological Confusion', *Agricultural History Review* 32, 113–23.

Ben-Amos, I. K. 2008. *The Culture of Giving. Informal Support and Gift-Exchange in Early Modern England,* Cambridge: Cambridge University Press.

Bennett, M. 2003. 'The Normans in the Mediterranean', in C. Harper-Bill and E. van Houts (eds), *A Companion to the Anglo-Norman World,* Woodbridge: The Boydell Press, 99–102.

Benson, J., and L. Ugolini (eds). 2002. *A Nation of Shopkeepers: Retailing in Britain, 1550–2000,* London: I. B. Tauris.

Berg, M. 2005. *Luxury and Pleasure in Eighteenth-Century Britain,* Oxford: Oxford University Press.

———. 2007. 'Cargoes: The Trade in Luxuries from Asia to Europe', in D. Cannadine (ed.), *Empire, the Sea and Global History. Britain's Maritime World, c. 1763–c.1840,* Houndmills: Palgrave Macmillan, 60–71.

———, and P. Hudson. 1992. 'Rehabilitating the Industrial Revolution', *Economic History Review* 45, 24–50.

Berger, J., and C. Offe. 1984. 'Die Entwicklungsdynamik des Dienstleistungssektors', in C. Offe, *"Arbeitsgesellschaft". Strukturprobleme und Zukunftsperspektiven,* Frankfurt, Main: Campus, 229–70.

Berger, R. M. 1980. 'The Development of Retail Trade in Provincial England, c. 1550–1700', *Journal of Economic History* 60, 123–28.

Berger, U., and C. Offe. 1984. 'Das Rationalisierungsdilemma der Angestelltenarbeit. Arbeitssoziologische Überlegungen zur Erklärung des Status von kaufmännischen Angestellten aus der Eigenschaft ihrer Arbeit als Dienstleistungsarbeit', in C. Offe, *"Arbeitsgesellschaft": Strukturprobleme und Zukunftsperspektiven,* Frankfurt, Main: Campus, 271–90.

———, and U. Engfer. 1982. 'Strukturwandel der gesellschaftlichen Arbeit', in W. Littek et al. (eds), *Einführung in die Arbeits- und Industriesoziologie,* Frankfurt, Main: Campus, 302–24.

Berghahn, V., and S. Vitols (eds). 2006. *'Gibt es einen deutschen Kapitalismus?' Tradition und globale Perspektiven der sozialen Marktwirtschaft,* Frankfurt, Main: Campus.

Berghoff, H., and J. Vogel. 2004. 'Wirtschaftsgeschichte als Kulturgeschichte. Ansätze zur Bergung transdisziplinärer Synergiepotentiale', in H. Berghoff and J. Vogel (eds), *Wirtschaftsgeschichte als Kulturgeschichte. Dimensionen eines Perspektivenwechsels,* Frankfurt, Main: Campus, 9–41.

Bermingham, A., and J. Brewer (eds). 1995. *The Consumption of Culture 1600–1800,* London: Routledge.

Bevir, M., and F. Trentmann (eds). 2004. *Markets in Historical Contexts: Ideas and Politics in the Modern World,* Cambridge: Cambridge University Press.

Beyer, J. 2006. *Pfadabhängigkeit. Über institutionelle Kontinuität, anfällige Stabilität und fundamentalen Wandel,* Frankfurt, Main: Campus.

Biernacki, R. G. 1995. *The Fabrication of Labor: Germany and Britain, 1640–1914,* Berkeley: University of California Press.

———. 2001. 'Labor as an Imagined Commodity', *Politics and Society* 29, 173–206.

———. 2004. *New Evidence on Schemas of Action in the Protestant Ethic. Havens Centre for the Study of Social Structure and Social Change,* University of Wisconsin, Madison (http://www. havenscenter.org/VSP/readings2sort/rtf/biernacki2.rtf, last accessed 3 October 2006).

Biggart, N. W. (ed.). 2002. *Readings in Economic Sociology,* Oxford: Blackwell.

Blake, R. (ed.). 1982. *The English World. History, Character and People,* London: Thames and Hudson.

Blanning, T. C. W. 2002. *The Culture of Power and the Power of Culture. Old Regime Europe 1660–1789,* Oxford: Oxford University Press.

Blaug, M. 1997. *Economic Theory in Retrospect,* 5th ed., Cambridge: Cambridge University Press.

Bloch, M. 1960. *Seigneurie français et manoir anglais,* Paris: Armand Colin.

———. 1964. *Feudal Society,* trans. by L. A. Manyon, vol. 2, Chicago: University of Chicago Press.

Block, F. 1994. 'The Roles of the State in the Economy', in N. Smelser and R. Swedberg (eds), *The Handbook of Economic Sociology,* Princeton, NJ: Princeton University Press, 691–710.

Blondé, B., P. Stabel, J. Stobart, and I. van Damme (eds). 2006. *Buyers and Sellers. Retail Circuits in Medieval and Early Modern Europe,* Turnhout: Brepols Publishers.

Bolte, K. M. 1979. *Leistung und Leistungsprinzip. Zur Konzeption, Wirklichkeit und Möglichkeit eines gesellschaftlichen Gestaltungsprinzips. Ein Beitrag zur Sozialkunde der Bundesrepublik Deutschland,* Opladen: Leske and Budrich.

Borsay, P. 1989. *The English Urban Renaissance: Culture and Society in the Provincial Town, 1660–1770,* Oxford: Oxford University Press.

———. 2002. 'Urban Life and Culture', in H. T. Dickinson (ed.), *A Companion to Eighteenth-Century Britain,* Oxford: Blackwell, 196–208.

———. 2003. 'The Rise, Fall and Rise of Polite Urban Space in England 1700–2000', in A. Fahrmeir and E. Rembold (eds), *Representations of British Cities. The Transformation of Urban Space 1700–2000,* Berlin: Philo, 30–48.

Bowen, H. V. 1995. 'The Bank of England during the Long Eighteenth Century, 1694–1820', in R. Roberts and D. Kynaston (eds), *The Bank of England. Money, Power and Influence 1694–1994,* Oxford: Clarendon Press, 1–18.

Brailsford, D. 1991. *Sport, Time, and Society. The British at Play*, London: Routledge.

———. 1994. 'England 1775–1815: A Time for Play', in I. Blanchard (ed.), *Labour and Leisure in Historical Perspective, Thirteenth to Twentieth Centuries. Papers Presented at Session B-3a of the Eleventh International Economic History Congress, Milan, 12th–17th September 1994*, Stuttgart: Steiner, 101–09.

Breen, T. H. 1988. '"Baubles of Britain": The American and Consumer Revolutions of the Eighteenth Century', *Past and Present* 119, 73–104.

Breward, C. 2003. 'Masculine Pleasures: Metropolitan Identities and the Commercial Sites of Dandyism', 1790–1840, *London Journal* 28, 60–72.

Brewer, J. 1982. 'Commercialization and Politics', in N. McKendrick et al., The Birth of a Consumer Society. The Commercialization of Eighteenth-century England, London: Hutchinson, 197–262.

———. 1990. *The Sinews of Power. War, Money and the English State 1688–1783*, Cambridge, MA: Harvard University Press.

———. 1994. 'The Eighteenth-Century British State. Contexts and Issues', in L. Stone (ed.), *An Imperial State at War. Britain from 1689–1815*, London: Routledge, 52–71.

———. 1995. '"The Most Polite Age and the Most Vicious". Attitudes towards Culture as a Commodity, 1660–1800', in A. Bermingham and J. Brewer (eds), *The Consumption of Culture 1600–1800*, London: Routledge, 341–61.

———. 1997. *The Pleasures of the Imagination. English Culture in the Eighteenth Century*, New York: Farrar Straus Giroux.

———, and E. Hellmuth (eds). 1999. *Rethinking Leviathan: The Eighteenth-Century State in Britain and Germany*, Oxford: Oxford University Press.

Briefs, G. 1952. *Zwischen Kapitalismus und Syndikalismus. Die Gewerkschaften am Scheidewege*, Bern: Francke.

Britnell, R. H. 1981. 'The Proliferation of Markets in England, 1200–1349', *Economic History Review* 34, 209–21.

———. 1991. 'The Towns of England and Northern Italy in the Early Fourteenth Century', *Economic History Review* 44, 21–35.

———. 1993. 'Commerce and Capitalism in Late Medieval England: Problems of Description and Theory', *Journal of Historical Sociology* 6, 359–76.

———. 1996. *The Commercialisation of English Society 1000–1500*, 2nd ed., Manchester: Manchester University Press.

———. 2003. 'England: Towns, Trade and Industry', in S. H. Rigby (ed.), *A Companion to Britain in the Later Middle Ages*, Oxford: Oxford University Press, 47–64.

———. 2006. 'Town Life', in R. Horrox and W. M. Ormrod (eds), *A Social History of England 1200–1500*, Cambridge: Cambridge University Press, 134–78.

———. 2006. 'Markets, Shops, Inns, Taverns and Private Houses in Medieval English Trade', in B. Blondé, P. Stabel, J. Stobart, and I. van Damme (eds), *Buyers and Sellers. Retail Circuits in Medieval and Early Modern Europe*, Turnhout: Brepols Publishers, 109–24.

———. 2011. 'Commerce and Markets', in J. Crick and E. van Houts (eds), *A Social History of England, 900–1200*, Cambridge: Cambridge University Press, 179–87.

Broadberry, S. 1998. 'How Did the United States and Germany Overtake Britain? A Sectoral Analysis on Comparative Productivity Levels, 1870–1990', *Journal of Economic History* 58, 375–407.

———. 2006. *Market Services and the Productivity Race, 1850–2000. British Performance in International Perspective*, Cambridge: Cambridge University Press.

————, and B. Gupta. 2006. 'The Early Modern Great Divergence: Wages, Prices and Economic Development in Europe and Asia', *Economic History Review* 59, 2–31.

Brodnitz, G. 1914. 'Die Stadtwirtschaft in England', *Jahrbücher für Nationalökonomie und Statistik* 102, 1–39.

Brodt, B. 2003. 'Authority – Loyalty – Autonomy, or the Archaeology of Power. English Provincial Capitals Reconsidered', in A. Fahrmeir and E. Rembold (eds), *Representations of British Cities. The Transformation of Urban Space 1700–2000*, Berlin: Philo, 18–29.

Buchheim, C. 1994. *Industrielle Revolution. Langfristige Wirtschaftsentwicklung in Großbritannien, Europa und Übersee*, Munich: Deutscher Taschenbuch Verlag.

Buck, P. 1977. 'Seventeenth-Century Political Arithmetic: Civil Strife and Vital Statistics', *Isis* 68, 67–83.

————. 1982. 'People Who Counted: Political Arithmetic in the Eighteenth Century', *Isis* 73, 28–45.

Budde, G. F. 1994. *Auf dem Weg ins Bürgerleben. Kindheit und Erziehung in deutschen und englischen Bürgerfamilien 1840–1914*, Göttingen: Vandenhoeck and Ruprecht.

Burke, P. 2001. *Papier und Marktgeschrei. Die Geburt der Wissensgesellschaft*, Berlin: Wagenbach.

Buß, E. 1973. *Der Wettbewerb. Eine rechtssoziologische Untersuchung*, Tübingen: Mohr.

Caenegem, R. C. van. 1973. *The Birth of the English Common Law*, Cambridge: Cambridge University Press.

Caillois, R. 2001. *Men, Play and Games*, Urbana and Chicago: Chicago University Press.

Cain, P. J., and A. G. Hopkins. 1986. 'Gentlemanly Capitalism and British Expansion Overseas, I: The Old Colonial System 1688–1850', *Economic History Review* 39, 501–25.

————, and ————. 1993. *British Imperialism. Innovations and Expansion, 1688–1914*, vol. 1, London: Longman.

Campbell, B. M. S. 2003. 'England: Land and People', in S. H. Rigby (ed.), *A Companion to Britain in the Later Middle Ages*, Oxford: Blackwell, 3–25.

————. 2006. 'The Land', in R. Horrox and W. M. Ormrod (eds). *A Social History of England, 1200–1500*, Cambridge: Cambridge University Press, 179–237.

————. 2009. 'Factor Markets in England before the Black Death', *Continuity and Change* 24, 79–106.

Cannadine, D. 1995. 'British History as a "New Subject"', in A. Grant and K. J. Stringer (eds), *Uniting the Kingdom? The Making of British History*, London: Routledge, 12–28.

————. 2008. 'Economy: The Growth and Fluctuations of the Industrial Revolution', in D. Cannadine, *Making History Now and Then, Discoveries, Controversies and Explorations*, Houndmills: Macmillan, 83–111.

Carlos, A. M., and L. Neal. 2006. 'The Micro-Foundations of the Early London Capital Market: Bank of England Shareholders during and after the South Sea Bubble, 1720–25', *Economic History Review* 59, 498–538.

Cassis, Y. 2007. *Metropolen des Kapitals. Die Geschichte der internationalen Finanzzentren 1780–2005*, Hamburg: Murmann Verlag.

Cecil, E. 1895. *Primogeniture. A Short History of its Development in Various Countries*, London: John Murray.

Cerman, M., and S. C. Ogilvie (eds). 1994. *Protoindustrialisierung in Europa. Industrielle Produktion vor dem Fabrikzeitalter*, Wien: Verlag für Gesellschaftskritik.

Chapman, S. 1992. *Merchant Enterprise in Britain. From the Industrial Revolution to World War I*, Cambridge: Cambridge University Press.

———. 1996. 'The Commercial Sector', in M. B. Rose (ed.), *The Lancashire Cotton Industry*, Preston: Lancashire County Books, 63–93.

Chartres, J. A. 1977. *Internal Trade in England 1500–1700*, London: Longman.

Chase, M. 2000. *Early Trade Unionism. Fraternity, Skill and the Politics of Labour*, Aldershot: Ashgate.

Chayanov, A. V. 1966. *The Theory of Peasant Economy*, D. Thorner (ed.), Homewood, Ill.: Irwin.

Chesterman, M. R. 1984. 'Family Settlements on Trust: Landowners and the Rising Bourgeoisie', in G.R. Rubin and D. Sugarman (eds), *Law, Economy and Society, 1750–1914. Essays in the History of English Law*, Abingdon, Oxon.: Professional Books Ltd., 124–68.

Chibnall, M. 2003. 'Feudalism and Lordship', in C. Harper-Bill and E. van Houts (eds), *A Companion to the Anglo-Norman World*, Woodbridge: The Boydell Press, 123–34.

Chinn, C. 1991. *Better Betting with a Decent Feller. Bookmaking, Betting and the British Working Class 1750–1990*, New York, London: Harvester Wheatsheaf.

Clark, Geoffrey. 1997. 'Life Insurance in the Society and Culture of London, 1700–75', *Urban History* 24(1), 17–36.

———. 1999. *Betting on Lives. The Culture of Life Insurance in England, 1695–1775*, Manchester: Manchester University Press.

Clark, Gregory. 1991. 'Labour Productivity in English Agriculture, 1300–1860', in B. M. S. Campbell and M. Overton (eds), *Land, Labour and Livestock: Historical Studies in European Agricultural Productivity*, Manchester: Manchester University Press, 211–36.

———. 2007. *A Farewell to Alms. A Brief Economic History of the World*, Princeton, NJ: Princeton University Press.

Clark, P. 1983. *The English Alehouse: a Social History, 1200–1830*, London: Longman.

———. 2000. *British Clubs and Societies 1580–1800. The Origins of an Associational World*, Oxford: Oxford University Press.

Clery, E. J. 1991. 'Women, Publicity and the Coffee-House Myth', *Women. A Cultural Review* 2, 168–77.

Cohen, D., and M. O'Connor. 2004. 'Introduction: Comparative History, Cross-National History, Transnational History – Definitions', in D. Cohen and M. O'Connor (eds), *Comparison and History. Europe in Cross-National Perspective*, London: Macmillan, IX–XXIV.

Cohen, J. 2002. *Protestantism and Capitalism. The Mechanisms of Influence*, New York: Aldine de Gruyter.

Coleman, D. C. 1975. *Industry in Tudor and Stuart England*, London: Macmillan.

———. 1983. 'Proto-Industrialization: A Concept Too Many', *Economic History Review* 36, 425–48.

Colón Semenza, G. M. 2003. *Sport, Politics and Literature in the English Renaissance*, Neward: University of Delaware Press.

Conrad, C. 2006. 'Vergleich und Transnationalität in der Geschichte', in A. Wirsching (ed.), *Oldenbourg Geschichte Lehrbuch: Neueste Zeit*, Munich: Oldenbourg, 317–32.

Convert, B. and J. Heilbron. 2007. 'Where Did the New Economic Sociology Come From?', *Theory and Society* 36, 31–54.

Cordery, S. 2003. *British Friendly Societies, 1750–1914*, Basingstoke: Palgrave Macmillan.

Cordes, A. 2005. 'The Search for a Medieval Lex mercatoria', in V. Piergiovanni (ed.), *From lex mercatoria to Commercial Law*, Berlin: Duncker and Humblot, 53–67.

Corfield, P. J. 1982. *The Impact of English Towns 1700–1800*, Oxford: Oxford University Press.

————. 1989. 'Dress for Deference and Dissent: Hats and the Decline of Hat Honour', in *Costume* 23, 64–79.

Coss, P. 2002. 'From Feudalism to Bastard Feudalism', in N. Fryde et al. (eds), *Die Gegenwart des Feudalismus,* Göttingen: Vandenhoeck and Ruprecht, 79–107.

————. 2006. 'The Age of Deference', in R. Horrox and W. M. Ormrod (eds), *A Social History of England, 1200–1500,* Cambridge: Cambridge University Press, 31–73.

Cotton, C. 1964 (1674). *The Compleat Gamester: or, Instructions How to Play at Billards, Trucks, Bowls, and Chess ... To Which is Added the Arts and Mysteries of Riding, Racing, Arching, and Cockfighting,* reprint of 2nd ed., Ithaka, NY: Cornell University Press.

Cowan, B. 2004. 'An Open Elite: The Peculiarities of Connoisseurship in Early Modern England', *Modern Intellectual History* 1, 151–83.

Coward, B. 1988. *Social Change and Continuity in Early Modern England 1550–1750,* London: Longman.

————. 1997. *Stuart England, 1603–1714. The Formation of the British State,* London: Longman.

Cox, N., and K. Dannehl. 2007. *Perceptions of Retailing in Early Modern England,* Aldershot: Ashgate.

Crafts, N. F. R. 1983. 'British Economic Growth 1700–1831: A Review of the Evidence', *Economic History Review* 36, 177–99.

Cranfield, G. A. 1962. *The Development of the Provincial Newspapers 1700–1760,* Oxford: Clarendon Press.

Crick, J., and E. van Houts (eds). 2011. *A Social History of England, 900–1200,* Cambridge: Cambridge University Press.

Cromartie, A. 2006. *The Constitutionalist Revolution. An Essay on the History of England, 1450–1642,* Cambridge: Cambridge University Press.

Crouch, C. 1993. 'Co-operation and Competition in an Institutional Economy: the Case of Germany', in C. Crouch and D. Marquand (eds), *Ethics and Markets, Co-operation and Competition within Capitalist Economies,* Oxford: Blackwell, 80–98.

————. 2005. 'Models of Capitalism', *New Political Economy* 10, 439–56.

Crump, J. 2005. 'The Perils of Play: Eighteenth-Century Ideas about Gambling', Gaming Research Weblog 27.1.2005 (http://www-histecon.kings.cam.ac.uk/docs/crump_perils .pdf, last accessed September 2012).

Dahlhaus, C., and H. H. Eggebrecht (eds). 1979. *Brockhaus Riemann Musiklexikon,* Mainz: Brockhaus.

Dahrendorf, R. 1979. *Lebenschancen. Anläufe zur sozialen und politischen Theorie,* Frankfurt, Main: Suhrkamp.

————. 1991. 'Die offene Gesellschaft und ihre Ängste', in W. Zapf (ed.) for the Deutsche Gesellschaft für Soziologie, *Die Modernisierung moderner Gesellschaften. Verhandlungen des 25. Deutschen Soziologentages in Frankfurt am Main 1990,* Frankfurt, Main: Campus, 140–50.

————. 1994. 'Das Zerbrechen der Ligaturen und die Utopie der Weltbürgergesellschaft', in U. Beck and E. Beck-Gernsheim (eds), *Riskante Freiheiten. Individualisierung in modernen Gesellschaften,* Frankfurt, Main: Suhrkamp, 421–36.

David, P. A. 1985. 'Clio and the Economics of QWERTY', *American Economic Review* 75, 332–37.

Davidoff, L., and C. Hall. 1987. *Family Fortunes. Men and Women of the English Middle Class, 1780–1850,* Chicago: The University of Chicago Press.

Davies, G. 2002. *History of Money. From Ancient Times to the Present Day*, Cardiff: University of Wales Press.

Davies, R. R. 1990. *Domination and Conquest. The Experience of Ireland, Scotland and Wales 1100–1300*, Cambridge: Cambridge University Press.

———. 2000. *The First English Empire. Power and Identities in the British Isles 1093–1343*, Oxford: Oxford University Press.

Davis, D. 1966. *A History of Shopping*, London: Routledge.

Davis, J. 2009. 'The Cross and the Pillory: Symbolic Structures of Commercial Space in Medieval English Towns', in S. Ehrich and J. Oberste (eds), *Städtische Räume im Mittelalter*, Regensburg: Schnell and Steiner, 241–59.

Davis, N. 1952. 'The Proxymate Etymology of Market', *Modern Language Review* 47, 152–55.

Deane, P. 1996. 'The British Industrial Revolution', in M. Teich and R. Porter (eds), *The Industrial Revolution in National Context. Europe and the USA*, Cambridge: Cambridge University Press, 13–35.

———, and W. A. Cole. 1967. *British Economic Growth 1688–1959: Trends and Structure*, 2nd ed., Cambridge: Cambridge University Press.

Defoe, D. 1719. *The Anatomy of Exchange-Alley; or a System of Stock-Jobbing. Providing the Scandalous Trade, as it is Now Carry'd on, to be Knavish in its Private Practice, and Treason in its Publick: ... By a Jobber*, 2nd ed., London: E. Smith.

———. 1726 (1725). *The Complete English Tradesman, in Familiar Letters; Directing Him in all the Several Parts and Progressions of Trade*, London.

Dickson, P. G. M. 1967. *The Financial Revolution in England: A Study in the Development of Public Credit, 1688–1756*, London: Macmillan.

Ditt, K., and S. Pollard (eds). 1992. *Von der Heimarbeit in die Fabrik. Industrialisierung und Arbeiterschaft in Leinen- und Baumwollregionen Westeuropas während des 18. und 19. Jahrhunderts*, Paderborn: Schöningh.

Dobson, C. R. 1982. *Masters and Journeymen. A Prehistory of Industrial Relations 1717–1800*, London: Croom Helm.

Dobson, R. B., and D. M. Smith (eds). 2006. *The Merchant Taylors of York. A History of the Craft and Company from the Fourteenth to the Twentieth Centuries*, York: Borthwick Publications.

Dockhorn, K. 1950. *Der deutsche Historismus in England. Ein Beitrag zur englischen Geistesgeschichte des 19. Jahrhunderts*, Göttingen: Vandenhoeck and Ruprecht.

Duffy, S. 2003. 'The British Perspective', in S. H. Rigby, *A Companion to Britain in the Later Middle Ages*, Oxford: Blackwell, 165–82.

Dyer, C. 1994. *Everyday Life in Medieval England*, London: Hambledon Press.

———. 1995. 'How Urbanized was Medieval England?', in J.-M. Duvosquel and E. Thoen (eds), *Peasants and Townsmen in Medieval Europe. Studia in honorem Adriaan Verhulst*, Gent: Snoeck-Ducajn and Zoon, 169–83.

——— (ed.). 2007. *The Self-Contained Village? The Social History of Rural Communities, 1250–1900*, Hatfield: University of Hertfordshire Press.

Ebeling, D., and W. Mager (eds). 1997. *Protoindustrie in der Region. Europäische Gewerbelandschaften vom 16. bis zum 19. Jahrhundert*, Bielefeld: Verlag für Regionalgeschichte.

Edwards, J. R. et al. 2002. 'British Central Government and "the Mercantile System of Double Entry" Bookkeeping: a Study of Ideological Conflict', in *Accounting, Organizations and Society* 27, 637–58.

Ehmer, J. 1991. *Heiratsverhalten, Sozialstruktur, ökonomischer Wandel. England und Mitteleuropa in der Formationsperiode des Kapitalismus,* Göttingen: Vandenhoeck and Ruprecht.

———. 1998. 'Traditionelles Denken und neue Fragestellungen zur Geschichte von Handwerk und Zunft', in F. Lenger (ed.), *Handwerk, Hausindustrie und die Historische Schule der Nationalökonomie. Wissenschafts- und gewerbegeschichtliche Perspektiven,* Bielefeld: Verlag für Regionalgeschichte, 19–77.

Eisenberg, C. 1986. *Deutsche und Englische Gewerkschaften. Entstehung und Entwicklung bis 1878 im Vergleich,* Göttingen: Vandenhoeck and Ruprecht.

———. 1999. *'English Sports' und deutsche Bürger. Eine Gesellschaftsgeschichte 1800–1939,* Paderborn: Schöningh.

———. 2003. 'Kulturtransfer als historischer Prozess. Ein Beitrag zur Komparatistik', in H. Kaelble and J. Schriewer (eds), *Vergleich und Transfer. Komparatistik in den Sozial-, Geschichts- und Kulturwissenschaften,* Frankfurt, Main: Campus, 399–417.

———. 2008 ff. *British History Compared: A Bibliography, Berlin* (http://www.gbz.hu-berlin.de/staff/staff/publications/bibliographien, last accessed 21 September 2012).

———. 2008. "Representing the Very Best': Anglo-German Competition and Transfers in Sport', in D. Geppert, and R. Gerwarth (eds), *Wilhelmine Germany and Edwardian Britain Essays on Cultural Contacts and Transfers,* Oxford: Oxford University Press, 393–413.

———. 2011. 'Playing the Market Game: Cash Prizes, Symbolic Awards and the Professional Ideal in British Amateur Sport', *Sport in History* 31, 197–217.

Eisenstadt, S. N. 1966. *Modernization. Protest and Change,* Englewood Cliffs: Prentice Hall.

Elias, N. 1994. *The Civilizing Process: the History of Manners and State Formation and Civilization,* Oxford: Blackwell, 1994.

Ellis, M. 2001. 'The Coffee-Women, The Spectator and the Public Sphere in the Early-Eighteenth Century', in E. Eger et al. (eds), *Women, Writing and the Public Sphere,* Cambridge: Cambridge University Press, 27–52.

———. 2004. *The Coffee-House. A Cultural History,* London: Weidenfeld and Nicolson.

———. 2008. 'An Introduction to the Coffee-House: a Discursive Model', *Language and Communication* 28, 156–64.

Epstein, S. R. 2000. *Freedom and Growth. The Rise of States and Markets in Europe, 1300–1750,* London: Routledge.

Ertman, T. 1999. 'Explaining Variations in Early Modern State Structure. The Cases of England and the German Territorial States', in J. Brewer and E. Hellmuth (eds), *Rethinking Leviathan: The Eighteenth-Century State in Britain and Germany,* Oxford: Oxford University Press, 23–52.

Eversley, D. E. C. 1967. 'The Home Market and Economic Growth in England, 1750–1780', in E. L. Jones and G. E. Mingay (eds), *Land, Labour and Population in the Industrial Revolution,* London: Hodder and Stroughton, 206–59.

Faber, K.-G., and C. Meier (eds). 1978. *Historische Prozesse,* Munich: Deutscher Taschenbuch Verlag.

Fahrmeir, A. 2003. *Ehrbare Spekulanten. Stadtverfassung, Wirtschaft und Politik in der City of London, 1688–1900,* Munich: Oldenbourg.

Feinstein, C. H. 1978. 'Capital Formation in Great Britain', in P. Mathias and M. M. Postan (eds), *Cambridge Economic History of Europe,* 7(1), Cambridge: Cambridge University Press, 28–96.

Field, A. J. 1985. 'On the Unimportance of Machinery', *Explorations in Economic History* 22, 378–401.

Finn, M. C. 2003. *The Character of Credit. Personal Debt in English Culture, 1740–1914*, Cambridge: Cambridge University Press.

Flotow, P. von, and J. Schmidt. 2003. 'Die 'Doppelrolle des Geldes' bei Simmel und ihre Bedeutung für Ökonomie und Soziologie', in O. Rammstedt (ed.), *Georg Simmels Philosophie des Geldes. Aufsätze und Materialien*, Frankfurt, Main: Suhrkamp, 58–87.

Floud, R., and P. Johnson (eds). 2004. *The Cambridge Economic History of Modern Britain, vol. 1: Industrialisation, 1700–1860*, Cambridge: Cambridge University Press.

———, and P. Thane. 2005. 'Sociology and History: Partnership, Rivalry, or Mutual Incomprehension?', in A. H. Halsey and W. G. Runciman (eds), *British Sociology. Seen from Without and Within*, Oxford: The British Academy by Oxford University Press, 57–69.

Flower, R., and M. Wynn Jones. 1974. *Lloyd's of London. An Illustrated History*, London: Lloyd's of London Press.

Fores, M. 1981. 'The Myth of a British Industrial Revolution', *History* 66, 181–98.

Forman-Barzilai, F. 2010. *Adam Smith and the Circles of Sympathy. Cosmopolitanism and Moral Theory*, Cambridge: Cambridge University Press.

Fourastié, J. 1989 (1949). *Le grand espoir du XXe siècle*, Paris: Gallimard.

Frisby, D. 1988. 'Die Ambiguität der Moderne: Max Weber und Georg Simmel', in W. J. Mommsen and W. Schwentker (eds), *Max Weber und seine Zeitgenossen*, Göttingen: Vandenhoeck and Ruprecht, 580–94.

Fulcher, J. 2004. *Kapitalismus*, Stuttgart: Reclam.

Galenson, D. W. 1994. 'The Rise of Free Labor: Economic Change and the Enforcement of Service Contracts in England, 1351–1875', in J. A. James and M. Thomas (eds), *Capitalism in Context. Essays in Economic Development and Cultural Change in Honor of R.M. Hartwell*, Chicago: The University of Chicago Press, 114–37.

Gebauer, G. 1972. '"Leistung" als Aktion und Präsentation', *Sportwissenschaft* 2, 182–203.

———, and C. Wulf. 1998. *Spiel, Ritual, Geste. Mimetisches Handeln in der sozialen Welt*, Reinbek: Rowohlt.

Gemmell, N. 1990. 'The Contribution of Services to British Economic Growth, 1856–1913', *Explorations in Economic History* 27, 299–321.

Georges, D. 1990. 1810/11–1993: *Handwerk und Interessenpolitik. Von der Zunft zur modernen Verbandsorganisation*, Frankfurt, Main: Peter Lang.

Ghosh, P. 2008. *A Historian Reads Max Weber. Essays on the Protestant Ethic*, Wiesbaden: Harassowitz.

Gillingham, J. 1996. 'Some Observations on Social Mobility in England between the Norman Conquest and the Early Thirteenth Century', in A. Haverkamp and H. Vollrath (eds), *England and Germany in the High Middle Ages*, Oxford: Oxford University Press, 333–55.

Gillmeister, H. 1995. 'Not Cricket und Fair play. Betrachtungen zum englischen Sportgedanken', in V. Gerhard and M. Lämmer (eds), *Fairness und Fair play: eine Ringvorlesung an der Deutschen Sporthochschule Köln*, 2nd ed., Sankt Augustin Academia Richarz, 127–37.

Glaisyer, N. 2006. *The Culture of Commerce in England, 1660–1720*, Woodbrige, Suffolk: Royal Historical Society and The Boydell Press.

Golby, J. M. and A. W. Purdue. 1984. *The Civilisation of the Crowd. Popular Culture in England 1750–1900*, London: Batsford Academia and Educational Ltd.

Goldstone, J. A. 1986. 'The Demographic Revolution in England: a Re-Examination', *Population Studies* 40, 5–33.

———. 1998. 'Initial Conditions, General Laws, Path Dependence and Explanation in Historical Sociology', *American Journal of Sociology* 104, 829–45.

Goltz, J. A. 2006. 'Publizieren im 18. und frühen 19. Jahrhundert. Deutschland und England im Vergleich. Eine Untersuchung der spezifischen Entwicklung des Autorenrechts anhand der Rechtsquellen des deutschen Urheberrechts und des englischen Copyright Law', Master's Thesis, Humboldt-Universität zu Berlin, Institut für Geschichtswissenschaften.

Gomes, L. 1987. *Foreign Trade and the National Economy. Mercantilist and Classical Perspectives,* London: Macmillan.

Goodhart, A. L. 1934. 'Precedent in English and Continental Law', *Law Quarterly Review* 50, 40–65.

Gorsky, M. 1998. 'The Growth and Distribution of English Friendly Societies in the Early Nineteenth Century', *Economic History Review* 51, 489–511.

Gosden, P. H. J. H. 1961. *The Friendly Societies in England, 1815–75,* Manchester: Manchester University Press.

Granovetter, M. S. 1973. 'The Strength of Weak Ties', *American Journal of Sociology* 78, 1360–80.

———. 1985. 'Economic Action and Social Structure. The Problem of Embeddedness', *American Journal of Sociology* 91, 481–510.

———, and R. Swedberg (eds). 2001. *The Sociology of Economic Life,* 2nd ed., Boulder, CO: Westview Press.

Grassby, R. 1970. 'English Merchant Capitalism in the Late Seventeenth Century. The Composition of Business Fortunes', *Past and Present* 46, 87–107.

———. 1999. *The Idea of Capitalism before the Industrial Revolution,* Lanham, MD: Rowman and Littlefield.

Graveson, R. H. 1941. 'The Movement from Status to Contract', *Modern Law Review* 4, 261–72.

Griffin, E. 2005. *England's Revelry: A History of Popular Sports and Pastimes, 1660–1830,* Oxford: Oxford University Press.

Gross, P., and B. Badura. 1977. 'Sozialpolitik und soziale Dienste: Entwurf einer Theorie personenbezogener Dienstleistungen', in C. v. Ferber and F.-X. Kaufmann (eds), *Soziologie und Sozialpolitik,* Opladen: Westdeutscher Verlag, 361–85.

Grossman, H. 1948. 'W. Playfair, the Earliest Theorist of Capitalist Development', *Economic History Review* 18, 65–83.

Habermas, J. 1989. *The Structural Transformation of the Public Sphere: An Inquiry into the Category of Bourgeois Society,* Cambridge: Polity.

———. 1990 (1962). *Strukturwandel der Öffentlichkeit. Untersuchungen zu einer Kategorie der bürgerlichen Gesellschaft,* Frankfurt, Main: Suhrkamp.

———. 1998. *Die postnationale Konstellation. Politische Essays,* Frankfurt, Main: Suhrkamp.

———. 1998. 'Konzeptionen der Moderne. Ein Rückblick auf zwei Traditionen', in J. Habermas, *Die postnationale Konstellation,* Frankfurt: Suhrkamp, 195–232.

Hall, P. A., and D. Soskice (eds). 2001. *Varieties of Capitalism. The Institutional Foundations of Comparative Advantage,* Oxford: Oxford University Press.

Hall-Witt, J. 2003. 'Reforming the Aristocracy: Opera and Elite Culture, 1780–1860', in A. Burns and J. Innes (eds), *Rethinking the Age of Reform. Britain 1780–1850,* Cambridge: Cambridge University Press, 220–37.

Hancock, D. 1995. *Citizens of the World. London Merchants and the Integration of the British Atlantic Community, 1735–85,* Cambridge: Cambridge University Press.

Hann, A. 2004. 'Modernity and the Marketplace', in S. Pinches, M. Whalley and D. Postles (eds), *The Market Place and the Place of the Market*, Leicester: Friends of the Centre for English Local History, 67–88.

———. 2005. 'Industrialisation and the Service Economy', in J. Stobart and N. Raven (eds), *Towns, Regions, and Industries: Urban and Industrial Change in the Midlands, c. 1700–1840*, Manchester: Manchester University Press, 42–61.

Hann, C., and K. Hart (eds). 2009. *Market and Society: The Great Transformation Today*, Cambridge: Cambridge University Press.

Harding, V. 2006. 'Shops, Markets and Retailers in London's Cheapside, c. 1500–1700', in B. Blondé et al. (eds), *Buyers and Sellers. Retail Circuits in Medieval and Early Modern Europe*, Turnhout: Brepols Publishers, 155–70.

Harley, C. K. 1982. 'British Industrialisation before 1841: Evidence of Slower Growth during the Industrial Revolution', *Journal of Economic History* 42, 267–89.

Harling, P., and P. Mandler. 1993. 'From "Fiscal-Military" State to Laissez-faire State, 1760–1850', *Journal of British Studies* 32, 44–70.

Harper-Bill, C., and E. van Houts (eds). 2003. *A Companion to the Anglo-Norman World*, Woodbridge, Suffolk: The Boydell Press.

Harris, B. 1996. *Politics and the Rise of the Press: Britain and France, 1620–1800*, London: Macmillan.

Harris, E. T. 2004. 'Handel the Investor', *Music and Letters* 85, 521–75.

Harris, R. 2000. *Industrializing English Law: Entrepreneurship and Business Organization, 1720–1844*, Cambridge: Cambridge University Press.

———. 2004. 'Government and the Economy, 1688–1850', in R. Floud and P. Johnson (eds), *The Cambridge Economic History of Modern Britain, vols 1: Industrialisation, 1700–1860*, Cambridge: Cambridge University Press, 204–37.

Harris, T. (ed.). 1995. *Popular Culture in England, c. 1500–1850*, London: Macmillan.

Hart, M. 't. 1991. '"The Devil or the Dutch": Holland's Impact on the Financial Revolution in England, 1643–1694', *Parliaments, Estates and Representation* 11, 39–52.

Hartmann, W. 1956. *Der Trust im englischen Recht*, Zürich: Juris-Verlag.

Hartwell, R. M. 1972. 'The Tertiary Sector in the English Economy during the Industrial Revolution', in P. Léon et al. (eds), *L'industrialisation en Europe au XIXe siècle. Carthographie et Typologie, Colloques internationaux du Centre National de la Recherche Scientifique*, Nr. 540, Paris: C.N.R.S., 213–31.

Harvey, A. 2004. *The Beginnings of a Commercial Sporting Culture in Britain, 1793–1850*, Aldershot: Ashgate.

Harvie, C. 1994. '"These Islands" und ihre Nationen: Das Dilemma "britischer" Geschichte', *Blätter für deutsche Landesgeschichte* 130, 49–63.

Hatcher, J., and M. Bailey. 2001. *Modelling the Middle Ages. The History and Theory of England's Economic Development*, Oxford: Oxford University Press.

Haupt, H.-G. (ed.). 2002. *Das Ende der Zünfte. Ein europäischer Vergleich*, Göttingen: Vandenhoeck and Ruprecht.

Haverkamp, A., and H. Vollrath (eds). 1966. *England and Germany in the High Middle Ages*, Oxford: Oxford University Press.

Hay, D. 2004. 'England, 1562–1875: The Law and its Uses', in D. Hay and Paul Craven (eds), *Masters, Servants, and Magistrates in Britain and the Empire, 1562–1955*, Chapel Hill, NC: University of North Carolina Press.

Heller, K. 1993. *Die Normannen in Osteuropa*, Berlin: Duncker and Humblot.

Hellmuth, E. 2002. 'The British State', in H. T. Dickinson (ed.), *A Companion to Eighteenth-Century Britain*, Oxford: Blackwell, 19–29.

Hesmondhalgh, D. 2002. *The Cultural Industries*, London: Sage.

Heyl, C. 2004. *A Passion for Privacy. Untersuchungen zur Genese der bürgerlichen Privatsphäre in London, 1660–1800*, Munich: Oldenbourg.

Hicks, M. 1995. *Bastard Feudalism*, London: Longman.

Hindle, S. 2004. *On the Parish? The Micro-Politics of Poor Relief in Rural England c. 1550–1750*, Oxford: Clarendon Press.

Hirsch, F. 1976. *Social Limits to Growth*, Cambridge, MA: Harvard University Press.

Hirschman, A. O. 1970. *Exit, Voice, and Loyalty. Responses to Decline in Firms, Organizations, and States*, Cambridge, MA: Harvard University Press.

———. 1977. *The Passions and the Interests: Political Arguments for Capitalism before its Triumph*, Princeton: Princeton University Press.

———. 1982. 'Rival Interpretations of Market Society: Civilizing, Destructive, or Feeble?', *Journal of Economic Literature* 20 (1982), 1463–84.

Hobsbawm, E., and T. Ranger (eds). 1983. *The Invention of Tradition*, Cambridge: Cambridge University Press.

Hollister, C. W. 1963. 'The Irony of English Feudalism', *Journal of British Studies* 11, 1–26.

Holt, R. 1989. *Sport and the British. A Modern History*, Oxford: Oxford University Press.

Holzer, B. 2006. *Netzwerke*, Bielefeld: Transcript.

Hont, I. and M. Ignatieff. 1983. 'Needs and Justice in the Wealth of Nations: an Introductory Essay', in I. Hont and M. Ignatieff (eds), *Wealth and Virtue: The Shaping of Political Economy in the Scottish Enlightenment*, Cambridge: Cambridge University Press, 1–45.

———, and ——— (eds). 1983. *Wealth and Virtue: The Shaping of Political Economy in the Scottish Enlightenment*, Cambridge: Cambridge University Press.

Hoppit, J. 1986. 'Financial Crises in Eighteenth-Century England', *Economic History Review* 39, 39–58.

———. 1986. 'The Use and Abuse of Credit in Eighteenth-Century England', in N. McKendrick and R. B. Outhwaite (eds), *Business Life and Public Policy. Essays in Honour of D. C. Coleman*, Cambridge: Cambridge University Press, 64–78.

———. 1987. *Risk and Failure in English Business 1700–1800*, Cambridge: Cambridge University Press.

———. 1990. 'Attitudes to Credit in Britain, 1680–1790', *Historical Journal* 33, 305–22.

———. 1996. 'Political Arithmetic in Eighteenth-Century England', *Economic History Review* 49, 516–40.

———. 2000. *A Land of Liberty? England 1689–1727*, Oxford: Oxford University Press.

———. 2002. 'Checking the Leviathan, 1688–1832', in D. Winch and P. O'Brien (eds), *The Political Economy of British Historical Experience, 1688–1914*, Oxford: Oxford University Press for the British Academy, 267–94.

———. 2002. 'The Myths of the South Sea Bubble', *Transactions of the Royal Historical Society* 6(12), 141–65.

———. 2006. 'The Contexts and Contours of British Economic Literature, 1660–1760', *Historical Journal* 49, 79–110.

Horrox, R. 2006. 'Conclusion', in R. Horrox and W. M. Ormrod (eds), *A Social History of England, 1200–1500*, Cambridge: Cambridge University Press, 473–79.

———, and W. M. Ormrod (eds). 2006. *A Social History of England, 1200–1500*, Cambridge: Cambridge University Press.

Houston, A., and S. Pincus. 2001. 'Introduction. Modernity and Later Seventeenth-Century England', in A. Houston and S. Pincus (eds), *A Nation Transformed. England after the Restoration*, Cambridge: Cambridge University Press, 1–19.

Houston, R. A., and K. D. M. Snell. 1984. 'Proto-Industrialization, Cottage Industry, Social Change and the Industrial Revolution', *Historical Journal* 27, 473–92.

Hudson, P. 1994. 'Proto-Industrialisierung in England', in M. Cerman and S. C. Ogilvie (eds), *Proto-Industrialisierung in Europa. Industrielle Produktion vor dem Fabrikszeitalter*, Wien: Verlag für Gesellschaftskritik, 61–78.

——— (ed.). 1989. *Regions and Industries. A Perspective on the Industrial Revolution in Britain*, Cambridge: Cambridge University Press.

Humphries, J. 2003. 'English Apprenticeship: A Neglected Factor in the First Industrial Revolution', in P. A. David and M. Thomas (eds), *The Economic Future in Historical Perspective*, Oxford: Oxford University Press, 73–102.

Hunter, D. 2000. 'Patronizing Handel, Inventing Audiences. The Intersection of Class, Money, Music and History', *Early Music* 18, 32–49.

Ibbetson, D. J. 1999. *A Historical Introduction to the Law of Obligations*, Oxford: Oxford University Press.

Ingham, G. 2004. *The Nature of Money*, Cambridge: Polity.

Ingram, W. 1999. 'The Economics of Playing', in D. S. Kastan (ed.), *A Companion to Shakespeare*, Oxford: Blackwell, 313–27.

Innes, J. 1994. 'The Domestic Face of the Military-Fiscal State. Government and Society in Eighteenth-Century Britain', in L. Stone (ed.), *An Imperial State at War. Britain from 1689 to 1815*, London: Routledge, 96–127.

Johnson, P. 2010. *Making the Market. Victorian Origins of Corporate Capitalism*, Cambridge: Cambridge University Press.

Jones, E. L. 1965. 'Agriculture and Economic Growth in England, 1660–1750: Agricultural Change', *Journal of Economic History* 25, 1–18.

———, and M. E. Falkus. 1979. 'Urban Improvement and the English Economy in the Seventeenth and Eighteenth Centuries', *Research in Economic History* 4, 193–233.

Jones, N. 1989. *God and the Moneylenders. Usury and Law in Early Modern England*, Oxford: Blackwell.

Jordan, S. (ed.). 2002. *Geschichtswissenschaft. Hundert Grundbegriffe*, Stuttgart: Reclam.

Kaelble, H. 1989. 'Was Prometheus most Unbound in Europe? The Labour Force in Europe During the Late XIXth and XXth Centuries', *Journal of European Economic History* 18, 65–104.

Kamphausen, G. 2002. *Die Erfindung Amerikas in der Kulturkritik der Generation von 1890*, Weilerswist: Velbrück.

Kavanagh, T. M. 1993. *Enlightenment and the Shadows of Chance: The Novel and the Culture of Gambling in Eighteenth-Century France*, Baltimore: Johns Hopkins University Press.

Keene, D. 2006. 'Sites of Desire: Shops, Selds and Wardrobes in London and other English Cities', in B. Blondé, P. Stabel, J. Stobart and I. van Damme (eds), *Buyers and Sellers. Retail Circuits in Medieval and Early Modern Europe*, Turnhout: Brepols Publishers, 125–54.

Kerr, C. 1929. 'The Origin and Development of the Law Merchant', *Virginia Law Review* 15, 350–67.

Kewes, P. 2001. 'Plays as Property, 1660–1710', in A. Houston and S. Pincus (eds), *A Nation Transformed. England after the Restoration*, Cambridge: Cambridge University Press, 211–40.

Kindleberger, C. P. 1975. 'Commercial Expansion and the Industrial Revolution', *Journal of European Economic History* 4, 613–53.

———. 1976. 'The Historical Background: Adam Smith and the Industrial Revolution', in T. Wilson and A. S. Skinner (eds), *The Market and the State. Essays in Honour of Adam Smith,* Oxford: Clarendon Press, 1–25.

King, S., and G. Timmins. 2001. *Making Sense of the Industrial Revolution. English Economy and Society,* Manchester: Manchester University Press.

Kneer, G. et al. (eds). 1997. *Soziologische Gesellschaftsbegriffe. Konzepte moderner Zeitdiagnosen,* Paderborn: Fink/UTB.

Kocka, J. 1990. *Arbeitsverhältnisse und Arbeiterexistenzen. Grundlagen der Klassenbildung im 19.* Jahrhundert, Bonn: Dietz.

———. 1996. 'Annäherung und neue Distanz. Historiker und Sozialwissenschaftler seit den fünfziger Jahren', in M. Hettling and P. Nolte (eds), *Nation und Gesellschaft in Deutschland. Historische Essays,* Munich: Beck, 15–31.

Körner, S. 1964. *The Battle of Hastings, England, and Europe 1035–1066,* Lund: Skanska Centraltryckeriet.

Kowalski Wallace, E. 2000. 'The Needs of Strangers: Friendly Societies and Insurance Societies in Late Eighteenth-Century England', *Eighteenth-Century Life* 24, 53–72.

Kramnick, J. B. 1998. *Making the English Canon. Print Capitalism and the Cultural Past, 1700–1770,* Cambridge: Cambridge University Press.

Kriedte, P. et al. 1977. *Industrialisierung vor der Industrialisierung. Gewerbliche Warenproduktion auf dem Land in der Formationsperiode des Kapitalismus,* Göttingen: Vandenhoeck and Ruprecht.

Krieger, K.-F. 2002. *Geschichte Englands von den Anfängen bis zum 15. Jahrhundert,* Munich: Beck.

Krippner, G. et al. 2004. 'Polanyi Symposium: a Conversation on Embeddedness', *Socio-Economic Review* 2, 109–35.

Kuchta, D. 2002. *The Three-Piece Suit and Modern Masculinity: England 1550–1850,* Berkeley: University of California Press.

Kurath S. H. (ed.). 1980. *Middle English Dictionary,* vol. O-P, Ann Arbor: University of Michigan Press.

La Vopa, A. J. 1988. *Grace, Talent, and Merit: Poor Students, Clerical Careers, and Professional Ideology in Eighteenth-Century Germany,* Cambridge: Cambridge University Press.

Laqueur, T. 1976. 'The Cultural Origins of Popular Literacy in England 1550–1800', *Oxford Review of Education* 2, 255–75.

Lake, P., and S. Pincus (eds). 2007. *The Politics of the Public Sphere in Early Modern England,* Manchester: Manchester University Press.

Lane, F. C. 1969. 'Meanings of Capitalism', *Journal of Economic History* 29, 5–12.

Langford, P. 2000. *Englishness Identified. Manners and Characters 1650–1850,* Oxford: Oxford University Press.

Lee, C. H. 1984. 'The Service Sector, Regional Specialisation and Economic Growth in the Victorian Economy', *Journal of Historical Geography* 10, 139–55.

———. 1986. *The British Economy since 1700: a Macroeconomic Perspective,* Cambridge: Cambridge University Press.

———. 1994. 'The Service Industries', in R. Floud and D. N. McCloskey (eds), *The Economic History of Britain since 1700,* vol. 2: 1860–1939, 2nd ed., Cambridge: Cambridge University Press, 117–44.

Leinwand, T. B. 1986. *The City Staged. Jacobean Comedy, 1603–1613,* Madison, WI: University of Madison Press.

———. 1999. *Theatre, Finance and Society in Early Modern England,* Cambridge: Cambridge University Press.

Lejeune, E. A. 1979. *The Gentlemen's Cubs of London,* London: Macdonald and Janes.

Lemire, B. 1988. 'Consumerism in Preindustrial and Early Industrial England: The Trade in Second Hand Clothes', *Journal of British Studies* 27, 1–24.

———. 1997. *Dress, Culture and Commerce. The English Clothing Trade before the Factory, 1660–1800,* Houndmills: Macmillan.

———. 2005. *The Business of Everyday Life. Gender, Practice and Social Politics in England, c. 1600–1900,* Manchester: Manchester University Press.

Lenger, F. 1994. *Werner Sombart 1863–1914. Eine Biographie,* Munich: Beck.

Léon, P. et al. (eds). 1972. *L'industrialisation en Europe au XIXe siècle. Carthographie et Typologie. Colloques internationaux du Centre National de la Recherche Scientifique,* Nr. 540, Paris: C.N.R.S.

Levy, H. 1920. *Soziologische Studien über das englische Volk,* Jena: Gustav Fischer.

———. 1932. 'Wirtschaftssprachliche Materialien aus der englischen Geschichte des 17. und 18. Jahrhunderts', *Neuphilologische Monatsschrift* 3, 109–22.

Lichtblau, K. 2000. '"Vergemeinschaftung" und "Vergesellschaftung" bei Max Weber: eine Rekonstruktion seines Sprachgebrauchs', *Zeitschrift für Soziologie* 29, 423–43.

Lieberman, D. 1995. 'Property, Commerce, and the Common Law. Attitudes to Legal Change in the Eighteenth Century', in J. Brewer and S. Staves (eds), *Early Modern Conceptions of Property,* London: Routledge, 144–58.

Lloyd-Jones, R., and M. J. Lewis. 1988. *Manchester and the Age of the Factory: the Business Structure of Cottonopolis in the Industrial Revolution,* London: Croom Helm.

Lottes, G. 1979. *Politische Aufklärung und plebejisches Publikum. Zur Theorie und Praxis des englischen Radikalismus im späten 18.* Jahrhundert, Munich: Oldenbourg.

———. 1984. 'Popular Culture and the Early Modern State in 16th Century Germany', in S. L. Kaplan (ed.), *Understanding Popular Culture. Europe from the Middle Ages to the Nineteenth Century,* Berlin: Mouton, 147–88.

———. 1995. 'Von "tenure" zu "property". Die Entstehung des Eigentumsbegriffes aus dem Zerfall des Feudalrechts', in G. Lottes (ed.), *Der Eigentumsbegriff im englischen politischen Denken,* Bochum: Brockmeyer, 1–23.

Lovell, M. C. 1957. 'The Role of the Bank of England as Lender of Last Resort in the Crises of the Eighteenth Century', *Explorations in Entrepreneurial History* 10, 8–21.

Lübbe, H. 1996. 'Netzverdichtung. Zur Philosophie industriegesellschaftlicher Entwicklungen', *Zeitschrift für philosophische Forschung* 50, 133–50.

Luhmann, N. 1978. 'Geschichte als Prozess und die Theorie sozio-kultureller Evolution', in K.-G. Faber and C. Meier (eds), *Historische Prozesse,* Munich: Deutscher Taschenbuch Verlag, 413–40.

———. 1979. *Trust and Power,* Chichester: Wiley.

Lyon, H. R. 1962. *Anglo-Saxon England and the Norman Conquest,* London: Longman.

Macfarlane, A. 1978. *The Origins of English Individualism. The Family, Property and Social Transition,* Oxford: Blackwell.

———. 1984. 'The Myth of the Peasantry; Family and Economy in a Northern Parish', in R. M. Smith (ed.), *Land, Kinship and Life-Cycle,* Cambridge: Cambridge University Press, 333–49.

———. 1987. 'The Peasantry in England before the Industrial Revolution – a Mythical Model?', in A. Macfarlane, *The Culture of Capitalism,* Oxford: Blackwell, 1–25.

———. 1988. 'The Cradle of Capitalism: The Case of England', in J. Baechler et al. (eds), *Europe and the Rise of Capitalism,* Oxford: Blackwell, 185–203.

———. 1992. 'On Individualism. Radcliffe-Brown Lecture in Social Anthropology', *Proceedings of the British Academy* 82, 171–99.

———. 1997. *The Savage Wars of Peace. England, Japan and the Malthusian Trap,* Oxford: Blackwell.

———. 2002. *The Making of the Modern World. Visions from the West and East,* Houndmills: Palgrave.

———, and G. Martin. 2003. *The Glass Bathyscaphe. How Glass Changed the World,* London: Profile Books.

Mackie, E. (ed.). 1998. *The Commerce of Everyday Life. Selections from The Tatler and The Spectator,* Boston, New York: Palgrave Macmillan.

Maddern, P. C. 2006. 'Social Mobility', in R. Horrox and W. M. Ormrod (eds), *A Social History of England, 1200–1500,* Cambridge: Cambridge University Press, 113–33.

Mahoney, J. 2000. 'Path Dependence in Historical Sociology', *Theory and Society* 29, 507–48.

Maine, H. S. 1965 (1861). *Ancient Law,* New York: Dutton.

Maitland, F. W. 1905. 'Trust und Korporation', *Grünhuts Zeitschrift für das Privat- und öffentliche Recht der Gegenwart* 32, 1–76.

Mann, M. 1994. *Geschichte der Macht, vol. 2: Vom Römischen Reich bis zum Vorabend der Industrialisierung,* Frankfurt, Main: Campus.

Margairaz, D., and P. Minard. 2006, 'Le marché dans son histoire', *Revue de synthèse* 5(127), 241–52.

Marquand, D. 1988. *The Unprincipled Society. New Demands and Old Politics,* London: Fontana Press.

Marx, K. and F. Engels. 2012 (1848). *The Communist Manifesto,* introduced by E. Hobsbawm, London: Verso.

Masschaele, J. 1997. *Peasants, Merchants, and Markets. Inland Trade in Medieval England, 1150–1350,* New York: St. Martin's Press.

———. 2007. 'Tolls and Trade in Medieval England', in L. Armstrong et al. (eds), *Money, Markets and Trade in Late Medieval Europe. Essays in Honour of John H.A. Munro,* Leiden: Brill, 146–83.

Mathias, P. 1969. *The First Industrial Nation. An Economic History of Britain 1700–1914,* London: Methuen.

———. 1988. 'The Industrial Revolution – Concept and Reality', in A. M. Birke and L. Kettenacker (eds), *Wettlauf in die Moderne. England und Deutschland seit der industriellen Revolution/The Race for Modernisation. Britain and Germany since the Industrial Revolution,* Munich: Saur, 11–30.

———, and P. K. O'Brien. 1976. 'Taxation in Britain and France, 1715–1810. A Comparison of the Social and Economic Incidence of Taxes Collected for the Central Government', *Journal of European Economic History* 5, 601–50.

Maurer, M. (ed.). 1992. *O Britannien. Von Deiner Freiheit einen Hut voll. Deutsche Reiseberichte des 18. Jahrhunderts,* Munich: Beck and Kiepenheuer.

Mayhew, N. 2007. 'Wages and Currency: The Case in Britain up to c. 1600', in J. Lucassen (ed.), *Wages and Currency. Global Comparisons from Antiquity to the Twentieth Century,* Berne: Peter Lang, 211–20.

McConahey, M. W. 1974. 'Sports and Recreations in Later Medieval France and England', PhD Thesis University of Southern California, Los Angeles: University of Southern California Press.

McFarlane, K. B. 1944. 'Parliament and Bastard Feudalism', *Transactions of the Royal Historical Society* 4(26), 53–79.

McGuinness, R. 2004. 'Gigs, Roadies and Promoters: Marketing Eighteenth-Century Concerts', in S. Wollenberg and S. McVeigh (eds), *Concert Life in Eighteenth-Century Britain*, Aldershot: Ashgate, 261–71.

———, and H. D. Johnstone. 1990. 'Concert Life in England I', in H. D. Johnstone and R. Fiske (eds), *The Blackwell History of Music in Britain the Eighteenth Century*, Oxford: Blackwell, 31–95.

McKendrick, N. 1974. 'Home Demand and Economic Growth: A New View of the Role of Women and Children in the Industrial Revolution', in N. McKendrick (ed.), *Historical Perspectives: Studies in English Thought and Society*, London: Europa Publications, 152–210.

———. 1982. 'The Consumer Revolution of Eighteenth-Century England', in N. McKendrick et al. (eds), *The Birth of a Consumer Society: The Commercialization of Eighteenth-Century England*, London: Hutchinson, 9–33.

———. 1982. 'The Commercialization of Fashion', in N. McKendrick et al. (eds), *The Birth of a Consumer Society. The Commercialization of Eighteenth-Century England*, London: Hutchinson, 34–99.

——— et al. 1982. *The Birth of a Consumer Society. The Commercialization of Eighteenth-Century England*, London: Hutchinson.

McLeod, C. 2004. 'The European Origins of British Technological Predominance', in L. Prados de la Escosura (ed.), *Exceptionalism and Industrialisation. Britain and its European Rivals, 1688–1815*, Cambridge: Cambridge University Press, 111–27.

McVeigh, S. 1993. *Concert Life in London from Mozart to Haydn*, Cambridge: Cambridge University Press.

Medick, H. 1974. 'Anfänge und Voraussetzungen des Organisierten Kapitalismus in Großbritannien', in H. A. Winkler (ed.), *Organisierter Kapitalismus. Voraussetzungen und Anfänge*, Göttingen: Vandenhoeck and Ruprecht, 58–83.

Melton, J. van Horn. 2001. *The Rise of the Public in Enlightenment Europe*, Cambridge: Cambridge University Press.

Mendels, F. 1972. 'Proto-Industrialization: the First Phase of the Industrialization Process', *Journal of Economic History* 31, 241–61.

Mergel, T. 1997. 'Geht es weiterhin voran? Die Modernisierungstheorie auf dem Weg zu einer Theorie der Moderne', in T. Mergel and T. Welskopp (eds), *Geschichte zwischen Kultur und Gesellschaft. Beiträge zur Theoriedebatte*, Munich: Beck, 203–32.

Michie, R. C. 1999. *The London Stock Exchange: A History*, Oxford: Oxford University Press.

Middleton, I., and W. Vamplew. 2003. 'Horse-Racing and the Yorkshire Leisure Calendar in the Early Eighteenth Century', *Northern History* 40, 259–76.

Miers, D. 1989. 'A Social and Legal History of Gambling: From the Restoration to the Gaming Act 1845', in T. G. Watkin (ed.), *Legal Record and Historical Reality. Proceedings of the Eighth British Legal History Conference, Cardiff 1987*, London: The Hambledon Press, 107–20.

Milgrom, P. R. et al. 1990. 'The Role of Institutions in the Revival of Trade: The Law Merchant, Private Judges, and the Champagne Fairs', *Economics and Politics* 2, 1–23.

Millward, R. 1981. 'The Emergence of Wage Labor in Early Modern England', *Explorations in Economic History* 18, 21–39.

Mokyr, J. 1984. 'The Industrial Revolution and the New Economic History', in J. Mokyr (ed.), *The Economics of the Industrial Revolution,* Totowa, N.J.: Rowman and Allanheld.

———. 1999. 'Editor's Introduction: The New Economic History and the Industrial Revolution', in J. Mokyr (ed.), *The British Industrial Revolution. An Economic Perspective,* Boulder, Co: Westview Press, 1–128.

———. 2002. *The Gifts of Athena. Historical Origins of the Knowledge Economy,* Princeton, NJ: Princeton University Press.

———. 2005. 'The Intellectual Origins of Modern Economic Growth', *Journal of Economic History* 65, 285–351.

———. 2009. *The Enlightened Economy. Britain and the Industrial Revolution,* London: Penguin, 2009.

Montesquieu, C. L. de Secondat Baron de. 1977. *Persian Letters,* trans. C. J. Betts, Harmondsworth: Penguin.

———. 1989. *The Spirit of the Laws,* A. Cohler et al. (eds), Cambridge: Cambridge University Press.

Morrison, K. A. 2003. *English Shops and Shopping. An Architectural History,* New Haven: Yale University Press.

Muldrew, C. 1998. *The Economy of Obligation. The Culture of Credit and Social Relations in Early Modern England,* London: Macmillan.

———. 1998. 'Zur Anthropologie des Kapitalismus: Kredit, Vertrauen, Tausch und die Geschichte des Marktes in England 1500–1750', *Historische Anthropologie* 6, 167–99.

———. 2000. 'From a 'Light Cloak' to an 'Iron Cage': Historical Changes in the Relations between Community and Individualism', in A. Shepard and P. Withington (eds), *Communities in Early Modern England. Networks, Place, Rhetoric,* Manchester: Manchester University Press, 156–77.

Mueller, H.-E. 1984. *Bureaucracy, Education and Monopoly. Civil Service Reforms in Prussia and England,* Berkeley: University of California Press.

Müller, S. O. 2006. 'Friction, Fiction and Fashion: German Perceptions of Music Life in Britain in the "Long Nineteenth Century"', in A. Bauerkämper and C. Eisenberg (eds), *Britain as a Model of Modern Society? German Views,* Augsburg: Wißner, 224–41.

Munro, J. H. 2000. 'English "Backwardness" and Financial Innovations in Commerce with the Low Countries, 14th to 16th Centuries', in P. Stabel et al. (eds), *International Trade in the Low Countries (14th–16th Centuries). Merchants, Organisation, Infrastructure,* Leuven-Apeldoorn: Garant, 105–67.

Munting, R. 1996. *An Economic and Social History of Gambling in Britain and the USA,* Manchester: Manchester University Press.

Musson, A. E. 1975. 'Continental Influences on the Industrial Revolution in Britain', in B. E. Radcliffe (ed.), *Great Britain and her World 1750–1914. Essays in Honour of W. O. Henderson,* Manchester: Manchester University Press, 71–85.

———. 1976. 'Industrial Motive Power in the United Kingdom, 1800–70', *Economic History Review* 29, 415–39.

Neal, L. 1990. *The Rise of Financial Capitalism. International Capital Markets in the Age of Reason,* Cambridge: Cambridge University Press.

———. 2004. 'The Monetary, Financial and Political Architecture of Europe, 1648–1815', in L. Prados de la Escosura (ed.), *Exceptionalism and Industrialisation. Britain and its European Rivals, 1688–1815,* Cambridge: Cambridge University Press, 173–90.

———, and S. Quinn. 2001. 'Networks of Information, Markets and Institutions in the Rise of London as a Financial Centre, 1660–1720', *Financial History Review* 8, 7–26.

Neckel, S. 2002. 'Ehrgeiz, Reputation und Bewährung. Zur Theoriegeschichte einer Soziologie des Erfolges', in G. Burkart and J. Wolf (eds), *Lebenszeiten. Erkundungen zur Soziologie der Generationen,* Opladen: Leske and Budrich, 103–17.

———, and K. Dröge. 2002. 'Die Verdienste und ihr Preis: Leistung in der Marktgesellschaft', in A. Honneth (ed.), *Befreiung aus der Mündigkeit. Paradoxien des gegenwärtigen Kapitalismus,* Frankfurk, Main: Campus, 93–116.

Nef, J. U. 1994 (1932). 'The Substitution of Coal for Wood', in R.A. Church (ed.), *The Coal and Iron Industries,* Oxford: Blackwell, 66–101.

Nietzsche, F. 1997. *On the Genealogy of Morality, ed. K. Ansell-Pearson,* trans. C. Diethe, Cambridge: Cambridge University Press.

Nightingale, P. 1983. 'The Ora, the Mark, and the Mancus: Weight-Standards and the Coinage in Eleventh-Century England (Part 1)', *Numismatic Chronicle* 143, 248–57.

———. 2004. 'Money and Credit in the Economy of Late Medieval England', in D. Wood (ed.), *Medieval Money Matters,* Oxford: Oxbow Books.

———. 2007. *Trade, Money, and Power in Medieval England,* Aldershot: Ashgate.

Nolte, P. 1997. 'Der Markt und seine Kultur – ein neues Paradigma der amerikanischen Geschichte?', *Historische Zeitschrift* 264, 329–60.

———. 2001. 'Modernization and Modernity in History', in *International Encyclopedia of the Social and Behavioral Sciences,* vol. 15, Amsterdam, 9954–61.

North, D. C. 1988. *Theorie des institutionellen Wandels,* Tübingen: Mohr.

———. 1990. *Institutions, Institutional Change and Economic Performance,* Cambridge: Cambridge University Press.

———, and R. P. Thomas. 1973. *The Rise of the Western World. A New Economic History,* Cambridge: Cambridge University Press.

O'Brien, P. K. 1988. 'The Political Economy of British Taxation, 1660–1815', *Economic History Review* 41, 1–32.

———. 1994. 'Central Government and the Economy, 1688–1815', in R. Floud and D. McCloskey (eds), *The Economic History of Britain since 1700,* vol. 1: 1700–1860, 2nd ed., Cambridge: Cambridge University Press, 205–41.

———. 1997. 'The Britishness of the First Industrial Revolution and the British Contribution to the Industrialization of 'Follower Countries' on the Mainland, 1756–1914', *Diplomacy and Statecraft* 8, 48–67.

———. 1998. 'Inseparable Connections: Trade, Economy, Fiscal State, and the Expansion of Empire, 1688-1815', in P. J. Marshall and A. Low (eds), *The Eighteenth Century* (= The Oxford History of the British Empire), Oxford: Oxford University Press, 53–77.

———. 1999. 'Imperialism and the Rise and Decline of the British Economy, 1688–1989', *New Left Review* 208, 48–80.

———. 2000. 'The Reconstruction, Rehabilitation and Reconfiguration of the British Industrial Revolution as a Conjuncture in Global History', *Itinerario* 24, 117–34.

———. 2006. 'The Divergence Debate. Europe and China 1368–1846', in G. Budde et al. (eds), *Transnationale Geschichte. Themen, Tendenzen und Theorien,* Göttingen: Vandenhoeck and Ruprecht, 68–82.

——— et al. 1991. 'Political Components of the Industrial Revolution: Parliament and the English Cotton Textile Industry, 1660–1774', *Economic History Review* 44, 395–423.

Offe, C. and K. Hinrichs. 1984. 'Sozialökonomie des Arbeitsmarktes: primäres und sekundäres Machtgefälle', in C. Offe (ed.), *"Arbeitsgesellschaft": Strukturprobleme und Zukunftsperspektiven,* Frankfurt, Main: Campus, 44–86.

Ogilvie, S. C. 1997. *State Corporatism and Proto-Industry: the Württemberg Black Forest, 1580–1797,* Cambridge: Cambridge University Press.

———. 1999. 'The German State: A Non-Prussian View', in J. Brewer and E. Hellmuth (eds), *Rethinking Leviathan: The Eighteenth-Century State in Britain and Germany,* Oxford: Oxford University Press, 167–202.

———. 2002. *A Bitter Living. Women, Markets, and Social Capital in Early-Modern Germany,* Oxford: Oxford University Press.

———. 2010 'Consumption, Social Capital, and the "Industrious Revolution" in Early Modern Germany', *Journal of Economic History* 70(2), 287–325.

———. 2011. *Institutions and European Trade. Merchant Guilds, 1000–1800,* Cambridge: Cambridge University Press.

Ormrod, D. 2003. *The Rise of Commercial Empires. England and the Netherlands in the Age of Mercantilism, 1650–1770,* Cambridge: Cambridge University Press.

Overton, M. 1996. *Agricultural Revolution in England. The Transformation of the Agrarian Economy 1500–1850,* Cambridge: Cambridge University Press.

Oz-Salzberger, F. 1995. *Translating the Enlightenment. Scottish Civic Discourse in Eighteenth-Century Germany,* Oxford: Clarendon Press.

Palmer, R. C. 1985. 'The Origins of Property in England', *Law and History Review* 3, 1–50.

———. 1985. 'The Economic and Cultural Impact of the Origins of Property: 1180–1220', *Law and History Review* 3, 375–96.

Pamuk, S. 2007. 'The Black Death and the Origins of the 'Great Divergence' across Europe, 1300–1600', *European Review of Economic History* 11, 189–317.

Parker, D. B., and A. R. Mellows. 1994. *The Modern Law of Trust,* ed. A. J. Oakley, London: Sweet and Maxwell.

Pawson, E. 1977. *Transport and Economy: The Turnpike Roads of Eighteenth Century Britain,* London: Palgrave.

Pearson, R. 2002. 'Shareholder Democracies? English Stock Companies and the Politics of Corporate Governance during the Industrial Revolution', *English Historical Review* 117, 840–66.

———, and D. Richardson. 2001. 'Business Networking in the Industrial Revolution', *Economic History Review* 44, 657–79.

Perkin, H. 1981. *The Origins of Modern English Society, 1780–1880,* London: Routledge.

———. 1989. *The Rise of Professional Society. England since 1880,* London: Routledge.

Pfister, U. 1998. 'Craft Guilds and Proto-Industrialization in Europe, 16th to 18th Centuries', in S. R. Epstein et al. (eds), *Guilds, Economy and Society,* Sevilla: Secretariado de publicaciones de la Universidad de Sevilla, 11–24.

Phillipson, N. 1983. 'Adam Smith as a Civic Moralist', in I. Hont and M. Ignatieff (eds), *Wealth and Virtue: The Shaping of Political Economy in the Scottish Enlightenment,* Cambridge: Cambridge University Press, 179–203.

Pincus, S. 2009. *1688. The First Modern Revolution,* New Haven: Yale University Press.

Pirker T. et al. (eds). 1987. *Technik und industrielle Revolution. Vom Ende eines sozialwissenschaftlichen Paradigmas,* Opladen: Westdeutscher Verlag.

Plumb, J. H. 1982. 'The Commercialization of Leisure', in N. McKendrick et al., *The Birth of a Consumer Society. The Commercialization of Eighteenth-Century England,* London: Hutchinson, 265–85.

Pocock, J. G. A. 1985. *Virtue, Commerce, and History. Essays on Political Thought and History, Chiefly in the Eighteenth Century,* Cambridge: Cambridge University Press.

Polanyi, K. 1944. *The Great Transformation,* New York: Rinehart.

Pollard, S. 1965. *The Genesis of Modern Management. A Study of the Industrial Revolution in Great Britain,* London: Edward Arnold.

———. 1973. 'Die Bildung und Ausbildung der industriellen Klassen Britanniens im 18. Jahrhundert', in R. Braun et al. (eds), *Gesellschaft in der industriellen Revolution,* Cologne: Kiepenheuer and Witsch, 147–61.

———. 1983. 'England: Der unrevolutionäre Pionier', in J. Kocka (ed.), *Europäische Arbeiterbewegungen im 19. Jahrhundert,* Göttingen: Vandenhoeck and Ruprecht, 21–38.

Pomeranz, K. 2000. *The Great Divergence. China, Europe, and the Making of the Modern World Economy,* Princeton, NJ: Princeton University Press.

———, and S. Topic. 1999. *The World that Trade Created. Society, Culture and the World Economy, 1400–the Present,* Armonk, NY: M.E. Sharpe.

Poovey, M. 1998. *A History of the Modern Fact. Problems of Knowledge in the Sciences of Wealth and Society,* Chicago: University of Chicago Press.

Porter, R. 1981. 'The English Enlightenment', in R. Porter and M. Teich (eds), *The Enlightenment in National Context,* Cambridge: Cambridge University Press, 1–18.

———. 1996. 'Material Pleasures in the Consumer Society', in R. Porter and M. M. Roberts (eds), *Pleasures in the Eighteenth Century,* New York: New York University Press, 19–35.

———. 2000. *The Creation of the Modern World. The Untold Story of the British Enlightenment,* New York: W.W. Norton and Company.

Postan, M. M. 1944. 'The Rise of a Money Economy', *Economic History Review* 14, 123–34.

Powicke, M. 1962. *Military Obligation in Medieval England. A Study in Liberty and Duty,* Oxford: Clarendon Press.

Prados de la Escosura, L. (ed.). 2004. *Exceptionalism and Industrialisation. Britain and its European Rivals, 1688–1815,* Cambridge: Cambridge University Press.

Price, J. M. 1989. 'What Did Merchants Do? Reflections on British Oversea Trade, 1660–1790', *Journal of Economic History* 49, 267–84.

Pückler-Muskau, H. Fürst von. 1985. 'J.-A. Barbey d'Aurevilly and C. Baudelaire', in G. Stein (ed.), *Dandy – Snob – Flaneur. Dekadenz und Exzentrik. Kulturfiguren und Sozialcharaktere des 19. und 20.* Jahrhunderts, Frankfurt, Main: Fischer, 19–23.

Pütz, M. 1984. 'Max Webers und Friedrich Kürnbergers Auseinandersetzung mit Benjamin Franklin. Zum Verhältnis von Quellenverfälschung und Fehlinterpretation', *Amerikastudien/American Studies* 29, 297–310.

Quesel, C. 2005. Pädagogik und politische Kultur in England 1870-1945, Berne: Peter Lang.

Ramsay, N. 1991. 'Introduction', in J. Blair and N. Ramsay (eds), *English Medieval Industries. Craftsman, Techniques, Products,* London: The Hambledon Press, XV–XXXIV.

Rashid, S. 1992. 'Adam Smith and the Market Mechanism', *History of Political Economy* 24, 129–52.

Razi, Z. 1980. *Life, Marriage and Death in a Medieval Parish: Economy, Society and Demography in Halesowen, 1270–1400,* Cambridge: Cambridge University Press.

Reddy, W. M. 1984. *The Rise of Market Culture. The Textile Trade and French Society, 1750–1900,* Cambridge: Cambridge University Press.

Reeves, C. 1995. *Pleasures and Pastimes in Medieval England,* Phoenix Mill, Gloucestershire: Anne Sutton Publishing Ltd.

Reininghaus, W. 1990. *Gewerbe in der frühen Neuzeit,* Munich: Oldenbourg.

Reith, G. 1999. *The Age of Chance. Gambling in Western Culture,* London: Routledge.

Rexroth, F. 2007. *Deviance and Power in Late Medieval London,* Cambridge: Cambridge University Press.

Ridder, P. 1976. 'Messung sozialer Prozesse', *Soziale Welt* 17, 144–61.

———. 2000. 'Kinetische Analyse historischer Prozesse. Modellfall Gesundheitssystem', *Historical Social Research* 25, 49–72.

Rigby, S. H. (ed.). 2003. *A Companion to Britain in the Later Middle Ages,* Oxford: Blackwell.

———. 2006. 'Introduction: Social Structure and Economic Change in Late Medieval England', in R. Horrox and W. M. Ormrod (eds), *A Social History of England, 1200–1500,* Cambridge: Cambridge University Press, 1–30.

Rose, M. B. 1996. 'Introduction: The Rise of the Cotton Industry in Lancashire to 1830', in M. B. Rose (ed.), *The Lancashire Cotton Industry,* Preston: Lancashire County Books, 1–28.

Rosseaux, U. 2007. *Freiräume. Unterhaltung, Vergnügen und Erholung in Dresden (1694–1830),* Cologne: Böhlau.

Rothenberg, E. A. 2006. '"The Diligent Hand Maketh Rich": Commercial Advice for Retailers in Late Seventeenth- and Early Eighteenth-Century England', in J. Benson and L. Ugolini (eds), *Cultures of Selling. Perspectives on Consumption and Society since 1700,* Aldershot: Ashgate, 215–35.

Rothschild, E. 2002. *Economic Sentiments. Adam Smith, Condorcet, and the Enlightenment,* Cambridge, MA: Harvard University Press.

Rowley, T. 2004. *The Normans,* Stroud: Tempus.

Rowlinson, M. 1999. '"The Scotch Hate Gold": British Identity and Paper Money, in E. Gilbert and E. Helleiner (eds), *Nation-States and Money. The Past, Present and Future of National Currencies,* London: Routledge, 47–67.

Rubinstein, W. D. 1991. '"Gentlemanly Capitalism" and British Industry, 1820–1914', *Past and Present* 132, 150–70.

———. 1998. 'The Weber Thesis, Ethnic Minorities, and British Entrepreneurship', in D. J. Jeremy (ed.), *Religion, Business and Wealth in Modern Britain,* London: Routledge, 170–81.

Samuel, R. 1977. 'Workshop of the World: Steam Power and Hand Technology in Mid-Victorian Britain', *History Workshop* 3, 6–72.

Saunders, A. (ed.). 1997. *The Royal Exchange,* London: The Typographical Society.

Scherer, F. M. 2001. 'The Evolution of Free-Lance Music Composition, 1650–1900', *Journal of Cultural Economics* 25, 307–25.

Schlie, F. 1988. 'Die Vielfalt der Leistungsbegriffe', in K.-O. Hondrich et al., *Krise der Leistungsgesellschaft? Empirische Analysen zum Engagement in Arbeit, Familie und Politik,* Opladen: Westdeutscher Verlag, 50–67.

Schmiechen, J., and K. Carls. 1999. *The British Market Hall. A Social and Architectural History,* New Haven: Yale University Press.

Schofield, P. R. 2003. 'England: The Family and the Village Community', in S. H. Rigby, *A Companion to Britain in the Later Middle Ages,* Oxford: Blackwell, 26–46.

Schröder, H.-C. 1977. 'Die neuere englische Geschichte im Lichte einiger Modernisierungstheoreme', in R. Koselleck (ed.), *Studien zum Beginn der modernen Welt,* Stuttgart: Klett, 30–67.

———. 1988. 'Der englische Adel', in A. von Reden-Dohna and R. Melville (eds), *Der Adel an der Schwelle des bürgerlichen Zeitalters 1780–1860,* Stuttgart: Steiner, 21–88.

Schulte Beerbühl, M. 1991. *Vom Gesellenverein zur Gewerkschaft. Entwicklung, Struktur und Politik der Londoner Gesellenorganisationen 1550–1825,* Göttingen: Vandenhoeck and Ruprecht.

———. 2007. *Deutsche Kaufleute in London. Welthandel und Einbürgerung (1660–1818),* Munich: Oldenbourg.

Shils, E. 1991. 'Henry Sumner Maine in the Tradition of the Analysis of Society', in A. Diamond (ed.), *The Victorian Achievement of Sir Henry Maine. A Centennial Reappraisal,* Cambridge: Cambridge University Press, 143–78.

Simmel, G. 1983 (1908). *Soziologie. Untersuchungen über die Formen der Vergesellschaftung,* 6th ed., Berlin: Duncker and Humblot.

———. 1989 (1900). *Philosophie des Geldes (Georg-Simmel-Gesamtausgabe,* vol. 6, ed. D. P. Frisby and K. C. Köhnke), Frankfurt, Main: Suhrkamp.

———. 1989 (1901). 'Philosphie des Geldes [self-advertisement of the book]', in G. Simmel, *Philosophie des Geldes* (Georg-Simmel-Gesamtausgabe, vol. 6, ed. D. P. Frisby and K. C. Köhnke), Frankfurt, Main: Suhrkamp, 719–23.

———. 2004 (1900). *The Philosophy of Money,* trans. T. Bottomore and D. Frisby, 3rd ed., London: Routledge.

Simpson, J. 2004. 'European Farmers and the British "Agricultural Revolution"', in L. Prados de la Escosura (ed.), *Exceptionalism and Industrialisation. Britain and Its European Rivals, 1688–1815,* Cambridge: Cambridge University Press, 69–85.

Slack, P. 1988. *Poverty and Policy in Tudor and Stuart England,* London: Longman.

———. 1990. *The English Poor Law 1531–1782,* Basingstoke: Macmillan.

Slater, D., and F. Tonkiss. 2001. *Market Society. Markets and Modern Social Theory,* Cambridge: Polity.

Slater, T. R. 2009. 'Social, Cultural and Politicial Space in English Medieval Market Places', in S. Ehrich and J. Oberste (eds), *Städtische Räume im Mittelalter,* Regensburg: Schnell and Steiner, 227–40.

Smelser, N. and R. Swedberg (eds). 2005. *The Handbook of Economic Sociology,* 2nd ed., Princeton, NJ: Princeton University Press.

Smith, A. 1981 (1776). *An Inquiry into the Nature and Causes of the Wealth of Nations,* ed. R.H. Campbell and A.S. Skinner, 2 vol., Indianapolis, IN: Liberty Fund.

———. 2005 (1776). *Untersuchung über Wesen und Ursachen des Reichtums der Völker,* trans. M. Streissler, Tübingen: Mohr Siebeck.

———. 2009 (1759). *The Theory of Moral Sentiments,* ed. R. P. Hanley, London: Penguin.

Smith, J. M. 1996. *The Culture of Merit: Nobility, Royal Service, and the Making of the Absolute Monarchy in France, 1600–1789,* Ann Arbor, MI: University of Michigan Press.

Smith, R. E. F. (ed.). 1986. *A. V. Chayanov on the Theory of Peasant Economy,* Madison, WI: University of Madison Press.

Smith, R. M. 1998. 'The English Peasantry, 1250–1650', in T. Scott (ed.), *The Peasantries of Europe from the Fourteenth to the Eighteenth Centuries,* London: Macmillan, 339–71.

Sokoll, T. 1983. 'Zur Rekonstruktion historischer Gemeinschaftsformen. Neuere sozialgeschichtliche Gemeindestudien in England', *Zeitschrift für Volkskunde* 79, 15–41.

Solar, P. M., and R. M. Smith. 2003. 'An Old Poor Law for the New Europe? Reconciling Local Solidarity with Labour Mobility in Early Modern England', in P. A. David and M. Thomas (eds), *The Economic Future in Historical Perspective,* Oxford: Oxford University Press, 463–78.

Sombart, W. 1910. 'Die Kommerzialisierung des Wirtschaftslebens', *Archiv für Sozialwissenschaft und Sozialpolitik* 30, 631–65, and 31, 23–66.

———. 1911. *Die Juden und das Wirtschaftsleben,* Jena: Duncker and Humblot.

———. 1915. *Händler und Helden. Patriotische Besinnungen,* Leipzig: Duncker and Humblot.

———. 1969 (1916). *Der moderne Kapitalismus. Historisch-systematische Darstellung des gesamteuropäischen Wirtschaftslebens von seinen Anfängen bis zur Gegenwart,* 3 vols, Berlin: Duncker and Humblot.

———. 2001. *The Jews and Modern Capitalism,* Kitchener, Ontario: Batoche Books.

Sommerville, C. J. 1981. 'The Anti-Puritan Work Ethic', *Journal of British Studies* 20, 70–81.

———. 1996. *The News Revolution in England. Cultural Dynamics of Daily Information,* New York and Oxford: Oxford University Press.

Stein, P., and J. Shand. 1974. *Legal Values in Western Society,* Edinburgh: Edinburgh University Press.

Steinert, H. 2010. *Max Webers unwiderlegbare Fehlkonstruktionen. Die protestantische Ethik und der Geist des Kapitalismus,* Frankfurt, Main: Campus.

Steinfeld, R. J. 1991. *The Invention of Free Labor. The Employment Relation in English and American Law and Culture, 1350–1870,* Chapel Hill, NC: University of North Carolina Press.

Steinmetz, W. 2002. *Begegnungen vor Gericht. Eine Sozial- und Kulturgeschichte des englischen Arbeitsrechts (1850–1925),* Munich: Oldenbourg.

Stigler, G. J. 1957. 'Perfect Competition, Historically Contemplated', *Journal of Political Economy* 65, 1–17.

Stobart, J. 1998. 'Shopping Streets as Social Space: Consumerism, Improvement and Leisure in an Eighteenth-Century Country Town', *Urban History* 25, 3–21.

———. 2005. 'Leisure and Shopping in the Small Towns of Georgian England', *Journal of Urban History* 31, 479–503.

Stöber, R. 2005. *Deutsche Pressegeschichte. Von den Anfängen bis zur Gegenwart,* Konstanz: UVK Verlagsgesellschaft.

Stone, D. 1997. 'The Productivity of Hired and Customary Labour: Evidence from Wisbech Barton in the Fourteenth Century', *Economic History Review* 50, 640–56.

Stone, L. 1969. 'Literacy and Education in England 1640–1900', *Past and Present* 42, 69–139.

Stratmann, S. 2000. *Myths of Speculation. The South Sea Bubble and 18th-Century English Literature,* Munich: Fink.

Strayer, J. R. 1970. *On the Medieval Origins of the Modern State,* Princeton, NJ: Princeton University Press.

Streissler, E. W. 2005. 'Einführung', in A. Smith, *Untersuchung über Wesen und Ursachen des Reichtums der Völker,* trans. M. Streissler, Tübingen: Mohr Siebeck/UTB, 1–31.

Styles, J. 2007. *The Dress of the People. Everyday Fashion in Eighteenth-Century England,* New Haven: Yale University Press.

Sugarman, D. 1997. 'In the Spirit of Weber: Law, Modernity and the "Peculiarities of the English"', in C. Peterson (ed.), *History and European Private Law. Development of Common Methods and Principles,* Lund: Institutet for Rättshistorisk Forskning Grandat av Gustav och Carin Olin, 217–62.

Swedberg, R. 1991. 'Major Traditions of Economic Sociology', *Annual Review of Sociology* 17, 251–76.

————. 1994. 'Markets as Social Structures', in N. J. Smelser and R. Swedberg (eds), *The Handbook of Economic Sociology*, Princeton, NJ: Princeton University Press, 255–82.

————. 1998. *Max Weber and the Idea of Economic Sociology*, Princeton, NJ: Princeton University Press.

————. 2000. 'Afterword: The Role of the Market in Max Weber's Work', *Theory and Society* 29, 373–84.

Szostak, R. 1991. *The Role of Transportation in the Industrial Revolution: A Comparison of England and France*, Montreal: McGill-Queen's University Press.

Tanner, J. 2004. '"Kultur" in den Wirtschaftswissenschaften und kulturwissenschaftliche Interpretationen ökonomischen Handelns', in F. Jaeger and J. Rüsen (eds), *Handbuch der Kulturwissenschaften. Themen und Tendenzen*, vol. 3, Stuttgart: J.B. Metzler, 195–224.

————. 2004. 'Die ökonomische Handlungstheorie vor der 'kulturalistischen Wende'? Perspektiven und Probleme einer interdisziplinären Diskussion', in H. Berghoff and J. Vogel (eds), *Wirtschaftsgeschichte als Kulturgeschichte. Dimensionen eines Perspektivenwechsels*, Frankfurt, Main: Campus, 69–98.

Tawney, R. H. 1937 (1922). *Religion and the Rise of Capitalism*, Harmondsworth: Penguin.

Thirsk, J. 1969. 'Younger Sons in the Seventeenth Century', *History. Journal of the Historical Association* 54, 358–77.

————. 1976. 'The European Debate on Customs and Inheritance, 1500–1700', in J. Goody et al. (eds), *Family and Inheritance. Rural Societies in Western Europe 1200–1800*, Cambridge: Cambridge University Press, 177–91.

————. 1978. *Economic Policy and Projects: the Development of a Consumer Society in Early-Modern England*, Oxford: Oxford University Press.

————. 1983. 'Introduction', in J. Thirsk (ed.), *The Agrarian History of England and Wales, 1640–1750*, vol. 5, Cambridge: Cambridge University Press, XIX–XXXI.

Thomas, B. 1986. 'Was there an Energy Crisis in Great Britain in the Seventeenth Century?', *Explorations in Economic History* 2, 134–52.

Thomas, H. M. 2008. *The Norman Conquest: England after William the Conqueror*, Lanham, MD: Rowman and Littlefield.

Thomas, K. 1986. 'The Meaning of Literacy in Early Modern England', in G. Baumann (ed.), *The Written Word: Literacy in Transition*, Oxford: Clarendon Press, 97–131.

————. 1991 (1971). *Religion and the Decline of Magic. Studies in Popular Beliefs in Sixteenth- and Seventeenth-Century England*, London: Penguin.

Thomas, M. 2003. 'The Service Sector', in R. Floud and P. Johnson (eds), *The Cambridge Economic History of Modern Britain, vol. 2: Economic Maturity 1860–1939*, Cambridge: Cambridge University Press, 99–132.

Thompson, E. P. 1991. *Customs in Common. Studies in Traditional Popular Culture*, New York: The New Press.

Thrupp, S. L. 1965. 'The Gilds', in M. M. Postan et al. (eds), *Cambridge Economic History of Europe*, vol. 3, Cambridge: Cambridge University Press, 230–80.

Tilly, R. 2003. *Geld und Kredit in der Wirtschaftsgeschichte*, Stuttgart: Steiner.

Tönnies, F. 2001 (1887). *Community and Civil Society*, J. Harris (ed.), trans. M. Hollis, Cambridge: Cambridge University Press.

Tribe, K. 1977. 'The "Histories" of Economic Discourse', *Economy and Society* 6, 314–44.

Tunzelmann, G. N von. 1978. *Steam Power and British Industrialization to 1860*, Oxford: Clarendon Press.

Underdown, D. 2000. *Start of Play. Cricket and Culture in Eighteenth-Century England*, London: Penguin.

Unwin, G. 1904. *Industrial Organization in the Sixteenth and Seventeenth Centuries*, Oxford: Clarendon Press.

Vanberg, V. 2001. 'Markets and the Law', in N. J. Smelser and P. B. Baltes (eds), *International Encyclopedia of the Social and Behavioral Sciences*, vol. 14, Amsterdam: Elsevier, 9221–27.

Volckart, O. 2001. 'Zur Transformation der mitteleuropäischen Wirtschaftsordnung, 1000–1800', *Vierteljahrschrift für Sozial- und Wirtschaftsgeschichte* 68, 277–310.

———. 2002. *Wettbewerb und Wettbewerbsbeschränkung im vormodernen Deutschland 1000–1800*, Tübingen: Mohr.

———. 2009. 'Regeln, Willkür und der gute Ruf: Geldpolitik und Finanzmarkteffizienz in Deutschland, 14. bis 16. Jahrhundert', *Jahrbuch für Wirtschaftsgeschichte*, 101–29.

Vries, J. de. 2008. *The Industrious Revolution. Consumer Behavior and the Household Economy, 1650 to the Present*, Cambridge: Cambridge University Press.

———, and A. van der Woude. 1997. *The First Modern Economy. Success, Failure and Perseverance of the Dutch Economy, 1500–1815*, Cambridge: Cambridge University Press.

Vries, P. 2003. *Via Peking Back to Manchester. Britain, the Industrial Revolution, and China*, Leiden: CNWS Publications.

———. 2010. 'Review Article of Jürgen Osterhammel, Die Verwandlung der Welt', *Comparativ* 20, 20–38.

Walker, S. 2006. 'Order and Law', in R. Horrox and W. M. Ormrod (eds), *A Social History of England 1200–1500*, Cambridge: Cambridge University Press, 91–112.

Wallerstein, I. 1983. *Historical Capitalism*, London: Verso.

Walter, J., and R. Schofield. 1989. 'Famine, Disease and Crisis Mortality in Early Modern Society', in J. Walter and R. Schofield (eds), *Famine, Desease and the Social Order in Early Modern Society*, Cambridge: Cambridge University Press, 1–73.

Walvin, J. 1997. *Fruits of Empire. Exotic Produce and British Taste, 1660–1800*, Houndmills: Macmillan Press.

Waugh, S. L. 1986. 'Tenure to Contract: Lordship and Clientage in Thirteenth-Century England', *English Historical Review* 101, 811–39.

Weatherill, L. 1986. 'The Business of Middlemen in the English Pottery Trade Before 1780', *Business History* 28, 11–76.

———. 1989. *Consumer Behaviour and Material Culture in Britain, 1660–1760*, London: Routledge.

Weber, A. F. 1967. *The Growth of Cities in the Nineteenth Century. A Study in Statistics*, New York: Macmillan Co. 1899, Reprint of 3rd ed. Ithaka, NY: Cornell University Press.

Weber, H. 1988. 'Common Law', in R. Sheyhing (ed.), *Ergänzbares Lexikon des Rechts* 1(270), 29 February 1988, Neuwied: Luchterhand, 1–4.

Weber, M. 1927. *General Economic History*, trans. Frank Knight, New York: Greenberg Publishers.

———. 1958. *The Protestant Ethic and the Spirit of Capitalism*, trans. T. Parsons with a foreword by R. H. Tawney, New York: Charles Scribner's Sons.

———. 1976. *Wirtschaft und Gesellschaft. Grundriß der verstehenden Soziologie, Studienausgabe*, 5th ed., Tübingen: Mohr.

———. 1988. 'Vorbemerkung', in M. Weber, *Gesammelte Aufsätze zur Religionssoziologie*, 9th ed., vol. 1, Tübingen: Mohr, 1–16.

————. 1999. *Essays in Economic Sociology*, R. Swedberg (ed.), Princeton: Princeton University Press.

Weber, W. 1992. *The Rise of Musical Classics in Eighteenth-Century England. A Study in Canon, Ritual, and Ideology*, Oxford: Clarendon Press.

Wehler, H.-U. 1975. *Modernisierungstheorie und Geschichte*, Göttingen: Vandenhoeck and Ruprecht.

Weisbrod, B. 1990. 'Der englische "Sonderweg" in der neueren Geschichte', *Geschichte und Gesellschaft* 16, 233–52.

Wellenreuther, H. 1992. 'England und Europa. Überlegungen zum Problem des englischen Sonderwegs in der europäischen Geschichte', in N. Finzsch (ed.), *Liberalitas: Festschrift für Erich Angermann zum 65. Geburtstag*, Stuttgart: Steiner, 89–123.

Welskopp, T. 2002. 'Die Theoriefähigkeit der Geschichtswissenschaft', in R. Mayntz (ed.), *Akteure – Mechanismen – Modelle. Zur Theoriefähigkeit makro-sozialer Analysen*, Frankfurt, Main: Campus, 61–90.

Westerfield, R. B. 1968. *Middlemen in English Business Particularly Between 1660–1760*, New Haven, CT: Yale University Press. 1915, Reprint New York: David and Charles Reprints.

Westhauser, K. E. 1994. 'Friendship and Family in Early Modern England: the Sociability of Adam Eyre and Samuel Pepys', *Journal of Social History* 27, 517–36.

White, E. W. 1983. *A History of English Opera*, London: Faber and Faber.

White, M. 2004. 'London Professional Playhouses and Performances', in J. Milling and P. Thomson (eds), *The Cambridge History of British Theatre, vol. 1: Origins to 1660*, Cambridge: Cambridge University Press, 298–338.

Wigglesworth, N. 1996. *The Evolution of English Sport*, London: Cass.

Williams, P. 1956. 'Lotteries and Government Finances in England', *History Today* 6, 557–61.

Williamson, J. G. 1990. *Coping with City Growth during the British Industrial Revolution*, Cambridge: Cambridge University Press.

————. 1984. 'Why Was British Growth so Slow During the Industrial Revolution?', *Journal of Economic History* 44, 687–712.

Wilson, C. 1966. *Anglo-Dutch Commerce and Finance in the Eighteenth Century*, Cambridge: Cambridge University Press.

Wilson, E. 2005. 'Fashion and Modernity', in C. Breward and C. Evans (eds), *Fashion and Modernity*, Oxford: Berg.

Wilson, R. G. 1971. *Gentlemen Merchants. The Merchant Community in Leeds, 1700–1830*, Manchester: Manchester University Press.

Winch, D., and P. O'Brien (eds). 2002. *The Political Economy of British Historical Experience, 1688–1914*, Oxford: Oxford University Press for The Boydell Press.

Withington, P. and A. Shepard. 2000. 'Introduction: Communities in Early Modern England', in A. Shepard and P. Withington (eds), *Communities in Early Modern England. Networks, Place, Rhetoric*, Manchester: Manchester University Press, 1–15.

Wong, R. B. 2002. 'The Search for European Differences and Domination in the Early Modern World: A View from Asia', *American Historical Review* 107, 447–69.

Wood, D. (ed.). 2004. *Medieval Money Matters*, Oxford: Oxbow Books.

Wood, E. M. 2002. *The Origins of Capitalism. A Longer View*, London: Verso.

Woodhall, R. 1964. 'The British State Lotteries', *History Today* 14, 497–504.

Woodward, D. 1980. 'The Background of the Statute of Artificers: The Genesis of Labour Policy, 1558–63', *Economic History Review* 33, 32–44.

Wordie, J. R. 1983. 'The Chronology of English Enclosure, 1500–1914', *Economic History Review* 36, 483–505.

Wrightson, K. E. 1989. 'Kindred Adjoining Kingdoms: An English Perspective on the Social and Economic History of Early Modern Scotland', in R. A. Houston and D. Whyte (eds), *Scottish Society 1500–1800*, Cambridge: Cambridge University Press, 245–60.

Wrigley, E. A. 1987. *People, Cities and Wealth. The Transformation of Traditional Society*, Oxford: Blackwell.

———. 1987. 'The Process of Modernization and the Industrial Revolution in England', in E. A. Wrigley, *People, Cities and Wealth. The Transformation of Traditional Society*, Oxford: Blackwell, 46–74.

———. 1987. 'The Supply of Raw Materials in the Industrial Revolution', in E. A. Wrigley, *People, Cities and Wealth. The Transformation of Traditional Society*, Oxford: Blackwell, 75–91.

———. 1987. 'A Simple Model of London's Importance in Changing English Society and Economy, 1650–1750', in E. A. Wrigley, *People, Cities and Wealth. The Transformation of Traditional Society*, Oxford: Blackwell, 133–56.

———. 1987. 'Urban Growth and Agricultural Change: England and the Continent in the Early Modern Period', in E. A. Wrigley, *People, Cities and Wealth: The Transformation of Traditional Society*, Oxford: Blackwell, 157–93.

———. 2004. *Poverty, Progress, and Population*, Cambridge: Cambridge University Press.

———. 2004. 'The Quest for the Industrial Revolution', in E. A. Wrigley, *Poverty, Progress and Population*, Cambridge: Cambridge University Press, 17–43.

———. 2004. 'The Divergence of England: the Growth of the English Economy in the Seventeenth and Eighteenth Centuries', in E. A. Wrigley, *Poverty, Progress and Population*, Cambridge: Cambridge University Press, 44–67.

———. 2004. 'City and Country in the Past: a Sharp Divide or a Continuum?', in E. A. Wrigley, *Poverty, Progress, and Population*, Cambridge: Cambridge University Press, 251–67.

———. 2004. '"The Great Commerce of Every Civilized Society": Urban Growth in Early Modern Europe', in E. A. Wrigley, *Poverty, Progress, and Population*, Cambridge: Cambridge University Press, 268–89.

Yamey, B. S. 1949. 'Scientific Bookkeeping and the Rise of Capitalism', *Economic History Review* 1, 99–113.

Zanden, J. L. van. 2009. *The Long Road to the Industrial Revolution. The European Economy in a Global Perspective, 1000–1800*, Leiden: Brill.

Zaret, D. 2000. *Origins of Democratic Culture: Printing, Petitions and the Public Sphere in Early-Modern England*, Princeton, NJ: Princeton University Press.

Zelizer, V. A. 1988. 'Beyond the Polemics of the Market: Establishing a Theoretical and Empirical Agenda', *Sociological Forum* 3(4), 614–34.

Zimmermann, R. 1993. 'Der europäische Charakter des englischen Rechts: Historische Verbindungen zwischen Civil Law und Common Law', *Zeitschrift für europäisches Privatrecht* 1, 4–51.

INDEX

www.ingramcontent.com/pod-product-compliance
Lightning Source LLC
Chambersburg PA
CBHW060042030426
42334CB00019B/2451